AF540307

NATURE AND SCOPE OF POLITICAL SCIENCE

NATURE AND SCOPE OF POLITICAL SCIENCE

Compiled & Edited
by
Dr. R.K. Pruthi

DISCOVERY PUBLISHING HOUSE
NEW DELHI-110002

First Published-2005

ISBN 81-7141-993-3

Published by

DISCOVERY PUBLISHING HOUSE
4831/24, Ansari Road, Prahlad Street,
Darya Ganj, New Delhi-110002 (India)
Phone: 23279245 • Fax: 91-11-23253475
E-mail:dphtemp@indiatimes.com

Printed at:
Arora Offset Press
Laxmi Nagar, Delhi 110 092.

Preface

Aim of this book is to introduce my readers to the discipline of political science. What is the definition and scope of political science? How the term political science has been found to be the most comprehensive and scientific term to describe this discipline? Which are the various conceptions of political science? The subject has been constantly evolving therefore the discussion on current trends in political science have been included.

The subject of this work will enable our readers to understand the changing conceptions of politics. It will describe the prevailing controversies regarding the standard nomenclature of political science. It will facilitate the identification of the major dimensions of the scope of political science and provide the current state of the subject. Some critical essays by the authorities on the subject and bibliography has been appended to facilitate further research in the topic.

We record our heartful acknowledgements to the authorities on the subject.

Librarians and their staff members deserve our thanks for help and cooperative.

My publisher and his staff have worked hard. They deserve the love and patronage of our readers.

R.K. Pruthi

Contents

1

Introduction

One of the most striking features of the contemporary social life, as you must have observed, is the increasing role of politics in all major spheres. The impact of politics, in some form or the other, is visible on economy, culture, social relations and even ethical norms. Disintegration of conventional forms of organisation, social and political revolutions and the aggravation of conflict at all levels have further placed politics at the centre of public life. This is, however, not to state that politics was non-existent or unimportant in earlier times. On the contrary, politics according to Aristotle and many other thinkers, is as old as human organisation. It has always played a decisive role in social life. This role has been constantly increasing in our times.

In conceptual terms also, politics has always occupied a significant place in both the East and the West. The conceptions of politics, however, have varied with time and place. Politics, for instance, was conceived as ethics by some in ancient Greece and India. During the medieval feudal ages, it was coloured in theological terms everywhere. The realistic orientation began in the West with Machiavelli in sixteenth century Italy, although in India it began much earlier with Kautilya and in Greece with Thrasymachus. State, Law, Sovereignty and related institutions as well as the structure and centre of power became the focal points of study. Karl Marx in the nineteenth century gave a revolutionary turn to social sciences, by giving politics a historico-economic interpretation. The third decade of the twentieth century witnessed the rise of 'Behaviouralism' in the USA, which dominated Political

Science, among other social sciences, till the last sixties. The Behavioural movement rejected all the major notions of traditional Political Science and advocated an empirical, scientific discipline of politics. Two decades later, however, restoration of values in political analysis became one of the major concerns of the leading contemporary movements such as post-Behaviouralism in the USA, revivalist-conservative movements in Europe, and Humanistic Marxism, currently popular in parts of America, Europe and Asia. Political Science, thus, is the sum of all that has happened in these preceding centuries.

The brief sketch outlined above should make it clear to you that there is no single definition of the subject matter of Political Science that is uniformly or universally accepted. There are different interpretations and approaches and therefore, a variety of definitions. In the following pages, we will discuss in detail, some of the major schools and their ideas. However, before doing so, let us briefly examine the controversies regarding the standard nomenclature of Political Science.

Politics

The term 'POLITICS' was used for the first time by Aristotle in a broad sense, so as to cover besides the ideal polis (the city-state), the structure of family, the control of slaves, the morphology of revolutions, comments on pure democracy, education etc. A definition of this kind was acceptable because Aristotle-conceived of the study of politics as the 'Master Science', as the science comprising not only the principles of governance, but also the ethical norms of conduct and social vision. In subsequent centuries, limitations of such perception were realized. Need for a narrower interpretation was felt in view of the growing areas of specialisation. The term 'politics' began to be used to mean political practice as distinct from political philosophy, which has ethical moorings or political theory. Sometimes, politics was, and is still, used as the technique of compromise or as the art of the possible or the method to capture power and retain it.

Frederick Pollock, in his famous study—Introduction to the History of the Science of Politics, has distinguished the theoretical study of politics from practical politics. In his view, a theoretical study of politics comprises theory of the state, government, legislation and the state as an artificial person. Practical politics includes actual forms of government, the working of government, administration, laws and legislation and international politics.

The above distinction made by Pollock is analytically useful. Political Science has travelled a long way since Aristotle's times, and the use of the term 'politics' as a standard nomenclature of Political Science, is marked by serious limitations. The term in its modern meaning is confined to practical aspects only. Consequently, it does not include conceptual and ethical dimensions of the discipline. Therefore, it is inadequate and inappropriate as a nomenclature of the subject.

Political Philosophy

The term 'Political Philosophy' was used inter-changeably with 'Political Science' till recent times. It was accepted as the foundation of Political Science, encompassing conceptual study of major institutions, theories and ideologies. In fact, analytically speaking, Political Philosophy is at once broader and narrower than Political Science. It is broader in that it is credited with a universalistic and holistic vision, whereas political analysis is specific and contextual. Philosophy is capable of transcending the limits of history, but political analysis may not do so. Political Philosophy is narrower in another sense: Political Science fruitfully combines political theory and political practice, but political philosophy remains confined to conceptual analysis.

The distinction between Political 'Science' and 'Philosophy' has been most strongly advocated by the Behavioural movement. The distinction is partly based on a presumed dichotomy of 'facts' and 'values', which you will study in Unit 2. Political Philosophy is concerned with clarification of concepts and a critical evaluation of beliefs. It tries to decide what is right or good for man and society and examines the rational justification of ideas and values. Therefore, Political Philosophy is primarily normative, prescribing what is good and addressing itself to questions of 'ought to be'. As against this, Political Science tries to analyse political phenomena in order to frame general laws. It tries to discover causal relationship for this purpose. In this sense, unlike philosophy, Political Science is more concerned with 'what is' than with 'ought to be'. It is more positive than normative. There is, however, an insistence on the inclusion of 'values' in the study of Political Science by contemporary schools of theory ranging from post-Behaviouralism to Marxist Humanism. They see the relationship between Political Science and Philosophy, not as a dichotomous relationship, but as a collaborative interaction.

Political Philosophy, on the whole, emphasises theoretical and philosophical postulates excluding the methodological and the practical aspects of political analysis. It is, therefore, considered unsuitable as a standard nomenclature of the discipline.

Theory of the State

The title 'Theory of the State' is more precise than both 'Politics' and 'Political Philosophy', in that it specifies and outlines the study of the state and related institutions as the focal unit of political study. Whereas 'Political Philosophy' is abstract, speculative and normative, 'Politics' primarily, is concrete and pragmatic. 'Theory of the State' is neither totally abstract nor pragmatic. It combines elements of both theoretical generalisations and details of practice. Yet, it does not cover the entire scope of political study. Significant practical dimensions of political activity which take place outside the institutional periphery of state are neglected if we call the subject, 'Theory of the State'. Fundamental philosophical principles with more universalistic implications than the state also suffer from similar neglect.

'Theory of the State', in brief, confines itself to the expression of the state's will, its contents and execution. Since, it excludes other relevant dimensions of political activity, it is not acceptable as a standard nomenclature of Political Science.

Political Science

The term 'Political Science' is the most inclusive and comprehensive compared to the preceding terms. The term includes study of state and related institutions, power-processes, dynamics of politics, philosophical and theoretical principles of political conduct. Political Science also compares political institutions across states. The emerging political trends in the post-World War II states of Asia and Africa have attracted the attention of political scientists in recent years. The study of relationships of political reality with the social, economic, cultural and other aspects of reality is now rightly claiming a central place in political analysis. These substantive dimensions of politics are studied through various approaches and methods such as philosophical, historical, institutional, empirical, behavioural and scientific. The study of Political Science, therefore, is inclusive of methodological techniques.

Thus, to conclude the discussion on standard nomenclatures, it may be stated that 'Political Science' is the most appropriate title for the discipline. It is also the generally accepted title.

The Classical Conceptions of Greece and Rome

The study of political ideas in the West begins with the ancient Greeks, because they are believed to be the first people to have applied critical and rational thinking to fundamental political questions. Major Greek political thinkers—Socrates, Plato and Aristotle—interpreted politics as an activity of the POLIS (City State). The POLIS was more than a State. It was a fused 'Society-State', as Earnest Barker in his Principles of Social and Political Theory, has characterised it. POLIS, in this sense was all-inclusive; that is, inclusive of economic, cultural, ethical and other aspects. Science of POLIS, that is Political Science was, therefore, logically described by Aristotle as a 'Master Science'. Politics, in other words, was not outside society. In fact, the individual, state and society were coterminous in Greek thinking. The governing ideals of politics, society and individual conduct were goodness, virtue and knowledge. The Greek conception of politics was, thus, primarily philosophical, idealistic and normative.

In contrast to the philosophical notions of the Greeks, the ancient Romans gave a justice or a legal interpretation of politics. Politics was an activity concerning the REGNUM (Empire). It was governed by a set of general and definite rules. Roman political theory was a continual attempt to bring the civil law close to the ideal of the natural law. The ancient Western world, in this way, had both the philosophical and the legal conceptions of politics.

During the middle ages, 'politics became a branch of theology'. In a sense, it was a form of dyarchy leaving two centres of authority—one for the worldly affairs and another for spiritual needs. Regnum or State was the political authority taking care of the material well-being of the society. Church was the supreme ecclesiastical or religious organisation. Political authority was subordinate to the authority of the Church. It was not autonomous. Medieval perception of politics was thus, basically, theological, prescriptive and narrow.

The Modern Liberal Conception

It was not until the sixteenth century, that is, with Niccolo Machiavelli, that politics acquired a realistic, pragmatic, secular and scientific orientation. Machiavelli enunciated the modern idea of 'power' as the central moving force of politics. 'State' now became the pivotal political organisation. For these unconventional ideas. Machiavelli is considered by many to be the father of modern political science. In the next century. Thomas Hobbes further developed the realistic and materialistic conception of politics. For him, politics operated not only through power, but also, through force. John Locke initiated the idea of constitutional institutionalisation of power, which could check indiscriminate use of force. Politics, in Locke's view, was legitimate within limits. Rousseau introduced the idea of popular sovereignty and democracy. This was translated into reality through the French Revolution (1789). Institutional politics was further strengthened. By the nineteenth century, politics was generally accepted as a pervasive phenomenon. Once political power came within the reach of the people, institutions such as state, government, semi-official associations, etc., began to be treated as centres of political activity. The role of political consciousness in deliberately changing the course of events acquired legitimate status. Rights to private property and individual liberty began to be asserted. Ideology played a vital role in expending this process. In the advanced liberal concept, the state is conceived as a positive welfare organ. Some of the liberal democrats regard the State as a mediator between diverse group interests or a best, as the final arbiter between them. Individualism, Liberalism and Socialism were some of the major ideologies having a decisive impact on world politics. Of all these Marxian Socialism, which arose as a protest against the capitalist world, is in marked contrast to the dominant western world-view. We will, therefore, take it up now.

Marxian Conception of Politics

Marxian conception of politics is based on the historical materialist approach propounded by Karl Marx and his collaborator Frederick Engels in the nineteenth century. Although, subsequent Marxist theoreticians have added their own interpretations, the basic assumptions of Marx's formulations have not changed to this day. According to Marx, the material conditions of the base very often determine the ideological superstructure in a given period of time. This does not preclude the possibility of the superstructure (viz., government, institutions, ideologies, laws etc.) influencing the base. Politics being conditioned by the economy serves it by supporting a corresponding social system. Any state has an apparatus of coercion as well as of administration; with which it protects and upholds the existing order. The social interests of classes, nations, groups and individuals are, thus, most clearly reflected in the sphere of political relations. Politics is the area where these interests compete and combine on the basis of the actual balance of forces in the civil society. Politics, finally, is the active sphere of social structure, affecting the latter directly and continually.

Marx, thus, rejected the existing formal and juridical approaches of conventional western political science and put forth a more comprehensive sociological analysis of politics. Some of the major tenets of Marxist conceptions of politics are: The concepts of base and superstructure, the Theory of class struggle and the Idea of the withering away of the State. You will study these in detail in later units.

Indian Conceptions

The study of politics was popular not only in the West, but

also in the East. There is an evidence of developed political thinking in China, Egypt and India. It is believed that political ideas were advanced in ancient India even a couple of centuries earlier than in Greece.

As in the West, in ancient India also, several nomenclatures were used for political study. Monarchy was the normal form of state and government; therefore, study of politics was called Rajadharma or Rajyashastra. Dandaniti and Nitishastra were other terms used for the subject; the former indicating the totality of social, political and economic relationships and sanctions; and the latter, a science of wisdom, moral principles and right course. In simpler terms, Dandaniti accepted punishment as a necessary element of politics, whereas Nitishastra emphasised the idealistic and ethical aspects of political conduct. The most effective term for the science of politics, however, was 'Arthashastra' which was defined by Kautilya as "The Science which deals with the acquisition and protection or governance of territory". All the above-mentioned schools shared a common emphasis on 'dharma'; that is, obligation to the doctrine of natural justice on the part of the ruler. Politics, in ancient India, remained ethical; despite overtones of pragmatism in Arthashastra or in Maharashtra. Brihaspati, Manu, Sukra and Kautilya could be cited as the builders of the classical tradition of political philosophy in India. Greece and Rome experienced diverse forms and ideologies of government, but ancient India from the very beginning experienced, with few exceptions, monarchical governments.

During the middle ages, under the Mughal empire, politics began to be perceived in terms of 'office' and 'authority'. The composite nobility of the day was purely 'official', because, there was no hereditary transmission of titles. After the death of a noble, his property was transferred to the state. The practice of decentralization in ancient India more or less continued through village panchayats. Politics, in medieval India, was, thus, more autonomous than in the medieval West.

With the advent of the British, there began a phase of the decline of conventional political institutions in India. For nearly two centuries, 'politics' was conceived as synonymous with subjugation, protest and nationalism. Philosophical orientation was replaced by 'activism' during the national freedom movement. The political ideas of Gokhale, Tilak, Gandhi, and Jaya Prakash Narayan amply confirm the need of the unity of political theory and practice in contemporary world context. Interestingly Karl Marx emphasised a similar necessity in another context.

Conceptions of politics in India, throughout the ages, have always contained some sort of ethical purpose and norms. Elements of realims as well as radicalism are also notable in some conceptions. Politics in its composite totality is perceptible in India political thinking as in the West.

The State

Study of the state remained the central and the most important preoccupation of political scientists till the end of the nineteenth century. However, if we note carefully, the word 'state' in its present sense is comparatively modern, not even more than four hundred years old. Probably, Machiavelli, who strove to establish a complete doctrine of the state was the first to use the term in is present sense. Earlier, the word had been used to denote status, commonwealth, community, etc.

You will study the state in detail in Unit 4. Here, it would be enough to note that the state is an organised group of people, habitually resident on a particular tract of land. It is part of the idea of the state that it should have exclusive rights on its own land. The people are governed by a supreme authority, commonly referred to as the 'sovereign'.

Being a focal point of political organisation, state has been interpreted in a variety of perspectives such as: state as force, consent, corporation, organism, a totalitarian evil and as an instrument of welfare. Whereas Machiavelli, Hobbes and Trietske conceived of the state as based on force. Locke, Mill and Green advocated consent as the basis of the state. The individualists thought of the state as a necessary evil, whereas the Collectivists glorified it as a positive institution. For the Anarchists, the state was unnecessary; for the Totalitarians, it was indispensable. In Marx's view, the state was an instrument of class-exploitation and would wither away with the development of communism. In Gandhian philosophy, state would justify its existence, by acting as a 'trustee' of the people.

However, it is generally agreed that the state is a necessary organisation, and should be used to promote social good on the largest possible scale. This, in other words, is the rationale of the welfare state, which you will study in detail later.

State, Society, Government and Nation

Functionally, the spheres of the state, society, government and nation are overlapping, but it is necessary as well as possible to distinguish them conceptually.

In distinguishing state and society, it is pointed out that the sphere of the state is not coextensive with society. It is organised within a society for specific ends. The state employs force as a legitimate sanction, whereas society works through voluntary action. Identifying the state with society can be dangerous, because it leeds to interference of state in every aspect of social life and paves the way for totalitarianism or authoritarianism.

Similarly, state is distinguishable from the government. Government is the agency of the state through which its will is formulated in the form of laws. This is usually done by the legislature. Laws are executed and interpreted by the executive and judicial bodies, bureaucracy and the courts. The state is a wider concept than the government. It is also more durable. A change in government does not mean change of the state.

The term 'nation' emphasises the consciousness of unity among its people, and according to an older view, a nation need not necessarily be a state. Since 1920, however, there has been a tendency both in theory and in practice to associate statehood with nationhood, to equate nation with a united people organised in a state. 'One nation one state', is a popular slogan and is the aim of the nationalist movements. But, it is possible to visualize a state comprising many nationalities, for example, the U.S.S.R. Many of the Asian-African states are nations in the making, trying to weld different ethnic communities into one nation.

Current Trends

Conventional political science, as the preceding discussion shows, emphasised either political ideas such as liberty, equality, justice or political institutions such as state, government, laws etc. This was till Karl Marx presented a radical alternative. Marxian philosophy, however, was largely rejected by liberal thinkers of Europe and pragmatic thinkers of America, although several notable thinkers in these continents continued to develop Marxist ideas in their own tradition.

The most dominant trend of twentieth century Political Science has been Behaviourism which you will study in detail in Unit 2. In 1908 Graham Wallas in his *Human Nature in Politics,* pioneered the study of political motivation as a new, non-institutional factor in political life. Stirred by Wallas, Bentley, Charles Merriam and George Catlin. Harold Lasswell interpreted politics as a System of relationships with respect to power. By the middle of the twentieth century, the view became widespread that, power, defined through the concept of 'decision' was the crux of politics. In 1953, David Easton enunciated the concept of 'Political System' replacing the earlier existing idea of state. He defined Political System as a network of inter-relations, in which authoritative decisions for society were formulated and carried out. Through the concept of power and political system. Behaviouralism sought to give operative meanings to politics. In simpler terms, the emphasis shifted from institutional and structural studies to studies of political activity, orientation, motivation and behaviour of men. The study of ideas was replaced by the study of facts and evidence. In reaction to the perceived weakness and inadequacies of Behaviouralism, a counter movement called Post Behaviourlism was started by Easton in 1969. Post-Behaviouralism was a modification of Behaviouralism. Rejecting the notion of pure science based on the artificially created fact-value dichotomy, post-behaviouralism advocated inclusion of values and ideals in scientific method. It was, thus, an attempt to synthesise the positive elements of both Traditional and Behavioural Political Science.

Both in Europe and India, similar advocacy of restoration of a synthesis or interaction between political analysis and practice, has been presisting for long. Humanists like Jean Paul Sartre and Gandhi, radicals like Mao, Marcuse and M.N. Roy and revivalist Philosophers like Oakeshott, Voegelin and Strauss—have all striven for ethical and just political order. A just political order, in their view, would ensure principled politics.

Currently, therefore, Political Science, is characterised by stimulating signs of growth and dynamism.

The scope and definition of Political Science has changed through the ages. Politics has been defined as institutional activity, as power and process, as idea and ideology, depending on the approach of study. Plato, Aristotle, Machiavelli, Rousseau and Marx are major builders of Western philosophical traditions of Political Science. Lasswell, Catlin, Easton, Dahl and Deutsch are notable Behaviouralists. Kautilya, Gandhi and M.N. Roy are among the notable Indian thinkers. European institutions, American pragmatism and Eastern philosophy have in their own ways contributed to the growth of Political Science. Political Science is the sum of all these ideas, institutions and activities. In Political Science, the State occupies the centre stage. Some consider man as a political being. Others hold that Political activities are not natural to man. These were artificially created.

2

Human Society: Its Development

Basic Concepts

Man is a social being and therefore cannot exist outside society. What is man and what is human society? What are the relations between them?

In order to exist people must eat and dress, have dwellings, and so forth. They produce their food and clothes and build dwellings with the help of instrument of labour. The production of the instruments of labour and everything else necessary for life is an eternal, natural and essential basis of man's existence.

In the process of production the human individual sets the instrument of labour, machines in motion and with their help acts upon metal, wood, soil and other objects of labour in order to obtain the necessary product. The employment of the instruments to labour to produce the required products is labour, i.e., the purposeful practical activity of a human individual. Not only man but some animals, too, possess the ability to create: birds build nests, beavers build long dams across rivers, and monkeys use sticks and stones for specific purposes. But not a single animal can improve or develop its "production". Only the history of man and humanity is characterised by a continuous improvement of the means of labour and ways of producing them.

What distinguishes human labour from the activity of animals is its conscious, purposeful character. Karl Marx wrote that what distinguishes the worst architect from the best of bees is that he raises his structure in imagination before he erects it in reality, while the bee builds its honeycombs instinctively. The bee does not have to be taught to build honeycombs. This knowledge is instinctive. All the other bees before it built exactly the same honeycombs.

Man, however, sets himself a goal, evolves a plan for achieving it and acts accordingly. This type of activity is characteristic of man only: it was inherent in him in the past, when he engaged in primitive hunting, and it is inherent today, when he controls the most sophisticated machinery.

We know that man's labour is connected with his consciousness. But consciousness in its turn is closely connected with speech, with language, by means of which man communicates with other human beings, expressing and conveying his thoughts to them. Articulate speech is characteristic of man alone, and each generation as it grows up has to learn a language in order to be able to participate in joint activity. Animals also emit sounds signalling food, danger, and so forth, but these sounds cannot be called speech. Speech is connected with man's ability to generalise, to think in abstract terms, i.e., to comprehend things and phenomena.

Thus *labour, consciousness and speech* are qualities which distinguish man from animals and endow him with the ability to engage in forms of joint activity inherent only in the human individual.

Insofar as people work and act jointly they enter into definite relations which are called social relations. *People with their activity and mutual relations comprise a society.* Since society can exist and develop only in the process of human activity, man can be only a social being. To understand a man, his way of life and thinking, it is necessary in the first place to determine the type of society in which he lives and what this society stands for. Therefore all social sciences are sciences about human beings.

Man studies life and cognises nature. Science has explored the atom, it is discovering ever new sources of energy and is studying celestial bodies. People must be armed with knowledge in order to apprehend the world in which they live and consciously to transform nature in the interests of mankind. At the same time man must possess knowledge about society, about himself. But mankind covered a long and different path of development before it witnessed the rise of social science giving people a true knowledge of the laws of social development.

This happened when the proletariat emerged as an active revolutionary force and placed the struggle for the socialist reconstruction of life on the agenda of historical development. The brilliant creators of this science were Karl Marx, Frederick Engels and Vladimir Lenin.

The Marxist science of society is called historical materialism. A study of this science discloses the substance of the historical process and its motive forces, the structure of society at various stages of history, the role played by the masses and the individual in social development and the place of socialism in human history and prospects of its further development. This knowledge is essential to everyone who wants to comprehend the surrounding world, the meaning of events and the significance of the struggle for humanity's better future—the communist future.

Social Formations, Production and the Laws of Its Development

The Concept of a Social Formation

Living conditions in various epochs and countries different substantially from each other, just as they do today, when there are about 200 states with an aggregate population of 3,700 million in the world. There are even some countries with remnants of the tribal system or those with feudal relations. People live in capitalist and socialist states, i.e., at different levels of social development.

A specific historical stage in the development of society is called a socio-economic formation. The history of mankind is not a conglomerate of incidental events, but a definite process leading from bottom to top, from the simplest to the more sophisticated types of socio-economic formations. In the course of its development from the lowest social formation, the primitive-communal system, to the communist formation, which is the highest and whose first stage is socialism, mankind passes through the slave-owning system, feudalism and capitalism. Each nation at a given period of its existence belongs to one or another formation, depending on the level of its socio-economic development.

However different are the history, culture and modes of life of such countries as the USA, FRG, Britain, France, Italy, Japan and Australia, all of them are capitalist countries where factories, land, roads, forests, mineral deposits, etc., are owned by the capitalists. That determines other aspects of life in capitalist society: political, for power likewise belongs to those who own the wealth, and intellectual, for science, culture and education are levers by means of which the ruling class strengthens its position.

A characteristic feature of socialist countries is the domination of public ownership of the means of production which engenders relations of co-operation between people and eliminates exploitation of man by man. Compared with capitalism, socialism is a higher stage of social development. It appeared as a result of socialist revolutions and subsequent economic, socio-political and cultural transformations.

We have already said that survivals of precapitalist formations stills exist in a number of countries, including some African ones, whose development has been greatly retarded as a result of protracted colonial rule of the imperialist states. The imperialists held on to these countries as sources of raw materials and cheap manpower for the advanced capitalist states. The majority of the formerly enslaved countries have already freed themselves of colonial domination. Given the necessary conditions they will be able to take the path of non-capitalist development; whether this will happen or not will depend on the outcome of the acute struggle between progressive and reactionary forces.

The economy and politics, the state and the law, technology and science, everything is interconnected in a human society, and changes in any one sphere engender changes in another. The interaction of all aspects of social life takes place on the basis of the production of essential material wealth.

Inasmuch as the history of mankind is a succession of socio-economic formations it is very important to have a thorough knowledge of structure of each of these formations, i.e., the interaction of all the forces operating in a society in a given period of time.

The Structure of Socio-Economic Formations

The existence of any human society depends on the production of material wealth. Production is a very broad concept. As a rule people engage in specific types of production. For instance, field husbandry, gardening, orcharding and animal husbandry are types of agricultural production. The extraction of coal, oil, and ore are branches of the mining industry. The heavy industry produces machines and other means of labour, while the light and food industry turns out fabrics, shoes and foodstuffs. All these branches are closely interconnected: industry supplies agriculture with machines, and agriculture supplies industrial enterprises with new materials.

Modern production is inconceivable without transport and communications, research and designing institutes and other branches of labour.

The chief element of any type of production is the means of labour, i.e., machines and mechanisms, fuel and other power resources, store-houses and factory buildings, everything that man uses to produce the necessary products and to act on nature. At the same time it is impossible to carry on production without people possessing adequate knowledge, experience and skill. The means of labour and people who use these means comprise society's productive forces.

In addition to making food, clothes, dwellings, means of labour and everything else that is necessary for life, people enter into what are called relations of production. Without these relations they would be unable to live together. The forces of production and the relations of production together define the mode of production.

Each socio-economic formation has its own mode of production: the feudal mode of production is the basis of the feudal formation, the capitalist mode of production is the basis of the capitalist formation, and so forth.

Why is the mode of production the determinative basis of life and social development?

Labour productivity and, consequently, society's wealth depend on the level of development of the means of labour and on how successfully people learn to master them. At the dawn of the human history instruments of labour were extremely primitive. The man employed stone axes, spears, bows and arrows and wooden hoes with which he hunted, fished, gathered fruits and engaged in primitive farming. Naturally, such a production base was not conducive to the rise of a prosperous and flourishing society.

The appearance of improved instruments of labour stimulated the development of society. A most important development in the productive forces was the transition from handicrafts tools, which people used over many centuries, to machine production which first appeared in England in the latter half of the 18th century. The improvement in production was so significant that it came to be known as the industrial revolution. The rapid and widespread introduction of machine production gave a powerful impetus to the development and consolidation of capitalist relations.

Thus each social formation rests on a definite level of development of the forces of production.

Social formations differ from the another in the first place in the relations of production. The relations of production are determined by the from of ownership of the basic means of production, i.e., the objects and means of labour. In Ancient Rome, for example, wealthy landowners possessed great landed estates (latifundia), the tools for cultivating the land and the slaves who worked on it. This from of ownership determined the relations between people in the process of production as relations between a slave and a slave-owner. The slave-owning form of ownership gave rise to the slave-owning social system

Under capitalism ownership has a different character. The capitalist owns only the means of production, while the worker is formally free, he can be neither bought nor sold. Yet, in order to exist, a worker is compelled to sell his labour power, to get a job at a capitalist enterprise where the capitalist is the owner and the worker does what he is hired to do, where the former gets the profits and the latter a wage. As a result society's main wealth accumulates in the hands of the capitalists.

The relations of production are called the economic basis of society. In other words, the basis is the economic system of a society at a given stage of its development. A corresponding superstructure arises on the basis. The conception "superstructure" also embraces a wide sphere of human relations. It is the political relations between various classes with their programmes of struggle for power; it is the state with all its instruments of compulsion in the form of the army, courts and prisons; it is the ideology of the various classes and social groups expressed in various forms—political, legal, moral, aesthetic, religious and philosophic. What unites all these heterogeneous phenomena?

They have at least two common features. First, they stem from the society's economic basis. Second, they serve to perpetuate, strengthen and develop the economic system on whose basis they have appeared, or to overthrow it, when they are the programmes and ideologies of the exploiting classes.

Let us examine the relation between politics and economy, for example. The politics of every class is determined chiefly by its economic interests. What is a capitalist's main interest? Since he owns property and money, he is concerned with preserving the social system which ensures his wealth and strengthening the relations which enable him to multiply his capital. It is this economic interest which above all determines the policies of the capitalist class and capitalist states, a policy of strengthening and consolidating the foundations of capitalism, a policy of fighting against the revolutionary and national liberation movement, a policy of anti-communism. This relation between politics and economy is definitely and concisely expressed in the Marxist formula: politics is the concentrated expression and consummation of economy.

Of course, politics is relatively independent with regard to economy and can exert great influence upon it. In order to explain the policy of a state we should have to take into account not only the economic interests of the ruling class in a given state, but also the latter's position in the system of other states, its historical and national traditions, the correlation of its social forces and many other factors. Still, the politics of a state depends in the first place on its economic situation and the economic interests of its ruling class.

Other superstructural phenomena are removed from economy further than politics and are not linked directly with economy. In the final count, however, the superstructure and all its components are either engendered by the economic basis, or are determined by it either directly or indirectly. We should always bear this in mind if we wish to examine scientifically the politics of one or another state, class or party, the essence of their political programmes and declarations, the character of the ideas dominating a given society.

Politics, being a concentrated expression of economy, serves it by supporting a corresponding social system. Any state has an apparatus of coercion and an apparatus of administration with which it protects and upholds the existing order. This means that elements of the superstructure engendered by economy are not passive, but forcefully act on the basis.

All the elements of the superstructure are connected by their common origin and their social function.

The basis and superstructure taken together characterises every social formation: the basis expresses its economic foundation, while the superstructure expresses its political and ideological forms. Thus, in a feudal state the nobility, land-owners and feudal lords held the dominating position. As a rule feudal states were monarchies. Society was divided into estates, each with its strictly defined rights, and transition from a lower estate to a higher one was almost impossible. The bourgeois state proclaimed the formal equality of citizens before the law and abolished the estates. In this state people were distinguished by their economic status, by their wealth, in the first place. Karl Marx used to say that a bourgeois carried his power in his pocket. This power is money. All the other distinctions between people recede into the background in the face of this chief idol of capitalist society.

It follows, therefore, that every society, i.e., every social formation, differs from another not only as regards its economic, but also as regards its political system.

The appearance of a socialist society gives rise to a qualitatively new type of state—the dictatorship of the proletariat, which gradually develops into a socialist state of the entire people.

Every social formation is dominated by ideas reflecting the interests of the ruling class. In the Middle Ages (6th-16th centuries), for instance, the Catholic Church was a tremendous social force in Italy, Spain, France, Germany, and some other countries and the religious Catholic ideology was predominant there. The Church subjugated everything: science and art, and morality, and was a great political force at the same time. Hence, it was only natural that the first actions undertaken by the bourgeoisie against feudalism had the form of religious movements, Further on, science joined the fight against feudalism. The most consistent struggle against the ruling religious ideology was waged by 17th-18th century materialist philosophers who attuned people's mentality for the impending bourgeois revolution.

Religion has lost its leading position in a bourgeois society, although it retains considerable ideological influence. Having cast off all the oppression of the Church natural science made great progress in their development. And an important role in bourgeois society is played by political and legal ideology.

This means that transition from one social formation to another is accompanied by important changes both in the basis and the superstructure, and these transformations attest to the birth of a new society.

As we have gathered from the above, the production of material wealth is the core of any social formation and, consequently, of all the important changes in the development of human society.

Society and Nature

In the process of labour man interacts with nature, which itself is a general object of labour. The process of labour is in fact the transformation of nature, the adaptation of natural objects to man's requirements. And so it follows that natural conditions influence the process of labour and can be either propitious or unfavourable. Yet people can surmount unfavourable effects of natural conditions. For instance, the rigorous conditions of the Far North with its long cold winters, long polar nights and permafrost deprive people of the possibility of engaging in agriculture and create great difficulties for the development of industry, trade and the construction of communications. It was due to these factors that the peoples of the Far North had remained at the level of the tribal system in their social development. The October Socialist Revolution and the assistance of the other peoples of the Soviet Union opened the road to modern forms of life for the ethnic groups of north and the rise of socialist relations among them.

While in the past the peoples of the Far North engaged solely in fishing and deer-breeding, now there are towns and a developing heavy industry inside the Arctic Circle. One such town in Norilsk. It has a mining and metallurgical combine, factories turning out pre-fabricated house parts, cement and ferro-concrete items and other industrial enterprises. It also has a college of mining and metallurgy, a repertoire drama theatre, etc. The Far North's immense natural wealth has promoted the rapid development of industry and construction. But in order to surmount the unfavourable influence of the natural conditions, man must have the necessary material means and a high level of production.

At the early stages of the development of human society, when the means of labour were extremely primitive, man depended to an enormous degree on nature, on the elemental forces. For example, he depended on whether his geographical environment was rich in fish, game and edible plants, inasmuch as his principal sources of livelihood were hunting, fishing and the gathering of edible plants. Later, when people began to cultivate land, their welfare depended largely on the climate and soil fertility. With the development of heavy industry which takes in metals, mineral raw materials, coal, oil, the energy of rivers and so forth in enormous quantities, territories abounding in these natural resources acquired the utmost importance. Today people utilise the earth's natural wealth in vast and ever increasing amounts; that means that the question of its economical and rational use is a matter of the greatest significance for the further development of human society.

Consequently, natural conditions can and do influence the development of production, either favourable or unfavourably, promoting the development of a given society or retarding its progress. At the same time the character and the strength of their influence depend on the level of a nation's social development.

Society not only experiences the influence of natural conditions, it also alters them. As the productive forces of society developed, people acquired increasingly powerful means of acting on their natural environment. They were able to transform nature to an ever greater degree and adapt it to their own requirements. Today nature in its primordial state has been preserved most probably only in the polar regions, in the impassable taiga and the ocean depths. The reason is obvious. A modern advanced state cannot exist without large towns, industrial complexes, a ramified system of railways and highways, numerous canals and man-made reservoirs, fields, orchards, and so forth.

Soviet socialist society has set itself the task of steadily transforming nature in the interests of man in order to create the most favourable conditions for his life and health.

But the relationship between man and nature is a many-sided, complicated problem, and society must foresee how its utilisation of natural resources effects nature itself. At times environmental changes favourable to man are accompanied by unexpected and harmful consequences. And the more powerful the means of man's acting on nature, the more adverse may be the impact if society fails to control its own interaction with nature.

This problem has never been as acute as it is today. Once it was generally believed that any harm which industry might cause nature was subsequently neutralised by the elements themselves. Reality, however, proved that this view was not only erroneous, but also dangerous, for changes harmful to man taking place in nature may prove to be irreversible. Today the air and water pollution from industrial waste, the destruction of forests and the contamination of huge areas with various waste have acquired such enormous proportions that without the effective and systematic work by society it is practically impossible to combat the harm caused to nature. Yet, the domination of private property in capitalist society inhibits the introduction of broad measures to protect and improve the natural environment, and the monopolists' thirst for profits leads to predatory utilisation of the natural wealth.

The problem of relations between man and nature, or the ecological problem, as it is called, is becoming more and more international in character. The most favourable conditions for its solution, naturally, exist in socialist countries whose planned economy is subordinated to the interests of the people. Obviously, it is impossible to solve all problems arising there immediately, for that would have entailed vast financial outlays. But the Soviet state is using the available possibilities to build installations at industrial enterprises to protect the atmosphere and water from pollution, rehabilitate forests, prevent soil erosion, improve urban life (planting of trees in streets, combating noise, etc.), and use natural resources more rationally. The Soviet Government has promulgated the law "On Measures of Further Improving the Protection of Nature and the Rational Utilisation of the Natural Resources". The protection of nature is not only the concern of society as a whole, but of each separate individual, too.

The Law of the Conformity of the Production Relations to the Productive Forces

The productive forces determine the development of society and define society's attitude to nature. Man's power over nature corresponds to the level of development of the forces of production.

Man's first tools were made of wood, stone and bone. Then people learned to smelt metal. The appearance of iron tools was a milestone in the development of the forces of production. "Today people employ not only the materials which they find in nature, but also create new, synthetic materials possessing properties which man needs.

Here is another example. At first people used their own muscular energy to set the instruments of labour in motion, then began to use the strength of animals. Gradually mankind learned to employ new types of energy: the energy of water and wind, steam and electricity, and now it also uses the energy of the atom.

The means of labour and the productive forces reflect the level of man's knowledge of nature and embody the production experience which he has accumulated. The level of development of the production forces is a gauge of society's progress.

Production is the basic form of human activity. The relations between people in the process of production do not depend on the will of the people and take shape in conformity with the character of the productive forces. The necessity that relations of production should be adapted to the productive forces arises from the very substance of production. It is just as impossible, for example, to build capitalism in the stone age, or to establish primitive-communal relations on the basis of large-scale industry, as to dress a full-grown man in baby clothes. If the productive forces correspond to the production relations then the former develop freely and society flourishes. But this conformity does not last for ever. The productive forces are in a state of constant change, for people are continuously improving the instruments of production. The development of productive forces can be very slow, so slow, in fact, that thousands of years pass by before any noticeable changes make their appearance, as was the case during primitive-communal system. It can also be relatively fast, even very fast, when perceptible changes in productive forces take place in the course of centuries and even decades.

The more sophisticated the means of production, the more advanced should be the production relations. This means that these relations must change. But in a capitalist as in any other exploiting society changes in the relations of production are inhibited by classes and groups which are not interested in seeing them change. The relations begin to lag behind the productive forces with the result that they not only do not promote the latter's development but, to the contrary, slow down their growth. This causes a conflict.

As a result it becomes necessary to replace the outmoded production relations with more progressive ones, and this means that the old social formation has outlived itself.

In an exploiting society such a situation calls not only for a change in the economic, but also in the political system inasmuch as the latter hinders the development of new production relations. Therefore the conflict between the new productive forces and the old relations of production is the economic foundation of social revolution which is the sole form of transition from one social formation to another.

Development of Socio-Economic Formations

Man has always been a social being. In primordial times people united according to their kinship into clans and tribes. Leading a nomad way of life they gathered edible plants, hunted and fished, Inside the clan matrimonial relations were prohibited and each clan united matrilinear relatives. Work was assigned according to the physical abilities of each individual. In other words, there existed a sex-age division of labour. All that people obtained through joint labour was equally divided between them and thus they were able to keep themselves alive.

What sort of production existed in those times?

The primitive man had such primitive tools that he could not exist by himself. This weakness of the individual in the face of nature was what forced people to unite. Only by living and working together could they stand up to nature and obtain food and other necessities. Evidently the primitive collective of people using individual primitive tools was the first productive force in human history. Collective labour and collective mode of life gave rise to equal distribution of products i.e., to such relations of production which precluded the possibility of exploitation.

Due to the extremely slow growth of the productive forces the production relations remained in conformity with the collective productive force of a primitive clan for many thousands of years. Gradually, however, some tribes, either as a result of favourable natural conditions, or for other reasons, began to attain a higher level of development of productive forces compared to the mass of humanity scattered throughout the world. Cropping and livestock breeding appeared. Stone tools gave way to bronze and then iron. People obtained more reliable sources of food, began to lay in food supplies and accumulate diverse types of material wealth, i.e., the productive forces reached a level at which it became possible to obtain surplus product. Surplus product is that part of the produced material wealth which remains after most essential requirements are satisfied. The surplus product gave rise to two important trends in social development.

First, it became possible to accumulate this product and redistribute it. In other words, there appeared an economic basis for the rise of inequality when some clans, tribes or individuals began to seize cattle, weapons, etc., while others lost them. Plunder and, consequently, wars for wealth became possible.

Second, exploitation came into being. Exploitation means the appropriation of the fruits of someone else's. So long as people produced only as much as they needed to survive, an individual could not exploit the labour of another individual. But as soon as man began to produce more than he needed to survive, he opened the road to exploitation. Thus slavery was established.

Although the instruments of labour became more productive, they remained adapted to individual use, and an individual or a family could produce all they needed for sustenance: plough the land and keep cattle. Interest in common tribal economy disappeared. On the other hand, as we have said earlier, people could now accumulate wealth. All this undermined the foundations of primitive collectivism and equality in distribution. Society split into the rich and the poor, into the slaves and the slave-owners Classes appeared. The primitive system gave way to a class society in which the economically dominant class lived at the expense of the labour of the oppressed class, thus engendering economic and social inequality and irreconcilable class contradictions.

The transition to a class society was a progressive phenomenon because it considerably accelerated the growth of the productive forces. The accumulation of wealth facilitated exchange and trade, and towns development as centres of trade and crafts. Groups of people who did not produce material wealth but devoted their time to diverse intellectual activity emerged in society. In other words, the era of the rise of a class society witness the separation of mental and physical labour, a most important precondition for the development of man's spiritual culture. The rise of classes was accompanied by the formation of states.

Social progress has a contradictory nature. When classes came into being, mankind began to advance at the expense of ruthless exploitation of the majority of the people, at the expense of the enslavement of the working people through sanguinary wars and plunder. Everything was placed on the altar of wealth and power; the basest human vices and instincts were rampant.

Such a society is called antagonistic.

History knows three antagonistic class societies: the slave-owning, feudal and capitalist.

Pre-capitalist class societies have one common feature: they have a primitive technical basis consisting of the wooden plough, hammer, axe, potter's wheel and other instruments of labour with which people obtained food and clothes, accumulated wealth, built houses, temples and sailing ships.

Very little could be done to improve on these tools: a hammer is a hammer and an axe is an axe whatever their shapes. With such a technical basis the labour productivity was very low and that accounted for the slow development of the slave-owning and feudal societies.

The technical basis of a developed feudal society was higher than that of the slave-owning society which existed, for example, in Ancient Greece or Rome. The status of the toiling people was also different. A slave was the chattel of the slave-owner. A slave had neither property, nor family nor a home and he was not interested in the result of his labour.

The chief productive force in a feudal society was the peasant who was personally dependent on the feudal landowner.

The most brutal semislave form of this dependence was serfdom. But a peasant had a home, family, tools and a plot of land, and although he was not a free man he was interested in obtaining more means for sustaining his family and himself, he had to pay labour rent (corvée), turn over a designated part of the harvest to the church, and so forth.

In the slave-owning and feudal societies the private character of the instruments of labour corresponded to the individual nature of the activity of a peasant or craftsman. Small-scale production and natural economy were predominant in both of them. The large-scale property of the slave-owner or the feudal lord developed on the basis of non-economic coercion, since neither the one nor the other could economically force the slave or the serf of work for him. Such were the main features of these formations. Their antagonistic nature manifested itself in an acute class struggle which at times took the form of armed uprisings, including such major ones as the slave revolt against Rome led by Spartacus (74-71 B. C.), the revolt in England led by Wat Tyler in 1381, the peasant wars in Germany (1524-25) and in Russia led by Stepan Razin (1670-71) and Yemelyan Pugachev (1773-75).

The level of social development was not the same throughout the world, for the human society advances unevenly. In ancient times and the Middle Ages a considerable portion of people in Asia, Africa, Australia and America still lived in tribal systems. When the feudal system became established in some European countries, the decaying slave-owning system still existed in other parts of the world. This uneven development is observed throughout the history of mankind.

The next stage in the development of class antagonistic society was capitalism.

Machine production became the technical basis of capitalism, although the first signs of capitalist relations appeared long before the machine acquired a leading place in production. The qualitative leap occasioned by the emergence of machine production had far-reaching consequences. This stage of development of productive forces was characterised by the introduction of scientific achievements in production, rationalisation and improvement of machines, technology and the organisation of production, and a continuous rise in the productivity of labour.

Under the system of capitalist ownership of the means of production, the owner of the capital economically forces the proletarian, a person who has no property, to work for him. Only vital necessity compels the worker to hire himself out to the capitalist.

Why does a capitalist hire workers? Not out of pity, of course, but to derive profit, of the workers create surplus value.

What is surplus value? It is the value of the product which a worker produces without compensation, since his wage is always smaller than the value of the commodity he has created. Theirin lies the essence of capitalist relations of production.

It is surplus value, which the capitalist receives in the form of profit by appropriating the product of the unpaid labor of workers, that is the chief stimulus of capitalist production. In their striving for profit the interests of the capitalists clash and a struggle for still greater profits begins. This struggle is called competition, and the winner is the capitalist whose production is better organised and who equips it with more sophisticated machinery and manages to sell his commodity more profitably. The race for profits and competition compel the capitalist to improve production and technology and turn out greater quantities of commodities. The production of more goods than can be purchased on the market leads to crises of overproduction.

These crises, however, do not in the least testify to an absolute excess of commodities. The demand for them still exists, but people cannot afford to purchase them because they do not have the money for it. Overproduction leads to the closure of factories and the dismissal of workers who swell the ranks of the unemployed. This still further narrows the demand for commodities. Crises are not of the most characteristic features of the capitalist system. Modern industrial production calls for a rational planned organisation which takes into account nation-wide demand and consumption.

Crises show that capitalism is unable to cope with this task.

The class struggle under capitalism becomes more acute. Workers unit and fight for better living and working conditions. This struggle takes the form of strikes, demonstrations and revolutionary uprisings.

Thus, ruthless competition, periodic crises and the unceasing class struggle attest to the contradictory nature of the capitalist system, the growing disparity between the productive forces and the production relations. The basic contradiction of capitalism is precisely the disparity between the nature of production and methods of appropriation of the fruits of production. The production process is social inasmuch as in present-day conditions millions of people bound by production relations jointly produce all the necessary commodities. But the product of this social production is appropriated by private owners.

Private property, however, can be turned into public property. Then not only the necessary but also the surplus product can be distributed in the interests of the whole of society. On the basis of public property it is possible to abolish competition, and effectively plan production on a scale corresponding to the entire society and in its interests. The social nature of production should be matched by public ownership of the means of production with its specific organisation of labour and forms of distribution. This, however, is possible only under socialism.

The bourgeoisie would like to resolve or at the least to smooth over the contradictions inherent in the capitalist system. Production is becoming increasingly socialised: individual capitalists are being replaced by associations of capitalists—firms, trusts and giant monopolies. Monopoly capitalism is developing and turning into state-monopoly capitalism, which is an indication of the recognition of the social character of the productive forces within the framework of the capitalist system itself. But the whole point is that monopoly property remains private capitalist in character, and monopoly profits are distributed among the shareholders. Monopolies do not abolish competition because they themselves compete on a world-wide scale. And the small and medium-size private enterprises, too, are locked in a sustained and embittered struggle for raw materials and consumer markets.

Monopoly capital is the source and the perpetrator of fearful crimes against humanity. It was responsible for the outbreak of two world wars which took a toll of dozens of millions of human lives. And it was monopoly capitalism that fathered fascism which is ever pregnant with the threat of reaction and violence.

Apologists of capitalism assert that the position which the working class in the advanced capitalist countries holds today does not permit the capitalists to cut wages impunely and compels them to pay fairly high wages to the workers, and therefore the class struggle is petering out. This is an illusion, an attempt at wishful thinking. The working people are winning their rights in the course of long years of fierce class struggle, at the cost of incalculable sacrifices. This struggle is not only continuing, it is becoming ever more acute.

Certainly, in developed capitalist countries such as the USA. the FRG, France and Britain a qualified worker receives a relatively high wage. He has also won other social rights, especially in the period following the Socialist Revolution in Russia in 1917. However, this does not mean that injustice, inequality and oppression have been wiped out in these countries. In capitalist society a person who works remains oppressed and is constantly aware of his dependence on the capitalist who can fire him at any moment and thus deprive him of shelter and food. Moreover, even in advanced capitalist countries the incomes of very many people are lower than the subsistence minimum.

For a long time capitalism exploited hundreds of millions of people in colonial countries. The colonial system collapsed but backwardness and poverty weigh heavily on the shoulders of toiling people in many African, Asian and Latin American countries. The peoples of the developing states are faced with the difficult problems of further development which are solved in the course of the struggle against imperialism and bitter social conflicts.

The development of state-monopoly capitalism did not smooth out, but exacerbated the internal contradictions of the capitalist system, and the scientific and technological revolution, that qualitatively new phase in the development of the modern forces of production, aggravated them to a still greater extent.

What is a scientific and technological revolution?

One of its features is that it radically alters the already developed industrial production, opening qualitatively new prospects before it. The chief trend in the transformation of technology is the creation of automated production, first partially and then fully. The prerequisites for such automation lie in the development of cybernetics and electronic computers with the help of which machines are able to control technological processes.

Another feature of the scientific and technological revolution is the growing implementation of scientific achievements in production, the transformation of science into an actual productive force, when modern equipment appears as the direct result of the development and application of science. The organic fusion of science and production as we are witnessing today has no precedent in history. And indeed, atomic energy, space flights, the production of synthetic materials with set properties, electronics, lasers, these and many other achievements arise from science and not merely as a result of the accumulated experience, as was the case in the past. The organic connection between scientific and technological progress is the distinguishing feature of the scientific and technological revolution.

Sophisticated technology makes it possible considerable to raise labour productivity and introduces serious in the very structure and organisation of production. But the most important result and the distinctive feature of the scientific and technological revolution is that it modifies man's role in production. On the basis of automated technology and the application of scientific methods, serial production will be increasingly guided by machines which do not require the direct participation of man in the technological process. His job will be controlling the operation of machines, handling repairs, designing and building new machines and performing other creative functions connected with production.

The craftsman set in motion his instruments of production chiefly by his own muscle energy, and in machine production, too, the worker became an appendage to the machine, but the machines created by the modern scientific and technological revolution will make man the master of the self-regulating (automatic) production process. Such is the prospect opened by the scientific and technological revolution. Today we are witnessing the beginning of this process for automated shops even in advanced countries have so far accounted for an insignificant part of the entire production.

The scientific and technological revolution will raise production to such a level that it will be possible to create the material and technical basis for the achievement of the maximum material wealth, reduce the working day and employ people's strength and abilities primarily in the field of creative work. But whether the achievements of the scientific and technological revolution will be employed to the benefit of the working man depends on the social system where it is developing—within the capitalist framework or in socialist society.

Capitalism takes advantage of the growth of the productive forces and the scientific and technological progress to intensify the exploitation of the working people and strengthen its system of domination and oppression. In capitalist conditions the scientific and technological revolution further strengthens the state-monopoly organisation which turns the working man into a particle, a tiny screw in the powerful capitalist machine.

As it promotes industrial development the scientific and technological revolution undermines capitalism, exacerbates its contradictions and increases the incompatibility of the growing productive forces with the narrow framework of the capitalist economy, with the character of the production relations, and engenders class conflicts.

The socio-economic system that corresponds to the modern character and prospects of further development of productive forces is socialist society. Socialism is the highest stage that mankind has so far achieved in its progress. And it is socialism that can make the best of the scientific and technological revolution and, most important, employ it in the interests of man.

Let us sum up all that has been said in this section.

Human history is movement from the lower to higher forms of social life and its leading force is the development of the productive forces. We have examined only the general aspects of the main line, the basic trend of social development. The knowledge of the stages of social development furnished by Marxist theory makes it possible to comprehend historical phenomena in their entire diversity, to analyse the past, assess the present and foresee the future.

At the same time the materialist theory of social development is not a fixed scheme; it calls for a concrete analysis of concrete historical phenomena. Historical progress is uneven and the rise of a new formation does not immediately cause the disappearance of the preceding one. Survivals of primitive-communal relations, for example, continue to exist for a long time in a class society. Survivals of feudalism are still found in some backward countries. Whole peoples, states and cultures perished in wars or disappeared due to other reasons. Many of the peoples which exist today passed over the above stage of social development. The Slav peoples, for instance, moved from primitive-communal relations directly into feudalism, bypassing the slave-owning formation. Many peoples living in the Soviet Union stepped from patriarchal, feudal relations into socialism, without passing through the capitalist stage of development. There are many similar examples.

The general theoretical principles, Lenin noted, are creatively applied to different countries inasmuch as each one has its historic, national, cultural and other features influencing its development. At the same time these general principles mirror the general laws of social development which determine the course of world history and which force their way through the numerous varieties of the concrete historical process. In our time it was the operation of these general laws that launched the capitalist social formation towards its inevitable end. A new, communist social formation is beginning to take shape and develop. This being the case, the contemporary epoch taken on the world historic scale is an epoch of transition from capitalism to socialism. The countries of the world socialist system are standing at the initial stage of the communist social formation.

What are the main features of a communist social formation?

The Communist Socio-Economic Formation

The economic basis of this formation is public ownership of the means of production. At the present stage public property has two forms: state property and co-operative and collective-farm property. It is this form of property that corresponds to the social nature of the production process and creates infinite opportunities for the growth of the productive forces.

The construction of communist society, as any other stage of historical development, is characterised by contradictions between the productive forces and the production relations. In this case, however, their solution is not attended by social conflicts and political revolution and is achieved as a result of conscious and planned improvement of the production relations. This is possible, first, because public property does away with exploitation of man by man, abolishes the exploiting classes, and the life of the entire society is guided by common interests; and, second, because the tasks and problems facing society can be resolved consciously and in a planned way. In a communist formation production, culture and social relations advance and improve at an especially rapid pace. Proof of this is the fact that the USSR developed into a mighty power with a highly advanced economy and culture in a mere 58 years.

The rise and development of the communist formation is a natural process. The material prerequisites for the transition to this formation are created in the depths of the capitalist system. The most important of them is modern production which unites the entire mass of the working people. The working class is the leading social force which consummates the socialist revolution in alliance with the working peasantry and lays the foundation of the communist social formation.

As it develops the communist social formation passes through several stages. The first is the transition period which begins with socialist revolution. In this period survivals of the overthrown classes (landowners and the bourgeoisie) are abolished and small peasant farms are transformation into large collective farms through cooperation and the development of the industrial base of the new society. In the sphere of social thinking the scientific ideology of Marxism-Leninism gained the dominating position, and the masses begin acquiring socialist consciousness.

Politically, the transition period is one of the dictatorship of the proletariat, i.e., the state power of the proletariat established after the bourgeois government is deposed.

After carrying through the socialist revolution the proletariat inevitably encounters the resistance of the overthrown classes which can be suppressed by force only. Therefore the establishment of the dictatorship of the proletariat is the main content of socialist revolution.

At the same time the dictatorship of the proletariat has an important creative mission. It is the chief instrument in the building of socialism. The dictatorship of the proletariat is a form of the political guidance of all sections of the working people by the working class. Its purpose is to win over the mass of working people and draw them into construction of the new society. In contrast to bourgeois rule, the dictatorship of the proletariat does not stand in opposition to the mass of people, but expresses their fundamental interests.

The dictatorship of the proletariat can be effected in various political forms depending on the specific conditions of the development of socialist revolution. One form of the dictatorship of the proletariat was the Paris Commune (March 18 to May 28, 1871). Though short-lived, it was of great significance for it was the first time in history that the proletariat had come to power. The Soviets, a new form of the dictatorship of the proletariat, appeared in the course of the revolution in Russia. Building upon the teaching of Marx and Engels about the dictatorship of the proletariat, Lenin substantiated the historical significance of the

Republic of Soviets, a state of a new type, of consistent and real democracy. People's Democracy, which appeared in the countries that took the road of socialist development after the Second World War, became another form of the dictatorship of the proletariat.

The transition period ends with the establishment of socialist social relations. Socialism, the first phase of the communist formation, fully abolishes private ownership of the means of production and the exploiting classes. Socialism stands for the complete socio-political and ideological unity of society, of all its classes, strata and social groups; it abolishes national oppression and establishes relations of friendship between peoples based on the principle of socialist internationalism.

Once socialism has won, the dictatorship of the proletariat develops into a state of the entire people. It performs a number of important and essential functions, economic and organisational in the first place. The state expresses the fundamental interests of the people, of the whole of society in the economic sphere; it plans and manages the national economy; it serves as the organising authority in the solution of the tasks facing society, protects public and personal interests of the working people and upholds socialist law and order. Relying on the support of all working people, the state of the entire people enforces measures of compulsion with regard to people violating the laws and principles of socialist society. The socialist state puts in a vast amount of works to promote public education, raise the cultural level of the working people, foster communist consciousness and create conditions for a continuous development of culture and science. The socialist state carries out the crucial function of protecting the country, defending the socialist gains of the working people and promoting friendship and co-operation between socialist countries; it supports the international revolutionary liberation movement and upholds the cause of peace and international security.

The victory of socialism, the first phase of communism, in the USSR was reflected in the new Constitution adopted in 1936. After that the socialist society developed on its own foundation. The growth of the socialist economy and culture was accompanied by consolidation of socialism and the further strengthening of the socialist state. As a result the Soviet people achieved the complete and final victory of socialism and the country entered a period of a developed socialist society.

As it continues to advance, the socialist system more fully discloses its advantages over the capitalist system. One of its most important advantages is the steadily increasing role of the people in the building of the new society. The 24th CPSU Congress (1971) set the people and the Oarty the task of using the advantages of socialism, combining them with the scientific and technological revolution and further improving the entire system of management in order to gain more efficacy of production and accelerate the growth of the material welfare and cultural level of the people.

Under developed socialism people are in a position to solve tasks which society was unable to fulfill in the past. As a result of the tremendous growth of industrial and agricultural production the Soviet Union can speed up the rates of growth of consumer goods production and increase investments into agriculture without lowering the rates of heavy industry development. Thanks to their dedicated labour in the socialist industry and agriculture the Soviet people fulfill the main task of the five-year plan, that of securing a considerable rise in the standard of living and the cultural level of the people. Today the Soviet state is in a position to channel increasing efforts and means into the development of public education, literature, and art and thus promote the growth of the intellectual wealth of society.

The further prospects for the development of socialist society are connected with the transition from socialism, the lowest stage in the development of the communist formation, to complete communism, its highest stage.

Wherein lies the distinction between socialism and communism? The chief distinction is society's level of economic and spiritual maturity.

One of the most important directions in the growth of the productive forces is that of intensifying production and raising the level of its socialisation. Production is being enlarged and links between factories, and the various branches of production are becoming more and more intricate and diverse. The employment of new materials, the automation of production, and broad introduction of scientific methods and technical means of organisation and management will eventually do away with heavy and monotonous works and as a result the majority of people will work in various fields of creative labour. All this is bound to cause enormous changes in their mode of life.

Under socialism material wealth is distributed among the members of society chiefly according to the quality and quantity of the work they perform for society, i.e., in line with the principle "From each according to his ability, to each according to his work".

Society takes care that people develop their abilities and for this purpose improves the system of education. The introduction of universal secondary education is a matter of very great significance for the intellectual development of all working people and their increasing participation in creative labour.

It is the concern of socialist society that each individual should work in a field where he can make full use of his abilities and thus be of the greatest service to society. This problem, naturally, still requires its ultimate solution, but socialist society considers it one of the most important.

The socialist principle of distribution according to the work done is embodied in the existing system of wages. A large and steadily increasing part of the material wealth and services in the USSR is distributed among people through public consumption funds regardless of the quantity and quality of work contributed by an individual. These funds account for free education and medical treatment, grants to mothers of large families, state-owned housing, numerous holiday facilities, and so on and so forth.

Under communism the level of development of productive forces and labour productivity must be high enough to ensure an abundance of consumer goods. A new principle of distribution, "From each according to his ability, to each according to his needs", will become effective in communist society. But before this happens society will have to attain a new level of development of production which will become the material and technical basis of communism. Man himself will rise to a higher stage in the new conditions. In socialist society distinctions still exist between urban and rural labour, between mental and physical labour, and unskilled manual labour is still needed. The survivals of the old division of labour and non-creative labour which restricts man's intellectual growth can be abolished only through a high level of technological development, introduction of science into all branches of production, the latter's complex mechanisation and automation and high productivity of labour. These are enormous and complicated taskes, but their solution will create the necessary material basis for man's all-round progress, for the burgeoning of his abilities in all spheres of creative labour.

Gradually labour will cease to be an obligation and a means of subsistence; it will become a prime necessity of life and the interest of the individual in the very process of labour will become predominant. Naturally, elements of such an attitude exist in socialist society and more appear with each passing year. For instance, the underlying principle of the movement for a communist attitude to labour, which has attained broad scope at Soviet industrial enterprises and offices, is "to learn to live and work the communist way". But only under communism, when society enters the highest stage of its economic and spiritual maturity, when all substantial distinctions between town and country and between mental and physical labour have been abolished, will the all-round development of the individual be accompanied by the consolidation of a communist attitude to labour in the whole of society.

Distinctions between the classes of workers and peasants and the 'intelligentsia continus to exist under socialism, but they will gradually disappear as society advances towards communism. The distinctions between workers and peasants will be gradually obliterated as agricultural labour develops into a variety of industrial labour. The introduction of the achievements of science into production and the growth of its machine-to-man ratio call for greater knowledge on the part of the worker so that the gap between physical and mental labour will gradually narrow. This will result in the formation of a socially homogeneous society, a classless society, not only because there will be no exploitation of man by man (this is achieved under socialism), but also in the sense that there will be no distinctions between the working classes.

The eradication of distinctions between classes and social groups does not mean levelling people and abolishing individual distinctions. On the contrary, the abolition of classes will offer every member of society equal opportunities and create all the essential conditions for the development of the individual and the formation of a harmoniously developed man.

Great changes will take place in the organisation and management of the economy and in the sphere of social relations. The working class is the one and only class known to history which takes power into its hands not in order to perpetuate its domination but so as to abolish classes in general.

As society advances towards communism moral principles will play an increasing role in guiding the behaviour of people, and each individual will voluntarily and consciously perform his duties in society. This will accelerate the development of communist social self-government and the withering away of the state. But the question of the withering away of the state has an external aspect as well as an internal one. The historical necessity of the existence of the state will disappear only when the threat of war and the social antagonisms existing in the world have been fully eliminated. These conditions will be created when the communist social formation is established throughout the world, or at least in the majority of countries.

The building of a communist society is the immediate practical task of the Soviet people. A developed socialist society is a society which is building communism. Its purpose is defined in the CPSU Programme: *"Communism is a classless social system with one form of public ownership of the means of production and full social equality of all members of society; under it, the all-round development of people will be accompanied by the growth of the production forces through continuous progress in science and technology; all the springs of co-operative wealth will flow more abundantly, and the great principle 'From each according to his ability, to each according to his needs' will be implemented. Communism is a highly organised society of free, socially conscious working people in which public self-government will be established, a society in which labour for the good of society will become the prime vital requirement of everyone, a necessity recognised by one and all, and the ability of each person will be employed to the greatest benefit of the people."*

The history of mankind knows no greater or more double aim than that of building communism. The opponents of Marxism, the enemies of communism, are endeavoring to portray it as wild fantasy. But reality has proved the untenability of their arguments.

The idea of socialism and communism was advanced and scientifically substantiated by the founders of Marxism in the 19th century. Today socialism is an historical reality which undeniably confirms the correctness of the scientific prediction of the proletariat's great teachers.

The ideas of communism do not clash with the objective trends of development of the contemporary forces of production, the prospects of the scientific and technological revolution; on he contrary, they fully correspond to them, which also confirms the viability of these ideas.

Communism stands not only for the comprehensive development of production, science and culture, but also for their utilisation in the interests of man, their subordination to the tasks of serving man. This cannot be attained under capitalism, which places science and technology in opposition to man. But this target becomes absolutely realistic under socialism and communism, for the communist formation erases social antagonisms and places all the achievements of the human genius at the services of man to promote his all-round development. It follows, therefore, that the communist ideal can be fully translated into reality.

The Activity of People in History

Factors Determining the Activity of People

History is made by people. But when we say that history is a consistent process we simultaneously assert that people cannot make history arbitrarily, according to their will and contrary to the requirements of social development. For example, the Soviet Union cannot at present effect distribution according to needs, for so far its economic and cultural development has not attained the level which would make it possible to implement this principle. Therefore distribution is effected according to the quantity and quality of the work done. This is in keeping with the level of economic development of the Soviet state and is one of the principles of socialism.

It is material conditions that determine the activity of people.

Does this, however, imply that man does nothing more than passively fulfil objective demands, that he automatically obeys the dictate of objective laws? Such understanding of the role played by people in history would be erroneous, one-sided, in other words, it would be fatalistic. The fact of the matter is that objective conditions and laws determine only the limits of the possible and the impossible in the given circumstances, and allow very considerable latitude for diverse activity. At the same time this latitude also depends on concrete circumstances.

The activity of people may differ in identical conditions, for it depends on their mentality and also on their desires, emotions and those intellectual and social values on which they rely and numerous other subjective factors.

Inasmuch as the actual course of history depends not only on objective conditions and the laws of development but also on the way of acting which is selected by people themselves and, therefore, is not predestined by fate, people create history in the true meaning of the word, and history is created in struggle, in collision of various social forces.

For instance, in present-day conditions there exist the possibility of an outbreak of a world nuclear conflict, for there are nuclear weapons, antagonistic contradictions and the aggressive forces of imperialism capable of precipitating it. On the other hand, the majority of people realise that a unclear war, if it does break out, will bring inestimable disaster to humanity. And since they do not want the war, there also exists the possibility of averting it. It is common knowledge that the Soviet Union is doing everything in its power to avert such a war and inhibit political adventurism.

In all historical conditions there are diverse possibilities that may determine the further course of developments. Which of these possibilities will gain the upper hand depends on the people themselves, on their activity and the balance of the opposing forces. Historical laws are enacted in the activity of the people and in no other way.

Marxism-Leninism gives people knowledge of the objective laws and motive forces of society, it explains the processes occurring in society and provides methods of analysing them. Obviously, the success of the activities of people depends on the degree of their congruity with specific conditions and their expediency within a definite period of time. In planning production, for instance, it is important to take account of internal production links, level of technology, scientific achievements, organisation of labour, system of management and a diversity of other factors which have a direct bearing on the rates of its development and determine its results. But first of all it is necessary to have a thorough knowledge of society's requirements. The compilation of such an optimal plan, especially for a large country, is a very difficult problem which cannot be solved without the help of science.

Marxist social science is revolutionary because it serves the achievement of a great aim—the creation of a new society, because it promotes the success of the revolutionary struggle of the working class and all working people for the emancipation of humanity from all forms of social, national and spiritual oppression.

Marxism-Leninism plays an enormous role in the life of people by making their activity more purposeful and reasonabl, thus helping them to make full use of the opportunities for promoting historical progress that are inherent in the existing conditions.

The already cognised laws of historical development are not always capable of showing man correct line of action in any given circumstances. The laws deal with objective trends and processes, whereas man operates in a concrete situation. Therefore when he reaches a decision he is largely guided by his experience, abilities, cultural level and moral qualities. The moral aspect is most important, for in identical circumstances a person can act either honestly or basely, do good or evil, be brave or cowardly, and so forth. Since this applies not only to individuals, but also to the activity of groups of people, it is necessary to take the psychology of these groups into account.

Politics, for example, cannot be only a science; it will always be an art, too. The adoption and implementation of political decisions depend to an enormous degree on the personal qualities of people, their abilities, experience, authority, character, and so forth.

Classes and Social Groups. The Struggle of Classes

Human activity has a great diversity of forms. People work in industry and agriculture. They produce material values.

People work at research institutes. They study nature and society, investigate their laws and furnish society with knowledge. This is scientific activity.

People create new machines, mechanisms, instruments, etc. This is engineering, designing activity.

People work at state institutions. This is administrative activity.

People work in the spheres of health service, education, culture and so forth.

All these types of activity are essential for society and they determine the division of people according to their occupations and specialities.

There are many other distinctions, too, including age, educational standard, wages, etc.

But the most important distinction between groups of people is the one between classes.

Class distinctions arise in the economic sphere. Classes are large groups of people differing from each other by the place they occupy in the system of production, but their relation to the means of production, by their role in the social organisation of labour and by the mode of acquiring income and its dimensions.

Every exploiting social formation known to history had its specific classes. Moreover, society developed in the course of the class struggle.

The interests of the individual, his mode of life and thinking essentially depend on the class to which he belongs.

The theory of classes and class struggle provides an understanding of the sources of the contradictory strivings of individuals and the causes for their thinking and acting differently.

What is the science of classes and class struggle all about in contemporary conditions?

In advanced capitalist countries the basic classes are the monopoly bourgeoisie and the proletariat. In addition, bourgeois countries have the peasantry (farmers), petty bourgeoisie (owners of small enterprises, shops and workshops). The intelligentsia, i.e., engineers, scientists, writers, men of arts and letters, and other mental workers, holds and important place in the class structure of the capitalist society. The intelligentsia is heterogeneous. It has absorbed representatives of various classes and forms a special social stratum.

Insofar as class interests are contradictory, their contradictions are manifested in the struggle of classes. For instance, workers organise strikes as they fight for higher wages. This is an economic form of struggle. But the actions of the workers, the intelligentsia and young people against aggressive wars, against militarism, are a political struggle because their purpose is to achieve definite political objectives. But the economic and political struggle is reflected in the collision of ideologies. Some theoreticians justify the actions of the bourgeoisie and the imperialist forces, others uphold the interests of the working class. The collision of opposing ideas also expresses antagonism between classes. Therefore, the ideological struggle is a form of class struggle between the proletariat and the bourgeoisie, between socialism and capitalism.

The political struggle is the main form of class struggle, because what class will gain political ascendancy and stand at the head of society depends on its outcome. Of course, the question of power is far from always posed directly, since various classes can put forward political demands which do not affect the political mainstays of a given society. The problem of power is of paramount importance in politics. When the bourgeoisie employs police to disperse a demonstration of working people, to smash organisations upholding the interests of the working class or to suppress strikes, it does so to assert its rule. Of course, besides direct political violence, the bourgeoisie resorts to economic, ideological and other methods. However, usually methods of political violence are widely employed in periods of the exacerbation of the class struggle. So, in order to wrest power from the bourgeoisie, the oppressed classes must also resort to violence.

An analysis of class struggle makes it possible to explain the existence of political parties in a modern society: in a political struggle each class defends its own interests. Therefore it is natural that there should be groups of people and organisations representing the interests of a given class and guiding its activity. These organisations are political parties. In bourgeois-democratic states there are various parties representing the interests of the basic classes and social groups, and representatives of various parties are elected to parliament. But this is merely formal democracy because the bourgeoisie with power and wealth concentrated in its hands always finds the ways and means of securing the parliamentary majority to support the policy advantageous to the ruling class.

Marxist-Leninist parties of the working class in bourgeois-democratic countries also participate in the political struggle by representing the workers in bourgeois parliaments. But their main mission is to uphold the interests of the working people, educate the working class in a revolutionary spirit and guide its activity against bourgeoisie and the capitalist system.

The political struggle has a variety of forms and methods. The reformists, Right opportunists, or simply conciliators and time-servers, deny the necessity of revolutionary struggle on the grounds that the working class should act in a "purely democratic" manner and achiever reforms by co-operating with the ruling class. There are also "Left"-wing opportunists, the extremists (champions of extreme measures), who believe that the working class will be able to attain its goals only through violence, and therefore reject peaceful forms of class struggle.

The correct standpoint is that a party of the working class should be prepared to employ all forms, legal and illegal, violent and non-violent, depending on the concrete situation and the resistance of the class adversary.

In its struggle each class seeks to win allies and enters in various blocs and agreements with other classes. These are questions of the strategy and tactics of the class struggle.

In the final count the objective of this strategy and tactics is to prepare the masses for revolution and secure victory over the forces of the old system.

What is revolution? Let us take a deeper look into this question. We have already said that social revolutions are a natural form of the transition from one socio-economic formation to another in the course of the progressive development of society; that their economic foundation is the deep conflict between the productive forces and the relations of production, when the latter begin to impede the development of the former; that this conflict assumes the form of a forcible political revolution because the ruling classes of the old society resist revolutionary changes, so that a revolution will be victorious only if the revolutionary forces seize power and employ it to suppress the resisting forces of the old society. This being the case, the question of power becomes the main issue of the revolution which itself becomes a political act. Such are the basic principles of the Marxist-Leninist theory of revolution.

The nature of the revolution depends on the type of production relations which it abolishes and the type of system for which it paves the way. There is a qualitative distinction between the bourgeois revolutions paving the way for the capitalist system, and the proletarian, socialist revolutions aimed at abolishing capitalism and all forms of exploitation and consolidating socialist relations. The motive forces of revolution are the classes and social groups which bring it to conclusion. The basic motive forces of socialist revolution are the working class and the peasantry. The working class is winning more and more allies and there is mounting protest against imperialist system, the oppressor of the broad masses.

If the peoples hate imperialism so intensely, why, then, have there been no revolution in many capitalist countries? The main reason is that general economic prerequisites alone cannot bring about a revolutionary explosion; the presence of a revolutionary situation is also essential.

A revolution matures only when society becomes entangled in economic contradictions and the situation of the masses drastically deteriorates. In some cases revolutionary situations were created by war. For instance, the 1905 Revolution in Russia was a result of the crisis caused by the Russo-Japanese War. The February1917 Revolution took place as a result of the sharp aggravation of social contradictions, discontent, poverty and hunger provoked by the First World War. In principal, however, a revolutionary situation does not necessarily develop as a result of war. It can be engendered by the exacerbation of society's internal contradictions.

Revolutions are not accidental phenomena, and neither are they made to order. Karl Marx and Vladimir Lenin, these great thinkers who dedicated their lives to the proletarian cause, always opposed those who believed a handful of conspirators detached from the movement of masses could consummate revolution and make people "happy". Such actions result only in defeat and always play into the hands of the reaction. Revolution cannot be exported to another country and imposed on another nation. It has to be prepared by the entire course of internal development of a country.

Building upon the Marxist theory of revolution Lenin showed that in imperialist conditions a socialist revolution could win first in one country. This idea was confirmed by the victory of the October Revolution in Russia. Later a number of other European and Asian countries and also Cuba took the road of socialist development. A world system of socialism, the chief revolutionary force of our time, came into being. Intricate processes are taking place in capitalist and Third World countries where new revolutionary forces are maturing.

The Communists are now striving to unite and rally all the forces capable of fighting imperialism, the main obstruction of historical progress, the basic force oppressing the peoples and a source of the threat of a nuclear war.

The problem of consolidating anti-imperialist forces—the working class, the peasantry, intelligentsia and various social strata—was raised as a most important political issue of the day at the International Meeting of Communist and Workers' Parties in Moscow in 1969.

Classes Under Socialism

Under socialism there are no antagonistic classes because the industry and the land belong to the socialist state and the exploiting classes have been eliminated. The building of socialist society is accompanied by the co-operation, or collectivisation of small peasant holdings. In other words, small private holdings of the peasants are united into the collective property of the collective-farm members, and the state turns over the land to the collective farms for permanent use.

Collectivisation gives rise to large-scale agricultural production employing modern machines and scientific achievements. The social character of the peasantry also changes.

The distinctions between the working classes—the workers and peasants—and between them and the intelligentsia—mental workers—continue to exist in socialist society, but they are not antagonistic because the basic interests of all social groups coincide: the entire nation is interested in strengthening and developing the socialist system, promoting society's economic and cultural growth and building communism.

The distinctions between classes will gradually disappear as socialist society continues to advance. Already today the scientific and technological revolution in agriculture is transforming it into a variety of industrial labour. Both in the way of life and culturally the countryside is approaching the urban level.

The present scientific and technological revolution makes for changes in society's social structure. The steady improvement of technology, the increasing application of science in production, the growth of automation and mechanization and the mounting demand for highly qualified labour dwindle the gap between mental and physical labour. The educational level of the entire people rises steadily. This means that distinctions between the intelligentsia and the rest of the working people are gradually being obliterated.

The Soviet people are building socially homogenous classless society. Classless society is the ultimate objective of the communist movement, for this society will be free from economic inequality and will provide for the all-round development of every individual. The only distinctions which will remain between people under communism will be talent, abilities, interests, level of knowledge and the like.

But so long as classes exist the working class, the most united and best organised class and the leading vehicle of the communist ideas, will play the principle role in society.

In socialist society the relations between classes and social groups are qualified as relations of socio-political and ideological unity. This unity is one of the greatest assets of socialism. It brings together the efforts of the whole nation in building communist society. In this sense the socio-political unity of society is one of the motive forces of the development of socialism.

Nevertheless, this does not mean that there are no contradictions in Soviet society. The building of a new society is invariably attended by unexpected developments and obsolection of things. Some contradictions disappear, while new contradictions associated with the development of society may emerge. But these contradictions are not antagonistic; the development and strengthening of the socialist society and the increasing social wealth create ever more favourable conditions for resolving contradictions.

Thus, socialism, being the initial phase of the communist social formation, is a society which has done away with exploiting classes and whose main objective is to create and develop conditions for surmounting the vestiges of class distinctions between the working classes and social groups and to create and develop conditions for the transition to communism.

Society, the Individual and the Collective

Although the course of history is set by the activity of large masses of people, and by classes when we refer to a class society, it does not mean that separate individuals play no part in it. History traces the activity of classes, nations and peoples, but it also records the feats of national heroes, the activity of heads of states and military commanders and discoveries made by great scientists and it brings to us the names of leaders of people's uprisings, and prominent figures in education, culture and art.

Historical science is interested in people who have left their imprint on human memory, whose personality influenced the course of developments, either by accelerating or retarding them. Who are these people? Socio-political developments are seriously influenced by people standing at the head of states, parties, movements, armies, etc. Indeed, an army which defeats another army owes its victory to many factors, not the least important the personality of its commander. A commander's abilities and personal qualities are a weighty factor in each concrete case.

The same applies to political leaders who have the backing of powerful parties or powerful states, and whose decisions can have a substantial impact on the course of history.

Why do certain individuals leave an imprint in history? Undoubtedly due to their outstanding intellect, talent and abilities and to the fact that their particular qualities fit in the particular period. The leaders of the popular movements of the past were people who had been singled out by the masses and enjoyed great authority. There can be no doubt that Stepan Razin and Yemelyan Pugachev, leaders of the peasant movements in Russia, were outstanding personalities who most fully expressed the interests and the characteristic features of the peasants of the period, their hatred for the oppression of the landowners, their love for freedom and their prejudices, such as their belief in a "benevolent" tsar.

Each class moulds its leaders in its own image. The revolutionary movement of the proletariat produced leaders of a qualitatively new type, well-educated people with outstanding personal qualities and a thorough knowledge of the interests and needs of the working class. The great leaders of the working class Karl Marx, Frederick Engels and Vladimir Lenin not only enormously influenced the course of history, but by their ideas and activity ushered in a new epoch in the struggle of the working class for socialism.

In the spheres of culture, science and arts, the life and consciousness of the masses are influenced by people whose discoveries enrich human knowledge, and who produce outstanding works of art and technical inventions.

Based as it is on the laws of historical development, social science seeks to explain the past and the present activity of the people and scientifically forecast the future. But the course of history depends not only on the operation of objective laws, but also on the activity of the makers of history themselves—the masses, classes and personalities standing at the head of various movements and especially on those who by virtue of their qualities and position are able to influence developments.

What about the personality of an "ordinary" person? Man, his development in history, his activity, have always been in the centre of social sciences. Marxist social science regards man as a social being in the first place. And man's biological nature is subordinated to this social beginning. At the same time man's social nature is not immutable. Man is both a social and historic being. His nature is determined by society in which he develops, lives and acts. Proceeding from this concept it is easy to understand why Marx defined the essence of man as "the ensemble of the social relations". In other words, in order to understand man it is necessary to study the society that produced him.

In primitive society man was a member of a clan, community or tribe and his consciousness was wholly determined by the conceptions prevailing in the clan. As the class society developed so did the class personality. It was the personality of a slave or a slave-owner, a feudal lord or a serf. In bourgeois society, where all people are formally equal, they are divided according to their wealth and property status. People are genuinely equal only under socialism and communism, since this society abolishes all privileges associated with the origin of a person and wealth. The communist society creates equal and favourable conditions for the all-round development of the individual. It will be a qualitatively new stage in the relations between society and the individual, where the individuality of a person will develop to a still greater extent. The greater the diversity of social life and the more abundant the cultural wealth of the people, the richer becomes the spiritual world of the individual and the more vivid his personality. In the past this process was extremely controversial because the exploiting classes appropriated the fruits of social and cultural progress, relegating the toiling masses to poverty and ignorance. Today workers in capitalist countries are subject to such forms of influence which are designed to educate submissive, socially passive people. Such achievements of human culture as the cinema, radio, television and the press are brought into play to divert the attention of the people from problems of reality, from the struggle for a better future. This is also the purpose of the developing "mass culture" which levels off or standardises human interests and consequently downgrades and coarsens the personality of man depriving it of genuine spiritual values.

Under socialism cultural development has the sole objective of moulding a vivid human personality. In this connection we should examine another important circumstance.

It is a fact that man is connected not only with the activity of society, of large social groups, but also with that of small groups which he is directly attached to, namely the body of his fellow workers and his family which greatly influence the formation of the personality.

A small group, or a collective, is a link between man and society. For instance, in the USSR man is connected with society in the production sphere through the collective in which he works, and his prestige in society depends on his prestige in the factory shop, collective farm, office or other place where he works. In a collective where man is in direct contact with other people there are specific relations and moral atmosphere which strongly influence labour productivity and the entire life and activity of the given group. Soviet society is interested in maintaining healthy relations among people, which would stimulate their labour and the intellectual development of the members of the collective body and improve them ideologically and morally.

Under socialism workers' collectives are the main cells of society and their further development is becoming an increasingly important factor of social progress. The combination of individual, collective and social interests, when the interests of the individual and the group are not opposed to each other and to the interests of society, encourages the progressive development of the entire country.

It is most important to promote the development of the human personality, for the richer the inner world of each person, the more diversified is the life of society.

Individuality should not be confused with individualism. Individualism is a bourgeois ideological and moral principle which sets the individual in opposition to society, to the collective, and puts personal interests and the striving for personal advantages in the forefront. This basically vicious principle does not reflect the interests of the individual in general, but the concrete interests of the bourgeoisie, whose property and power is defended by the bourgeois system. The principle of individualism is alien to the working class because it disunites people. In contrast to bourgeois individualism, the proletarian outlook and communist morality assert the principle of collectivism making it incumbent on the individual to concert his interests and behaviour with the interests of his collective, class and society.

Does socialist collectivism run counter to the moulding of the individuality and freedom of the individual? Not at all. A person finds the necessary means for development only in a collective. Therefore, the emancipation of the collective is a factor of the emancipation of the individual. This task, i.e., the emancipation of the collective, is fulfilled by socialist revolution. Under socialism, which promotes the rapid growth of education, culture and welfare, the collective and society acquire truly limitless opportunities for progress. It can be confidently stated that no other society in the world has done so much for the promotion of the spiritual development of the masses as has socialism. Socialist collectivism brings to the surface the most realistic ways for the development of the individual and individuality when "the free development of each is the condition for the free development of all".

Of course, socialist society cannot immediately offer such an opportunity. At first it is necessary to raise sufficiently production and culture, surmount the survivals of the old social division of labour and eliminate the demand for unskilled and semi-skilled labour. The creation of conditions for the all-round development of the individual is an historical process which socialism is carrying out at present. This process shows that only socialist society is directing all its material and spiritual means to mould a harmoniously developed man.

Spiritual Life of Society

In everyday life we easily distinguish existing objects from their ideal images, from what takes place only in our mind. For instance, a person recalls his home and dreams and thinks of visiting it. All this takes place in the mind. It is a totally different thing when this takes place in reality, when a person has come home, met his near and dear ones, and so forth.

Materialist philosophy has proved that the material, i.e., real, existence of things does not depend on consciousnenss and that sensations, concepts, nations, all that we call consciousness, are a reflection of the material and secondary to consciousness.

The line between the material and the ideal (mental) is present in society, too. When people produce the necessary material values and use them, i.e., when they interact with nature and with each other, this is their social being.

Social being is the material life of society. But public life is not the same thing as social being. People are conscious beings and when they work they do not act like automation but consciously set themselves specific aims and seek to attain them. This means that the mental element, the aim, is always present even in the simplest of jobs. The aim is determined by man's requirements, his interests, the specific conditions of his activity, etc. It follows, therefore, that the aim is secondary to the conditions of activity, it derives from them. Furthermore, people, once they have set themselves a specific aim, consciously select the means with which to attain it. In other words, the purposeful character of human activity is connected with the consciousness which enables man to understand the surrounding world and act accordingly.

In order to work together people must develop patterns of behaviour to regulate their relations. These patterns are also factors of social consciousness.

Finally, the birth of consciousness in people is accompanied by the rise of their spiritual requirement which, just as material requirements, have to be satisfied, for as the saving goes: "Man shall not live by bread alone." The level of these spiritual requirements differs in various periods and depends on the level of the spiritual development of society or its individual sections. And yet spiritual requirements have always existed and this is proved by primitive paintings, or the history of the development of poetic folklore.

Thus, spiritual life is correlated with material life, and social consciousness with social being. The material, or in this case social being determine the ideal, or social consciousness. The latter is a reflection of the people's social being and as such is secondary to it. Their interaction, however, does not end there. Social consciousness, its various forms such as science, art, morality, accumulate a certain amount of ideas and concepts with which each new step in the development of social consciousness is connected. In other words, the relation of social consciousness to social being is always seen in the light of concepts and ideas already formed earlier. Social consciousness is relatively independent of social being. It can either lag behind social being or, on the contrary, overtake it, reflect it correctly or distort, create a scientific concept of reality or all sorts of illusions. What imprint, and why precisely this particular one reality leaves on social consciousness, are questions which require scientific study.

Social consciousness is influenced not simply by the interests of separate individuals but the interests of large social groups, or classes. The systems of ideas expressing the interests of classes and reflecting reality and social relations in the light of these interest constitute ideologies. Ideology is an element of social consciousness which in a class society is most directly and intrinsically linked with classes, their interests and struggle.

Ideologies play a major role in the life of society, guiding parties and classes that defend their interests in confrontations with other classes. In our day the main ideologies are the communist, Marxist-Leninist ideology of the working class, and the reactionary bourgeois ideology with all its variations (liberal, fascist and others).

Why is bourgeois ideology reactionary? In the first place because it reflects the interests of the reactionary exploiting class. History does not stand still, and the assertion and development of socialist relations correspond to its objective laws and demands. But the bourgeoisie wants to thwart the victory of socialism, preserve the bourgeois system under which it holds the leading position, and retain its power and wealth. Hence, the interests of the bourgeoisie contradict historical progress and inhibit it, and bourgeois ideology sanctifies these interests. Hence its reactionary nature.

Unlike bourgeois ideology, Marxist-Leninist proletarian ideology is progressive and revolutionary because it serves the demands of historical development, the revolutionary transformation of capitalist relations who socialist. It is a scientific ideology that correctly reflect reality and its laws; it expresses the interests of the progressive class, the interests of the working people for whom a correct understanding of reality, and a sober, realistic, scientifically-based approach to social problems and contradictions and to prospects of social development are questions of especial importance. Marxist-Lenininst ideology is winning its difficult struggle against world imperialism because it is genuinely scientific.

Besides ideology, which is a system of political and legal concepts, moral ideals and principles, artistic trends, religious dogmas and philosophical ideas, there are other systems of knowledge and ideas whose direct and main purpose is to satisfy the requirements of the developing productive forces. In the first place these systems are natural, precise and technical sciences. The laws of nature which they study do not depend on society, on the activity of people and can be cognised either approximately or more precisely. Science is committed to the truth, it discovers the truth and employs objective knowledge to improve production, and society's practical activity.

The attitude to any science, including sciences studying nature, depends on class interests. The bourgeoisie seeks to place science at its service, for without science modern production cannot develop. Moreover, the ruling circles in capitalist countries use scientific achievements to step up exploitation, intensify labour and strengthen their own military-political domination.

Natural science cannot be disconnected from ideology, from the ideological struggle. Bourgeois ideologists are endeavouring to interpret science in a way that would preclude any materialistic conclusions and make it impossible to employ it in the struggle against religion. They portray science not as objective knowledge of the laws of nature, but as a man-created system of views and ideas devoid of the objective truth.

If science does not convey the objective truth then it is impossible to distinguish the real from the falls, scientific knowledge from religious or any other dogma.

Thus, while being interested in implementing science in industry, the bourgeoisie fights the system of views which is based on science.

Under socialism science serves the whole of society, the working people, and there are all conditions for promoting science and its all-round application in the interests of historic progress.

The fusion of science, of scientific and technological progress with the gains and advantages of the socialist system of economy is one of the primary sources of society's progressive development.

Social consciousness is a complicated manifold phenomenon. We have seen that it includes both ideology, with all its diverse forms, and non-ideological forms of consciousness. Besides, the psychology of society, class or social groups, i.e., social psychology constitutes a distinctive part of social consciousness. We often hear about "petty-bourgeois psychology", "proletarian psychology", etc.

Social psychology is moulded under the impact of the direct living conditions of people and their everyday activity. For instance, petty-bourgeois psychology is a term describing the qualities characteristic of a petty proprietor, a moneygrubber, a person whose interests are concentrated only on his property and the narrow world in which he exist.

In this case it is not a question of a particular person, but rather of a definite social type, of the psychology of a certain type of individual, of attitudes, traditions and sentiments prevailing in a specific social milieu, all the things which are specifically refracted in the psychology of individuals.

In *What Is To Be Done?* Lenin wrote that the immediate living conditions of the working class under capitalism give rise to a specific psychology, specific consciousness. On the one hand, living and working conditions develop in the workers a sense of solidarity, firmness, stamina, discipline and organisation.

On the other hand, life in a bourgeois society instils in them what is called trade union mentality, awareness of the need to wage an economic struggle to improve their material conditions within the capitalist framework. Such is the psychology of a worker which is moulded by the conditions of his life in bourgeois society.

It expresses the class interest of the worker, but in a very narrow and restricted form: the worker is unaware of the antithesis of his interests and those of the bourgeoisie.

This awareness is cultivated in the proletariat by an ideology built by the theoreticians of working class on the achievements of science and social thinking. It is introduced into the ranks of the working class by its conscious vanguard—the party.

This comparison of the psychology and ideology of the proletariat also discloses the significance and the poverty of psychology. It is significant because it is fertile soil for the assimilation of the scientific revolutionary ideology, and its poverty lies in that it does not give the worker the understanding of his general class interests.

It can be said, therefore, that psychology pertains to the sphere of ordinary consciousness which guides people in their everyday activity. Ideology, on its part, comes to the forefront when it is necessary to solve crucial social problems in the course of the class struggle.

Each new generation finds that it has at its disposal the productive forces and relations of production created by the preceding generations. This makes for continuity in the sphere of society's production activity and social being. At the same time each new generation assimilates and further improves the system of knowledge and ideas of the world and society, the patterns and rules of behaviour, or, in other words, the spiritual culture it has inherited. Otherwise there can be no progress.

Not only material wealth but intellectual as well is unequally distributed in all antagonistic societies. The rich have every opportunity to raise their cultural level, while the mass of the working people oppressed by poverty and constant fear of the future, and due to their inferior education or complete illiteracy, find it difficult to do so.

Prior to the socialist revolution the vast majority of the population in Russia could neither read nor write. The abolition of illiteracy become one of the most important objectives of the socialist revolution. With this aim in view Lenin set the task of carrying through a cultural revolution which included a broad programme for surmounting the cultural backwardness of the masses and moulding a new, people's intelligentsia.

The cultural revolution was essential for the construction of socialist society.

The building and development of socialism goes hand in hand with rapid industrial progress, the introduction of new, more sophisticated equipment, and consequently with a vast growth in the demand for highly qualified specialists.

In the course of socialist construction socialist democracy develops further on, and an increasing number of people are drawn into the administration of state affairs. But to be able to do so a person has constantly to raise his level of political knowledge and culture.

Finally, as we have already said, the ideal of socialism and communism is an individual with an all-round development who participates in creative activity.

This, however, is impossible without a high level of culture of the masses. Consequently, the solution of all problems of the building and the further development of socialism is inseparable from the continuous growth of the cultural level of the masses and the shaping of the communist world outlook in all people.

3

The Nature, Scope and Methods of Political Science

Political Science is a science which deals with the State and Government. It had its origin in the city-states of ancient Greece. The Oriental people had speculated on the State and its problems even before the time of the Greeks. But they did not develop political science in its pure and systematic form. It was mixed up with a great deal of mythology and superstition. Religion and politics were so closely intertwined that no attempt was made to develop an independent science of politics. The social sciences were treated as a branch of theology. The task of separating politics from religion, superstition, and mythology first fell to the lot of the Greeks. Thus it was that the Greeks were the first people to develop political science in its pure and systematic form. They were eminently fitted for this task by the rational and social outlook which characterised all their thinking.

TERMINOLOGY

A difficulty which confronts us at the very outset in undertaking a study of political science is as regards the precise meaning of such terms as Politics, Political Science, Comparative Governments, etc. We can not hope to go very far in understanding problems pertaining to the State, unless we make clear to ourselves what these terms mean. Although political science has its roots in the Greek past, it is in its modern form a comparatively new science. Consequently, it has not yet acquired a definite terminology of its own. In France and Germany however, it seems to have attained a greater degree of perfection than in the Anglo-Saxon countries.

1. Politics

Earlier writers on the subject simply use the term Politics in describing the entire science of the State. Aristotle's celebrated treatise has for its title the simple name *Politics*. The term Politics is derived from the Greek words *Polis* or 'City State' and *Politeia*. In the view of the Greeks, Politics embraces everything that touches the life of the State. Used in that sense it is the equivalent of Political Science. Writers of an earlier generation like Jellinek Holtzendorff, and Sidgwick prefer the term Politics to 'Political Science' which is in current use to-day. Among modern writers there is a distinct aversion to using the term 'Politics' in its wide sense to cover a study of the phenomena relating to the State and Government. Politics, as ordinarily used to-day, refers either:

1. To practical politics, as meaning 'the art of controlling a party and securing the nomination and election or the appointment of particular persons to office' or
2. To the art of Government, the art of directing or guiding the policy of the Government towards a particular goal.

Sir Frederick Pollock, using the term Politics in its broad sense, divides it into Theoretical Politics and Practical or Applied Politics. Under the first head he includes:

(a) Theory of the State,

(b) Theory of Government,

(c) Theory of Legislation, and

(d) Theory of the State as an artificial person.

Under the second division he includes:

(a) The State (actual forms of Government),

(b) Government (the working of Government, Administration, etc.)

(c) Laws and Legislation (Procedure, Courts, etc.), and

(d) The State personified (Diplomacy, Peace, War, and International dealings).

Theoretical politics deals with the basic problems of the State, without concerning itself with the activities of any particular Government or the means by which the ends of any particular States are attained. Practical politics, on the other hand, deals with 'the actual working of Governments and the various institutions of political life'. It will no doubt be generally agreed that this is both a useful and convenient distinction, but many would prefer the term 'Political Science' to 'Politics' in the present context.

2. Political Science

The term 'Political Science' in its current usage is much more comprehensive than the term 'Politics'. It connotes the whole range of knowledge regarding the State and embraces the theory of the State. It includes both 'Theoretical Politics' and 'Practical' or 'Applied Politics'. On the theoretical side, it is concerned with questions like the nature, origin, purpose and justification of the State and is known as the Theory of the State or Political Philosophy. On the practical side, it is concerned with the structure, functions, and forms of political institutions and is known as Comparative Politics of Constitutional Government. A succinct definition of Political Science is given by Paul Janet, a distinguished French writer, who says that Political Science is 'that part of social science which treats of the foundation of the State and the Principles of Government'. According to Gettell, Political Science is 'a historical investigation of what the State has been, an analytical study of what the state is, and a politico-ethical discussion of what the State should be.'

3. Political Philosophy

Political Philosophy is another term which gives rise to confused thinking in studying the phenomenon of the State. To some English political thinkers, political philosophy is the major portion of political science; political philosophy being that part of philosophy which deals with the State, is a part of the universe with which philosophy proper is concerned. This view is due to the belief that philosophy, being the unifier of all knowledge, should regard the study of the State as one of its sub-divisions. We differ from this point of view, because the modern age of specialisation calls not so much for a synthesis of all knowledge as for an analysis of it. Progress in political thinking, just as much as in other fields of thought, calls for specialisation and delimitation of the various fields.

The distinction between political science (Staatwissenschaft) and political theory or political philosophy (Staatslehre or Staatsphilosophie) is generally observed by Continental writers, though it is difficult to point to the exact line of demarcation. Political Science, as we use the term to-day, is broader in scope than political philosophy and carries with it a greater precision of meaning. 'Political Philosophy deals with the fundamental problems of the nature of the State, citizenship, questions of duty and right, and political ideals'. 'It is in a sense prior to political science, for the fundamental assumptions of the former are a basis to the latter.' Nevertheless, if Political Philosophy is not to become vague and imaginative, it must use the material supplied by Political Science. Political Theory and objective political conditions act and react upon one another.

4. Theory of the State

This term is in many ways preferable to the term political philosophy, although the subject matter of both is much the same. Political philosophy tends to suggest something abstract and speculative, but the theory of the State or political theory is much clearer and its boundaries are better marked. It is not a study of the structure of the forms of government nor a comparison of the various forms of government. These are dealt with in that branch of political science known as comparative government. The theory of the State, likewise, is not a study of the historical development of the State or of law. Nor is it an attempt to discover the ideal State. Neither is it a study of the art of governing or of administration. It no doubt presupposes some knowledge of all these things as a necessary pre-requisite. But it is not concerned with the structure and activities of any one State. It deals with the essentials of the State and is based upon a study of the State both as it is and as it has been.

Value of Political Thought

There is a disposition in some quarters to-day to minimise the value of a study of political theory as being an abstract and a barren subject. This under-estimation is largely due to the habit of laughing at all theory a habit which seems to be a feature of the matter-of-fact, mechanical, and industrialised society of to-day. We agree with Mr. Ivor Brown when he says that 'Sensibly handled with a common-sense attitude to the real value of social life, it (political theory) is both a concrete and a fruitful study'.

In his *History of Political Thought,* Prof. Gettell carefully sums up the arguments for and against a study of political thought, which we shall run over as briefly as possible. It is often said that political theory has little relation to reality, that it cannot be applied in practice, that it deals with legal fictions and absolute concepts, that it is inexact, that it is incapable of giving definite answers to disputed questions, and that it is sometimes disastrous to actual politics. The opponents of political theory might very well use the aphorism of Emerson that there is 'nothing new, nothing true, and nothing matters'.

To counteract the above charges, certain values of a study of political theory may be enumerated. It gives precision and definiteness to the meaning of political terms. It is conducive to clarity and honesty of thought. It is an aid to the interpretation of history. A knowledge of past political thought is an invaluable help in understanding present-day politics and international relations. Constructive political progress rests upon a sound and comprehensive political theory; applicable to present-day conditions and needs. Political thought represents a high type of intellectual achievement. Finally, if government can be shaped and improved by human ingenuity, no study is more valuable than a study of political theory. Political theory is thus intensely practical and intensely important. It is the abstract treatment of a concrete subject.

The charge that political theory is too far removed from actual conditions is not true. We need accurate definition and close analysis. Wise statesmanship requires more than mere hazy and often conflicting intuitions. It requires a sound philosophy, a scheme of moral values, and that is exactly what political theory endeavors to give. Statesmanship is essentially a moral task. That some political theorists have been mere pedants is no reason for condemning political theory wholesale. By its very nature political theory cannot always give us clear-cut answers. While it may not lead to unity in political discussion, it will at least be an aid to mutual respect and toleration. If it is true that where there is practice, there should be theory also, a study of political theory is invaluable to political practice.

Scope of Political Science

Prof. Goodnow claims that political science divides itself into three distinct parts, *viz.*

1. The expression of the State will;
2. The content of the State will as expressed; and
3. The execution of the State will.

The first division includes political theory and the network of extra-legal customs and extra-legal organisations which influence the political system of a country. The second is practically a synonym for law. The third deals with the ascertainment and application of the correct principles of administration.

Suffice it to say that Prof. Goodnow conceives the scope of political science rather narrowly. His description does not seem to include such questions as the nature and characteristics of the State and the relation between authority and obligation.

Relation of Political Science to Allied Sciences.

Political science does not stand alone, since it is not the only science which concerns itself with men in organised society. Being one of the many sciences dealing with relations of man to man, it has its close connections with other social sciences. Thus Paul Janet remarks that political science is 'closely connected with political economy or the science of wealth; with law, either natural or positive, which occupies itself principally with the relations of citizens to one another; with history, which furnishes the facts of which it had need; with philosophy, and especially with morals, which gives to it a part of its principles'.

1. Political Science and History

These two sciences are very intimately connected. As Seeley puts it: 'History without political science has no fruit. Political science without history has no root' To quote the same writer again: 'Politics are vulgar when not liberalized by history, and history fades into mere literature when it loses sight of its relation to politics. History provides the raw material for political science. According to Seeley, political science and history will ultimately become identical with one another. But this seems improbable, if not impossible. Though both sciences are inter-dependent and mutually complementary, there are some fundamental differences between them.

(a) *In their method of treatment*—History being narrative deals with facts in their chronological order, whereas political science finds out such events only as relate to political evolution. The method of political science is reflective. Using the material provided by history, it seeks to discover general laws and principles.

(b) *In scope*—History is more comprehensive because it deals with the economic, religious, and military aspects of the social life, whereas political science is not interested in them except in so far as they throw some light on the nature of the State and the development of political control.

(c) *In their end*—History is much less philosophical than political science. History deals with concrete facts and political science deals with ideals and abstract types. Political science deals with the state as it ought to be, whereas history deals with the State as it is and has been.

The conclusion, then, is that Political Science must make use of history only to transcend it. The historian's task is not to pacs moral judgments, but the political scientist is bound to make such judgments. It is there that political science joins hands with ethics and parts company with economics and sociology

Lord Bryce claims that 'political science stands midway between history and politics, between the past and the present. It has drawn its materials from the one, it has to apply them to the other'.

2. Political Science and Economics

Political science and economics are very closely related. They exert considerable influence on each other and cover a common ground to a large extent. Production and distribution of wealth are affected by the regulations of the State. All economic activity is carried on within the State on conditions laid down by the State through laws. Political movements, on the other hand, are profoundly influenced by economic causes. Our economic life is conditioned by political institutions and ideas. Some of the important questions of present day politics are at the same time questions which vitally concern economics e.g. questions relating to tariff laws, labour legislation, government ownership, etc. The relation between the two sciences is so great that a century ago scientific writers regarded economics as a branch of political science, and the subject itself was described as political economy. As late as the eighteenth century, political economy was regarded as 'a branch of statesmanship'.

Although the two sciences are so closely related, there are still some fundamental differences between them. Commenting upon the question, Ivor Brown remarks that economics is concerned with things, while political science is concerned with people; one deals with prices and the other with values. If economics is concerned with people, it is not with people as ends in themselves, but only in relation to the things they make, sell, and use. Political science also takes things into account, but this it does only in relation to human or moral values. Thus it is that political science easily becomes a normative science while economics remains a descriptive science. As someone has humorously remarked that an economist is one who knows the price of everything but the value of nothing.

It is a welcome sign of the times that economics is becoming more and more a normative science, concerning itself not merely with the production of wealth, but also with its just distribution.

3. Political Science and Sociology

What philosophy is to the mental sciences, sociology is that to the social sciences. Both of them aim at a unification of the subject matter which belongs to the several allied subjects, Thus both of them possess an all-embracing character. Political science is narrower than sociology and is, in a general sense, a sub-division of sociology. Sociology is the fundamental social science. The field covered by sociology is so vast that present-day writers prefer to limit it to the study of certain phases of the life of society, other than for its political aspects.

(a) Sociology in its widest significance denotes a study of society in all its manifestations, while political science is only a study of the State and Government. Putting the same thought in other words, we may say that while sociology deals with man in all social relations, political science deals with man in his political alone. This may not be true of the State in its early stages, but it is emphatically true of the modern State. In its early stages, the State was more a social than a political institution. In the words of Gilchrist, 'Sociology is the science of society; political science is the science of the State, or political society. Sociology studies man as a social being, and as political organisation is a special kind of social organisation, Political Science is a more specialised science than Sociology.' Or, as Kranenburg puts it, 'while sociology examines the formation and operation of groups as such, political theory focuses its attention on a special group, namely the State.'

(b) Sociology deals not only with organised communities but also with unorganised communities. The concern of political science is only the former. It deals only with societies which have received the impress of political organisation. Thus it is later in origin than sociology.

(c) Sociology deals with the legal and coercive relationships of man with his fellows as well as with the evolution of customs, manners, religion, and economic life. Political science deals only with the former.

(d) Unlike political science which treats only of the conscious activities of man, sociology treats of unconscious social activities as well.

(e) Political science starts with the assumption that man is a political being. Sociology goes behind this assumption and seeks to explain how and why man became a political animal.

(f) Sociology is concerned with what has happened or does happen, and not with what ought to happen. Political science, at least in one of its aspect, is concerned with what ought to be done.

4. Political Science and Ethics

Political science is the science of the political order and ethics is the science of the moral order. Both have to deal with questions of right and wrong. The relation between the two is so close that Plato considered politics a sub-division of ethics. The State, he believed, should train men in a life of virtue. The capital advance made by Aristotle upon Plato is said to be his separation of ethics and political. But this separation turns out to be one of methodology rather than of substance. Aristotle, too, posits a close relation between ethics and politics and allows political questions to be influenced by man's highest moral judgment. The end of the state is, according to him, good life or a community of well-being.

Machiaveli is the first writer of any note in the western world to sharply separate politics from ethics. To him religion and morality are not the masters of the State, not even safe guides, but useful servants and agents.

The modern view is, on the whole, in favour of maintaining a close relation between ethics and political science. Lord Acton goes so far as to say: 'The great question is to discover, not what Governments prescribe, but what they ought to prescribe.' Another writer holds that to separate ethics and politics is disastrous to both. Politics divorced from ethics rests on a foundation of shifting sand; ethics divorced from politics is narrow and abstract. Ivor Brown maintains that the difference between politics and ethics is one of quantity, not of quality; for 'politics' is but ethics writ large. He goes on to say: 'Ethical theory is incomplete without political theory, because man is an associated creature and cannot live fully in isolation; political theory is idle without ethical theory, because its study and its results depend fundamentally on our scheme of moral values, our conceptions of right and wrong.

The ultimate justification of the State is determined by the moral end or purpose which the State serves. Thus the ideals of both ethics and political science must be in agreement. Yet the bulk of the material with which the two sciences deal is distinct. Catlin contends that from ethics the statesmen may learn which courses among several are desirable and from political science he may learn which among several may be feasible.

5. Political Science and Psychology

Psychology, as we know it today, is a comparatively new science and its advocates are trying to apply psychological methods to every part of man's individual and social life. E. Barker apply remarks: 'The application of the psychological clue to the riddles of human activity has indeed become the fashion of the day. If our fathers thought biologically, we think psychologically.' There can be little doubt that the psychological approach to politics, upon which much insistence is placed these days, is under valuable. It may be that politics has been too long under the sway of philosophy and has not given enough attention to the facts of human behaviour. We need to reinvigorate our minds from the wells of direct observation. We cannot go very far in our study of political science without understanding the way in which human beings behave as individuals and as members of society when subjected to various kinds of stimuli. We need to 'study such factors as habit and instinct, imitation and suggestion, if we are to understand human behaviour aright. Government to be stable and really popular must reflect and express the mental ideas and moral sentiments of those who are subject to its authority; in short, it must be in harmony with what Le Bon calls the 'mental constitution of the race.' A study of mob psychology and of such factors as the prestige complex and the psychology of the oppressed can help us to understand recent events in Europe.

At the same time it is necessary to remember that it is easy to exaggerate the importance of psychology to political science. E. Barker, in his *Political Thought in England from Spencer to To-day,* clearly brings out the limitations of the psychological method as follows:

1. The psychologist does not and cannot deal in terms of value. Values belong to the moralist. Psychology deals with things as they are; ethics with things as they ought to be. Therefore political theory should look to ethics rather than to psychology for constructive help.

2. Psychology seeks to explain to civilized life in terms of savage instinct—the higher by the lower. This does not seem to be the correct evolutionary method. The right procedure would be to explain the lower by the higher. Man explains the monkey, and not monkey the man. It is illogical to explain civilized life by the conditions of life in pre-historic times. Reason is none the less reason when it is not conscious inference. Habit and instinct, suggestion and imitation exist, but they exist in connection with intelligence. Just because a thing is primitive, it does not mean that it is final.

3. A well-known psychologist, like McDougall gives al full account of the origin of instincts that act *in* society, but he hardly shows how they issue *into* society. 'He seems to do a

great deal of packing in preparation for a journey on which he never starts.' The fundamental question is after collecting all the necessary psychological facts what are we to make of them? On this psychology is rather silent.

4. According to Catlin, psychology is concerned with mental acts which must be considered in relation to the observable, individual mind. Politics is concerned with the impulsive or willed relations as such of social beings.

6. Political Science and Law

The Sate is both a social phenomenon and a legal institution and any attempt to explain the State in its entirety must include both these points of view. From the legal standpoint, the State is a person in the sense that it is a subject of rights and duties. It can sue and be sued at a law court. Or, to put it in the form of a definition, it is 'a corporation composed of men domiciled upon a particular territory and endowed with original ruling power.'

Jurisprudence may be defined as the science of Law. Although, strictly speaking, a subdivision of political science, it is studied as a separate branch of study owing to the vastness of its scope and its technical nature.

Constitutional defines the organs of the State, their relations to one another, and the relations of the State of the individual. International law regulates the relations of states to one another.

7. Political Science and Geography

Man is, to a considerable extent, influenced by this physical environment and the geographical conditions under which he lives. It is easy to exaggerate the influence of the climate, topography, and physical features of a country upon the character, institutions and accomplishments of a people. While these external factors play an important part in man's life, it is necessary to remember that civilised man is not a mere passive tool of Nature. Like the lower animals he does not blindly allow himself to be adapted to nature. By the use of intelligence and forethought he adapts nature to his purposes.

Aristotle was one of the earliest writers to give attention to the influence of geography upon the political institutions and the national character of a people. Among modern writers, Bodin in the sixteenth century gave close attention to this subject. After him, Rousseau worked out a co-relation between climate and forms of Government. He held that despotism was most natural for warm climates, barbarism for cold climates, and good polity for moderate climates. He held also that the best form of Government for small countries was democracy and for large countries, monarchy.

In the middle of the last century, Thomas Buckle in his *History of Civilisation* exaggerated the relation between physical environment and national character, contending strongly that geographical influences were most important factors in moulding the character and institutions of peoples. He gave particular attention to the influence of climate, food, soil, and the 'general aspect of nature'. His extreme position is not shared by many today.

After making due allowance for exaggeration, it remains undoubtedly true that geographical conditions have influenced in considerable measure the determination of national politics and to some extent the character of political institutions. At the same time we are safe in saying that geography is a much less important factor in moulding social and political institution to-day than it was in earlier times.

Methods of Political Science

It is admitted by all writers that political science is an inexact science. It does not aim at absolute truth. It aims at relative truth. Consequently there is bound to be difference of opinion with regard to almost all political questions. What is sound politically today may not be sound a hundred years hence. No theory of the State can be considered as ultimate truth.

Because of these limitations some thinkers even refuse to give the name 'science' to a study of political theory. It is true that political science is not exact like mathematics, physics or chemistry. Two plus two makes four everywhere in the world except in a lunatic asylum. Two atoms of hydrogen and one of oxygen produce water whenever they chemically combine. These are universal and unvarying laws. But such laws we do not find in studying social sciences owing to the instability of human behaviour. It is difficult, if not impossible, to draw precise conclusions from political phenomena or to make exact forecasts about the future. Still, by a close and prolonged observation of political phenomena we can arrive at general laws and principles which can be of real help to us in solving the practical problems of government.

We cannot experiment with human society or the political order in the way in which a scientist can experiment with physical or chemical substances. We cannot at will introduce democracy in one state and aristocracy in another in order to study the effects of these respective forms of government. Physical phenomena and social phenomena differ fundamentally. Nevertheless, every law passed is an experiment, and a careful student can arrive at general conclusions based on particular phenomena. A study of political theory, thus, does not enable us to reach conclusions with mathematical precision. 'However, it can help us to discover probable truths, and "probability" as Samuel Butler remarks, "is the guide of life", prediction in physics may be certain; in politics it can at best be no more than probable.'

A great many modern thinkers have given their thought and attention to the methods by which political phenomena can be collected and classified, with a view to reaching practical results. According to Augustus Comte, the principal methods are *observation experiment* and *comparison*. Bluntschli holds that the true methods are philosophical and historical. To a great many among present-day thinkers, inductive and pragmatic methods are more sure to lead to positive results in political science than deductive and dogmatic methods. The methods which are generally favoured by them are:

1. The experimental method,
2. The historical method,
3. The comparative method,
4. The method of observation, and
5. The philosophical method.

The first four of these methods have a great deal of similarity and so can be easily bracketed together. The fifth method belongs to a category of its own. A combination of these two types of methods alone can lead to valuable results. The inductive and deductive methods are complementary to one another.

1. The Experimental Method

As seen already, there is no much room for conscious experimentation in a field where we have to deal with human beings. Human motives and human values cannot be weighted and tabulated like a chemical substance. Nevertheless, every Law passed, every new policy enunciated, and every political system instituted is an experiment, and by a study of such experiments the political scientist can reach positive conclusions. It is his task to take note of the political experiments and happenings that go on around him all the time and make his deductions. Governments all the time try experiments on the community. History is experimentation on a very vast scale.

In the modern world, we do not rely on more unconscious experimentation. We make conscious political experiments, in the light of past experience, when and where circumstances permit. Witness, for example, the grant of responsible self-government to Canada based on the Durham Report of 1839 and the constitutional reforms granted to India and the transfer of complete power done by constitutional methods. Thus there is a definite and distinct place for the experimental method in political science.

2. The Historical Method

This may be regarded as a form of the experimental method. A proper study of history is an invaluable aid to the student of political science. It is a corrective to hasty and one-sided conclusions in politics. The value of studying the origin, growth and development of political institutions is that from such a study we can draw conclusions for future guidance. History not only explains the past, but also contains the key for interpreting the future.

The historical method is mainly inductive in character. It is based on observation and study of historical facts. Its chief limitation is that it cannot, and does not, deal in values. So it has to be supplemented by the philosophical or ethical method which looks to ultimate ends and values. Yet indirectly the historical method does enable us to judge the goodness of badness of actions.

In using the historical method, there are certain precautions that the student will do well to take:

(a) He should guard himself against superficial resemblances and parallels.

(b) He should not let the present and the future be determined solely by the past. The historical method should not become a synonym for hidebound conservatism. Just because a thing has been thus and so in the past, it does not follow that it should be thus and so at present.

(c) He should avoid the temptation to make history support his preconceived notions. And to do that he should be altogether objective or scientific in his outlook.'

(d) He should remember that the oft-quoted saying that history repeats itself is only a half-truth. The other half-truth is that history never repeats itself. Historical conditions never exactly reproduce themselves. 'One cannot step twice into the same river.'

3. The Comparative Method

This method supplements the historical method. It goes back to the time of Aristotle and has been used effectively in modern times by De Tocqueville, Bryce, and others. Study of history is useless if we cannot make valid comparations. The comparative method helps us to relate events, to establish caused and effect, and to arrive at general principles. It gathers together the multiplicity of phenomena, arranges them in order, and selects the elements common to them.

If this method is to be usefully employed, we must take into account not only resemblances but also differences. We are not to be in a hurry to come to conclusions. The phenomena from which the common elements are to be selected must not be too different in character. Comparisons must not be pushed too far and analogies must not be farfetched. Generalizations of a vague and broad character should be avoided. It is profitable on the whole to confine our investigations to the states which have sprung from a common historical background and which are relatively near together in point of time.

A particular form of the comparative method is the analogical method. It is very useful in political science, provided analogy is not pushed to the limit of identity. To establish an analogy between two things is not to establish their identity. Analogy is not proof. It can give us probability, but not certainty.

4. The Method of Observation

Like the foregoing methods, it is an inductive method. It was followed by Lord Bryrce to a very great extent. It rests upon an observation of the actual working of political institutions at close range, before undertaking his monumental works. The *American Commonwealth* and *Modern Democracies,* Lord Bryce visited the countries concerned and based his conclusions upon personal conservations with public men and the observation of governments at work. A method like this, based as it is on direct observation and reflection, has much to commend it. It is practical and concrete and has a refreshing sense of reality about it. It is in living touch with facts and is free from the charge of being abstract and doctrinaire. Nevertheless, it is a method which has to be used with caution. When the facts are very many and often conflicting, only a man with a trained eye and mature judgment can arrive at sound conclusions. One must have the ability to sift evidence and rightly interpret one's data There is a danger of seeing the things that one wants to see and leaving out those things of which one chooses to be oblivious. Likewise, there is a danger of missing the wood for the trees. The first desideratum is no doubt to get at facts. But facts are of little use in and by themselves. We need a penetrating and understanding mind to interpret them aright and make them real and living.

5. The Philosophical Method

Unlike the foregoing method, this method is of a deductive or a *priori* kind. Its chief exponents are Rousseau, Mill, and Sidgwick. On philosophical and ethical grounds it first determines the nature and end or purpose of the State and then casts about for the best forms of political institutions for the realisation of this end. It begins with abstract concepts, and then attempts to harmonize them with the actual facts of history. The chief danger of this method is that it may easily become imaginative and visionary, as seen in More's Utopia and, to some extent, in Plato's Republic. It may not have any basis whatever in historical facts and may thus sink into mere ideology. Attempts to construct an ideal type of State have engaged the attention of thinkers from the days of Greek philosophy, through the scholasticism of the Middle Ages down to the present day.

Conclusion

The careful student would seek to combine the historical and philosophical methods. He would test and correct his deductive principles by the actual facts of human experience and interpret the facts of life in the light of abstract or *a priori* principles. While his feet stand four square on solid facts, his head would soar high into the skies. He would seek to bring about a happy blend of realism and idealism. He would have no use for that type of realism which does not look much beyond one's own nose, nor for that type of idealism which loses itself in the clouds. He would follow the footsteps of men like Aristotle and Burke who combine in their writing the historical and philosophical methods.

Select Readings

Barker. E.—*Political Thought in England from Spencer to To-day*—Chs. 5 and 6.

Barnes, H.E.—*Sociology and Political Theory*—Ch. 2.

Brown, Ivor—*English Political Theory*—Ch. I.

Catlin, G.E.G.—*The Science and Method of Politics*—Chs. 1-3.

Garner, J.W.—Political Science and Government—Chs. 1-3.

Gettell, R.G.—*Introduction to Political Science*—Ch. 1.

Gettell, R.G.—*Readings in Political Science*—Introduction.

Gilchrist, R.N.—*Principels of Political Science*—Chs. 1.

Leacock, S.—*Elements of Political Science*—pp. 3-12.

Merriam, C.E.—*New Aspcts of Politics*—Chs. 3-4.

Pollock, G.—*Introduction to the History of the Science of Politics*—Ch. 1.

Seeley, S.—*Introduction to Political Science*—Lectures 1 and 2.

Sidgwick, H.—*Elements of Politics*—Ch. 1.

Willoughby, W.W.—*The Nature of the State*—Ch. 1.

4

The Purpose of The State

Divergent Views

What is the purpose of political organisation? There are perhaps as many answers to this question as there are writers on Politics. We shall cite a few, beginning with Aristotle.

To understand Aristotle's thought on the subject, we must start with his proposition that man is by nature a political animal. This means, first, that the social instinct is implanted in all men by nature, and that man can rise to his full stature only through the State. The State, Aristotle tells us, which originated for the sake of life, continues 'for the sake of the best life'. The end of the State is, therefore, ethical. As Newman puts it, the State exists (according to Aristotle) for the sake of that kind of life which is the end of man—not for the increase of its population or wealth or for empire or the extension of its influence. It exists for the exercise of the qualities which make men good husbands, fathers and heads of households, good soldiers and citizens, good men of science and philosophers. When the State by its education and laws, written and unwritten, succeeds in evoking and maintaining in vigorous activity a life rich in noble aims and deeds, then and not till then has it fully attained the end for which it exists. The ideal State is that which adds to adequate material advantages the noblest gifts of intellect and character and the will to live for their exercise in every relation of life, and whose education, institutions and laws are such as to develop these gifts and to call them into play. We may add that good life is life lived according to reason; 'the function of reason in ethics consists in the direction of conduct by a rule, the rule, namely, of the mean's; in politics, reason prescribes co-operation with one's fellow citizens in promoting the welfare of the State.

The ethical end of the State is subordinated to convenience in Locke. His concern is not with the 'good' but with the 'convenient'. 'The great and chief end of men uniting into commonwealths and putting themselves under government is the preservation of their property'—which is Locke's general name for 'lives, liberties and estates'. In the state of nature, these are not safe owing to the want of a settled known law, a known and indifferent judge, and a common Executive. The better preservation of these natural rights is therefore the purpose of political society; the exercise of power by a Government is conditioned by that purpose. Locke, it will be remembered, does not make his natural man surrender his natural rights even to the community; only the right of enforcing the law of reason is given up. The end of the State, as defined by Locke, is intelligible when it is remembered that the 'provocation' for his *Two Treatises of Civil Government* was the arbitrary exercise of power by the Stuart kings, and that its aim was to justify the principles of the Bill of Rights and the 'Glorious' Revolution of 1688.

Adam Smith (1723-90) in his *Wealth of Nations* (1776) laid down the following proposition:—The sovereign has only three duties to attend to: the duty of protecting society from the violence and invasion of other independent societies; secondly, the duty of protecting, as far as possible, every member of society from the injustice or opposition of every other member of it, or the duty of establishing an exact administration of justice; and, thirdly, the duty of erecting and maintaining certain public works and certain public institutions, which it can never be for the interest of any individual, or small number of individuals, to erect and maintain, because the profit yielded would never repay the expense to any individual or small number of individuals, though it might frequently do much more than repay a great society.

The process of the narrowing down of the purpose of the State reaches its culmination in Herbert Spencer (1820-1903).

According to him, the State is nothing but a natural institution for preventing one man from infringing upon the rights of another; it is a joint-stock protection company for mutual assurance.

"THE STATE IS AN END IN ITSELF'

Locke, Adam Smith and Spencer agree that the State is a means to an end, the end being a better life for the individual, whether conceived in ethical terms or not, whether the State is to interfere more or less. The opposite view that the State is an end in itself has had its exponents too, and is perhaps best illustrated by the school of thinkers known as Idealists, especially by Hegel. Hegel's argument is somewhat as follows:—Men want to be free; they are free only when they do what their reason recommends. Individual reason is not, however, trustworthy, because it is particularistic and moved by temporary and irrelevant considerations. The existence of some entity, whose will is universal and as acceptable to individuals as the voice of reason itself, is necessary. Such an entity is the State. It is a person and has a will of its own. It has ends of its own divorced from, and superior to, those of the individual human beings subjected to its authority. It carries out the dictates of universal reason and is therefore impelled by its own nature and destiny to seek its own perfection. 'The State, being an end in itself, is provided with the maximum of rights over against the individual citizens, whose highest duty it is to be members of the State." True freedom, therefore, consists in conformity to law; every law is a veritable freedom. The same trend of thought is illustrated in fascism and nazism. Thus:

'The Italian nation is an organisation having ends, a life and means superior in power and duration to the single individuals or groups or individuals composing it.'

It is noteworthy that those who claim that the State is an end in itself also take their stand on the idea that the individual is fleeting, the State is everlasting; the leaves wither, the tree stands. Says the fascist:

'Society is an imperishable organism, whose life extends beyond that of the individuals who are its transitory elements.

These are born, grow up, die and are substituted by others, while the social unit always retains its identity and its patrimony of ideas and sentiments, which each generation receives from the past and transmits to the future.'

The individual cannot therefore be considered as the ultimate end of society. Society has its own purposes of preservation, expansion and perfection, and these are distinct from, and superior to, the purposes of the individuals who at any moment compose it. In the carrying out of its own proper ends, society must make use of individuals; the individual must subordinate his own ends to those of society.

It sounds grandiose to say that the State has 'ends superior to those of the single individuals composing it'. But what are those ends? What should the individual subordinate his own ends to those of the State? No conclusive answer has been given. Answers involving words and phrases like 'universal reason', 'spirit', 'idea', 'real will' are only evasions of the issue. One suspects that these phrases are only meant to justify the acquisition of power and prestige for the State, i.e. for the glory of the ruler, and to commend to the ruled the sacrifice which this necessarily involves for them. The theory is but one way of justifying absolutism. It is founded on assumptions which are contrary to human experience.

'It regards humanity as something more than men,' writes R.M. MacIver; 'nationality as something more than the members of a nation. It suggests that it is possible to work for humanity otherwise than by working for men, to serve nationality otherwise than by serving the members of a nation. In so far as the end and value of society are regarded as other than the ends and values of its members taken as a whole, the latter count for less than before. Not only can we not give meaning and concreteness to such a value, but the postulation of it deprives of actuality the values we actually know.'

No. The formula laid down by Kant is as true now as when it was laid down: The individual is the end and cannot be considered as a means to an end. The State may rightly be considered only as a means to the enrichment of individual personality.

THE GREATEST HAPPINESS OF THE GREATEST NUMBER

An answer, more satisfactory than most of the answers given above, has been provided by the Utilitarian school, of which Jeremy Bentham (1748-1832) and John Stuart Mill (1806-73) are the best-known exponents. Briefly, their point of view is this:—All men desire happiness, which may be defined as the surplus of pleasure over pain. Pleasure and pain are therefore the main springs of human action.

'Nature has placed man under the governance of two sovereign masters, pain and pleasure. It is for them alone to point out what we ought to do, as well as to determine what we shall do . . . . We owe to them all our ideas; we refer to them all our judgements, and all the determinations of our life'. (Bentham) The sources of pleasure and pain are physical (e.g. good scenery) political (e.g. good laws), moral (public opinion) and religious (relations with God). It is the task of the legislator to manipulate these 'sanctions' to promote human happiness, individual and social. In the calculus of happiness, everybody is to count as one and nobody for more than one. To the individual the value of a pleasure or pain taken by itself depends on a number of factors including its duration, intensity, certainty (or uncertainty) and nearness (or remoteness). In dealing with a group the number of persons affected is another factor. So it is a matter for hedonistic calculus, summing up pleasures and pains in any particular case and balancing the pleasures against the pains, considering the number of persons affected and seeing whether the law contemplated produces the greatest happiness of the greatest number.

Utilitarianism has been subjected to a number of criticisms. It assumes that the business aspect of human affairs alone governs man's conduct; it does not seem to appreciate pure disinterestedness, which it ultimately resolves into the pursuit of individual pleasure. Again, a sum of pleasures may be an attractive phrase; but when it comes to estimates of human happiness or misery, arithmetic in politics is not much more helpful than politics in arithmetic; for there is no proof that by pursuing the happiness of the greatest number, we shall produce, or help to produce, the greatest happiness. If men were all equal, it would be simple political philosophy, because it is nothing more than simple arithmetic, to conclude that the greater the number of men made happy, the greater the resulting sum of happiness. But men are not equal; Bentham himself admitted that the dogma of the equality of men was an 'anarchic fallacy'. As men are not equal, and the same pleasure may be felt by different men unequally it would be difficult to calculate the greatest happiness of the greatest number, with any assurance of success.

But in spite of all this criticism, the formula of the greatest happiness of the greatest number still remains valuable in Politics. It supplies a 'slogan' which gets imprinted in the popular mind and supplies a standard, a touchstone, with which one can judge State actions. The basic idea of Utilitarianism (distinguished specially from Idealism) is simply this: all actions must be judged by their results, by their fruitfulness in pleasure, and this pleasure must find actual expression in the lives and in the experience of definite individuals. And above all, to use Pollock's metaphor, the formula of the greatest happiness can be made a hook to put in the nostrils of the leviathan [the State], that he may be tamed and harnessed to the chariot of utility. The criterion of unity serves to simplify the problem of Politics. Bentham said, 'let the State act to remove disabilities'; in so doing the rulers would be forwarding the welfare of their subjects. But if the authorities failed in this purpose, they could claim no rights of sanctity. The claims of legality could not stand for a moment against the claims of morality, and the claims of morality were summed up in the happiness of the people.

'A public judgement of happiness, expediency, well-being, or whatever else we call it, is in the nature of human affairs a rough thing at best; and there is plenty of work to be done which ought to be done on any possible view of the nature of duty. The main point was to rouse the State to consciousness of its power and its proper business; and by persistent and confident iteration, Bentham did this effectually.

A Modern View

One of the best statements in recent times regarding the purpose of the State is made by Laski in *A Grammar of Politics:* The State is an organisation to enable the mass of men to realize social good on the largest possible scale. It exists to enable men, at least potentially, to realize the best that is in themselves. Men can be enabled to realize the 'best that is in themselves' only if the State provides 'rights'. Rights are those conditions of social life without which no man can seek in general to be himself at his best. They have a content which changes with time and place. They are prior to the State in the sense that, recognized or no, they are that from which its validity derives. Rights are, therefore, the groundwork of the State.

To illustrate: the citizen has a right to work. Society owes the citizen the occasion to perform his function, for to leave him without access to the means of existence is to deprive him of that which makes possible the realization of personality. The right to work involves the right to maintenance in the absence or work. The right to an adequate wage, the right to reasonable hours of labour, and the right to be concerned in the government of industry are other economic rights which are necessary to provide decent conditions of life and work. The citizen has a right to such education as will fit him for the tasks of citizenship.

A group of other rights are necessary to enable the citizen to have a share in the government of his State, itself a necessary condition for the realization of his best self: the right to vote, periodical elections, the right to stand as a candidate for election, equal eligibility to government office (if the necessary qualifications are fulfilled), and freedom of speech, press and association. They enable the citizen to contribute his instructed judgement for the public good, to elect his rulers and call them to account for their conduct in office. They enable him, too, to work with like-minded men for the promotion of these purposes in life which he deems necessary for realizing his own personality.

And, finally, a third group of rights which Laski calls *private* is essential. Under this head he includes the right to reasonable access to judicial remedy, freedom of religion and a limited right of property. These are necessary to give the citizen a sense of personal security and freedom of conscience.

These rights, it is hardly necessary to mention, are not absolute rights: the rights of one are limited by the rights of others. They have also to be defined in detail from time to time in relation to social conditions. Moreover, which it is true that the State must give the citizen these conditions, without which he cannot be that best self that he may be, this does not mean the guarantee that his best self will be attained. It means only that the hindrances to its attainment are removed as far as the actions of the State can remove them. But the State must do its duty; since it exists to enable men to realize their best, it is only by maintaining rights that its end may be attained.

Laski, it ought to be added, is careful to point out that his way of stating the purpose of the State is only a special adaptation of the Benthamite theory to the special needs of our time. It follows Bentham in its insistence that 'social good is the product of co-ordinated intelligence', and that social good means the avoidance of misery and the attainment of happiness. It differs from the Utilitarian outlook in its rejection of the egoistic nature of the human impulse and of the elaborate calculus of pains and pleasures.

'Our view', concludes H.J. Laski, 'is rather, first, that individual good cannot, over a long period, be usefully abstracted from the good of other men; and, second, that the value of reason is to be found in the degree to which it makes possible the future, not less than the immediate, harmony of impulses'.

The view outlined above has the great merit of being simple, realistic, and intelligible. It is broader than the views of Locke and Spencer. It is clearer and safer than the Idealist view; clearer because it does not take shelter behind big phrases like 'cosmic reason' and 'the personality of the State', and safer because it leaves the judgement of the performance of the State to the average man and women who are subject to its laws. It is not static, but takes note of changes in time and place. Above all, it makes the individual the end, and the State the means. It puts the State on trial; for, over any long period, the State can win the allegiance of its citizens only by the efforts it makes to give their rights increasing substance.

Political Obligation

If now we ask ourselves the question: 'Why do men obey the state?' the answer is clear. In rational terms, men obey the State because they stand to gain by doing so. They are conscious that the State has a rational purpose; that purpose is the promotion of social good on the largest possible scale; the achievement of that purpose demands their willing co-operation and obedience to laws. But the same view also tells them that, in certain circumstances, they may deem it their duty to withdraw their co-operation and resist the State, viz. when the mischiefs of obedience are greater than the mischiefs of disobedience. They obey the State because, by doing so, they hope to be provided with those conditions of social life which are necessary for the realization of their own personalities; it is the duty of the State to recognize their rights and give them increasing substance. When there is clear evidence that, over a reasonable period, the State is not doing its duty—in our words, when its actions are not in accordance with its purpose—the individual has a duty to ask himself why he should continue to render obedience. There is a moral right to resist.

The right to resist the State, however, is itself limited by conditions, as indeed all rights are. First, the individual must not resist the State if reaonsble grounds exist to show that it is seeking to play its part, even though it has not achieved its object as quickly as he might wish. Second, he must have reasonable ground for the belief that the changes he advocates are likely to result in the end he has in view. Third, he must try constitutional methods of agitation before resorting to resistance; for, very often, by themselves they may be sufficient to gain the objective. Further, resistance can be resorted to only for the vindication of significant issues, as distinguished from minor details of no moment. The gist of these limitations is that, as Burke said, the right to resist is the medicine of the constitution and not its daily bread. This is a necessary caution because, while the conscientious individual who leads the resistance may often be motivated by the highest moral purpose, he must remember that he may be followed by others less conscientious who may take advantage of the opportunity to gain their selfish ends.

This is purely a rational view of the problem of political obligation and, therefore, inadequate. Graham Wallas has taught us that the play of reason in politics is restricted by the strength of emotions and instincts in the mental life. As Laski suggests, the State as it was and is has found the roots of allegiance in all the complex facts of human nature. This nature is a mixture of impulses and reason. The satisfaction of man's primary wants—hunger, drink, sex, clothing and shelter—involves associated life; and associated life implies the necessity of government.

"The activities of a civilized community are too complex and too manifold to be left to the blind regulation of impulse; and even if each man could be relied upon to act consistently in terms of intelligence, there would be need for a customary standard by which the society in its organized form agreed to differentiate right from wrong.'

Some obey through fear of the punishments which disobedience to law involves. Further, men are born in the State; obedience to the State becomes with most men an habit, and few expend the effort to scrutinize its foundations. And those who reflect on the nature of the State would find it an organisation to enable the mass of men to realize social good—an instrument to further men's happiness and would render obedience to it to the extent it realizes its purpose.

To enable the State to fulfil its purpose, it is endowed with force, with coercive power. But force is not the essence of the State but only its criterion. The Government, as the agency of the State, is vested with coercive power in order to compel obedience to its law for the preservation of order and for the common good of the community. The purpose of force is to prevent individuals and associations of individuals from taking the law into their own hands and to insist on a peaceful settlement of their differences. As A.D. Lindsay puts it, most people usually wish to obey the law.

Everybody has to obey it always. The force of the State is necessary to fill up the margin between 'most people' and 'everybody', between 'usually' and 'always'. But force, essential as it is, is not the *basis* of the State. It is assigned to the Government as upholders of law; and the law itself must be such as to command the general consent of the people. This point is well brought out in Green's famous statement: 'Will, not force, is the basis of the State'.

Select Bibliography

Aristotle, *Politics* Bk. I, 'Everyman's Library', Dent W.L. Davidosn, *Political Thought in England: Bentham to Mill,* 'Home University Library', Oxford, 1915.

R.G. Gettell, *Political Science,* ch. XXI, Ginn, 1933.

H.J. Laski, *A Grammar of Politics,* ch. I, Allen & Unwin, 1948.

W.W. Willoughby, *An Examiantion of the Nature of the State,* ch. XII, Macmillan, 1922.

———, *The Ethical Basis of Political Authority,* chs. XIV & XV, Macmillan, 1930.

5

The Nature of The State

The State is the most universal and most powerful of all social institutions. Whether human beings have lived together for any length of time, there we find organisation and authority. And where we find organisation and authority, there we have the nucleus of the State. The only outstanding example of a people who form a society but do not constitute a State is that of the Eskimps.

As the Greek writers have taught us to think, the State is both a natural and a necessary institution. Headache may be natural, but is not necessary. The State is natural in the sanse that it has arisen out of the primary instincts of man and is a gradual growth. Aristotle declares that man by nature is a political being. The development of the original family, according to him, meant a village, and when many villages joined together there came into being the city of State. Each city is a 'work of Nature'. To Aristotle, to live in the State and to be a man were identical, for whoever was not a member of the State or was not fit to be one was either a God or a beast; he was either above the State or below it. Modern writers sometimes speak of the political instinct of man? By that they mean that the State has its roots in the natural impulses of man and that it cannot be easily eradicated. The State grows, is permanent, and reappears when it is destroyed. If it is claimed that the State is not natural in the sense in which the family is natural and that it is the artificialisations of some human need, our answer is that 'it is natural for human beings to be artificial'. But our contention is that the State is not an artificial creation. We are born into the State. We do not ordinarily choose it and cannot, of right, claim dissociation from it. Spencer is mistaken when he says that the indiciual has a 'right to ignore the state'.

The State is necessary for man's growth and development. Without it man cannot reach the height of his perfection. Aristotle holds that the State first came into being in order that we might live, but is continued in order that we may live happily. In his own words, 'the State comes into existence originating in the bare needs of life, and continuing in existence for the wake of a good life'. In other words, satisfaction of economic wants is the chief reason why the State first came into being. But its continuance lies in the fact that it is indispensable to good life, *i.e.,* to a life of happiness and nobility. Aristotle's teacher, Plato, finds the necessity for the State in the fact that no man is sufficient unto himself. The need of man for social co-operation and social endeavour, at a certain stage of a development, express itself in the State.

The State, we have said, is the most universal and most powerful of all social institutions, and is natural and necessary. What then is the State?

1. The State and Society

The State is not identical with society. To the early Greek thinkers the State was indistinguishable from society. This identification of the State with society is to be explained by the peculiar circumstance that prevailed in the Greek city-state. The city-state was small in size and compact in population. The citizens knew one another personally and met together in common assemblies to pass laws and choose magistrates. They were knot together by common interests. The problems with which they were faced were simple in character. In these circumstances it was natural for the Greek to consider the city as including the whole life of man. 'She is ours and we are hers' was the characteristic attitude of the Greeks towards their city or State. The city performed multifarious functions. It was the State, the Church, and the School, all in one. The social life was, to the Greek, a life of citizenship.

Whatever justification the Greeks may have had for the identification of the State with society, we, to-day, have no such justification. Interpreted strictly, the State is a political organisation. It is society politically organised. Society is both broader and narrower than the State. It may be used to describe the whole community of mankind just as much as a small social group of a village. In his broader sense, 'it transcends the individual state and crosses state boundaries without regard to their existence', e.g., the Islamic Society and the Free Mason Brotherhood.

The State is part of society, but is not a form of society. It is more than a number of loosely connected individuals who happen to live together. It is a number of people associated together politically, organised under and through some form of Government, occupying a definite portion of the earth's surface. Society exercises authority largely through customs. The State exercises authority through laws enacted and enforced by Government. The State is the only instrument which can legitimately use force. Society can only use moral persuasion or influence and social ostracism or expulsion. It cannot imprison a man for the violation of its requirements. To use the language of E. Barker, the area of society is voluntary co-operation, its energy that of goodwill, its method that of elasticity; while the area of the State is rather that of mechanical action, its energy force, its method rigidity. In the words of MacIver, 'the State is a structure not coeval and co-extensive with society but built within it as a determinate order for the attainment of specific ends'. The importance of the State to society is clearly brought out by E. Barker when he says, 'Society is held together by the State; and if it were not thus held together, it could not exist'. Society may be compared to the many planks which comprise a wooden barrel, and the State to the iron band which goes around them holding them together in their proper places.

2. The State and Government

In our ordinary conversation we use the two terms interchangeably. Yet a moment's reflection is enough to show that they are not only and the same. Government is the instrument of the State. In the words of Rousseau, it is 'a living tool'. It is the practical organisation of the State through which the will of the State is 'formulated, expressed and realized'. The ends and purposes of the State are executed through the instrumentality of the government. Without government the State has no existence. The State is largely an abstraction, but government is concrete. The State is permanent and fixed while government is transitory. Changes in the form of the government do not mean changes in the continuity of the State.

The principal ways by which the State may cease to exist are:

1. Conquest followed by incorporation
2. Voluntary choice.
3. Distruction of the land or the people of a state. Examples of these are:
   (a) The incorporation of the Kingdom of Hangover into Prussia after its conquest in 1866.
   (b) Union of the small states of Italy into the Kingdom of Italy,
   (c) The threat of William of Orange that he would cut the dykes of Netherlands and destroy the country rather than see it conquered by the Spaniards:

The authority of the Government is not original. It is derived from the state. The functions of any Government are executive, legislative, and judicial. Government is an expression of the genius of a people.

3. The State, Nation, and Nationality

In Political Science these terms have often been used as synonymous terms. Even today, political thinkers in general do not make a careful distinction between Nation and Nationality. For the sake of clarity of meaning and precision in the use of words, it is wise to employ these terms to describe distinct things. The State, as we have already seen is a political organisation. It may or may not be co-existent with Nationality. Where a State is exclusively composed (or nearly so) of one nationality we get a nation-State. But where we have a State which consists of more than one nationality, or where a nationality is spread over several States, the State and nation do not coincide. Nation means a self-governing nationality. Or, as Gilchrist puts it, a nation equals State plus nationality. The same writer goes on to say that the term nation today has acquired a definitely political meaning. 'It stands for the unity of the people organized in one State and acting spontaneously as a unity'. Nationality is primarily a cultural and ethical term. It is a spiritual sentiment or principle. Factor which make a people a nationality are factors like geographical unity, common racial stock, common culture, common language, religion, customs and traditions, common history, common economic interests and political associations, common hopes and aspirations, etc. It is not necessarily that every one of these factors should be present in order that a people may become a nationality. Still without at least some of these factors nationality unimaginable. On the political side, nationality is defined as the disposition to act together politically.

Since the early part of the nineteenth century, there has been a growing feeling that every group of people who claim to be a nationality should be allowed to have an independent political organisation. This movement received an impetus in the World War I and expressed itself in such potent ideas as the 'self-determination of Nations' and 'one nation, one State'. Whether this is the goal towards which political progress should be directed is a question which will claim our attention later.

The distinction that we have drawn between a 'nation' and a 'nationality' is not the one which is usually drawn. Gettell observes: Considerable confusion arises from the fact that publicists do not agree in their usage of the terms 'nation' and 'nationality'. Some use the term 'nation' to mean a population of ethnic unity, regardless of its political affiliation; others widen the term to mean a population having also political unity and identity of 'nation' and 'state'. Some use the term 'nationality' to signify the principle or characteristic that creates a nation. Others distinguish nation and nationality by using the former to mean a population of the same race, language and tradition inhabiting the same territory and constituting the larger part of its population and the latter to mean one of several distinct ethnic groups scattered over an area and forming but a comparatively small part of its population.

Vico in 1725 said that nation 'is a natural society of men who by reason of unity of territory, origin, custom, and language are drawn into a community of life and of conscience'.

4. One-sided or False Views of the State

There is scarcely any term in political science which has given rise to more confused thinking than the primary term 'State'. Practically every writer of political science gives his own definition of the 'State', and there are hardly any two thinkers who agree on what they consider to be a satisfactory definition of the 'State'. MacIver in his *Modern State* sums up views of the State which are either narrow and one-sided or altogether false.

1. According to writers like Oppenheimer, the author of *The State,* the State is essentially a class-structure, 'an organisation of one class dcminating over the other classes'. Or, as another writer puts it: 'The State is the formal staff of the class which owns economic power'. It is needless to say that this is a caricature of the State rather than a correct view of it. It is in line which the teaching of Karl Marx, according to whom the modern State is an agency for the exploitation of the poor by the rich. As a definition of the State, Oppenheimer's definition may be true of certain states at certain times, but we object to making it apply to all states at all times. It applies more to a diseased State than to a normal one. In a normal or well-ordered State individual or class interests are duly subordinated to the general interest or common good.
2. Some interpret the State as a power-system. They interpret it exclusively in terms of might. Machiavelli is the forerunner of this point of view. Professor T.N. Carver holds that the State is force and nothing but force. Many German writers such as Treitschke uphold the same view during the Great War I. We totally disagree with this view. Force is no doubt an essential part of the State, but is not the foundation of the State. Might never makes anything right. It is right which can lend support to might. When used in the interest of right,

might may be justifiable. T.H. Green aptly remarks, 'Will, not force, is the basis of the State'; Force is the distinguishing mark of the State. But the reason why we as enlightened citizens obey a well-ordered State is that we are conscious that in obeying the State we obey the best in ourselves, we obey our own individual wills purged and purified of their selfishness. Obedience to the State is highly justifiable when it arises out of the consciousness that, in obeying the will of the well-ordered State, one promotes a common good of which the individual good is an intrinsic part.

3. To thinkers like Grotius and Althusius the State is a welfare-system. One form of this theory is that the State is in the nature of a public utilities company. We have no hesitation in saying that this is too narrow a view of the State. Promotion of public welfare is undoubtedly a very important duty of the State. But to identify the State with a public utility company, like the U.P. Electric Supply Company, is clearly a mistake. The State is not like a company at all. Membership in it is not voluntary. We are born members of the State. We cannot enter the State when we like and leave it when we like. Further, the view of the State under consideration ignores the fact that besides being a welfare-system, the State has a life, will, and personality of its own, which, in some ways are different from the life, will, and personality of the individual members comprising it.

4. There are a few writers, whose number is happily diminishing to-day, to whom the State is in the nature of a mutual insurance society for purposes of mutual protection. Herbert Spencer was a staunch advocate of this theory. To him, the State is 'a joint stock protection company for mutual assurance'. We have already seen that the State cannot be compared to a company, much less can it be compared to an insurance company. Views like this do scant justice to the organic nature of the State, according to which, individual good and social good are intimately related and are not two clearly separable entities. if mutual protection is the only purpose for which the State exists, what is there to deny the name 'State' to group of brigands who band themselves

together against the rest of society? Any self-defence group would be entitled to describes itself as a State.

5. Some interpret the State as entirely a legal construction. To them the State is a community 'organized for action under legal rules'. Once again, we would say that this is a very narrow view of the State. There is no doubt whatever that the legal aspect of the State is a very important aspect, but it is not the only aspect. The State guarantees to is citizens rights and enforces duties. But that does not exhaust the nature of functions of the State. The legal view of the State ignores the higher life of the State altogether. 'The State', says Hegel, 'is the world the spirit has made for itself'. Miss Follett in her *New State* remarks: 'The home of my soul is in the State. The State is, to our way of thinking, as much of a spiritual entity as a legal construction.

6. The individualists consider the State as a necessary evil. They regard every action of the State as a subtraction from the freedom of the individual. Hence, they say, the State is an evil, although it is rendered necessary by the selfishness and rapacity of man. If each individual were left to himself, they argue, he would seek his own self-aggrandizement at the expense of others and there would be no social peace and no social order. The State thus becomes a concession to human weakness. Spencer and even such an enlightened thinker as Bentham uphold this point of view. As for ourselves, we believe that it is a mistake to consider the State an evil, or even a necessary evil. We agree with the idealists when they say that the State is a positive good. It is man's truest fried, for the fullest and freest development of human personality is impossible without the instrumentality of the State.

7. The mild anarchists modify the position of the individualists to the extent of holding that the State is an evil, but that some day it will be unnecessary. They rely unduly upon the changeability of human nature, believing that with the increasing moral development of man the State will become less and less necessary and will eventually 'wither away'.

The extreme anarchists such as those who subscribes to anarchistic communism hold that the State is an unmitigated evil, and, therefore, the sooner we get rid of it the better it will be for the moral growth of man. While there is much that is admirable in the anarchist position, we must admit that it does scant justice to the fact that the State has its roots in human nature. The anarchist has to persuade our instincts as well as our reason that the State is an evil which carries with it no compensating factor. A contention which we shall attempt to establish in a later chapter, is that obedience to authority is natural and that authority and liberty are complementary, and not antithetical to one another.

8. Some modern writers prefer to regard the State as one in the order of 'corporations'. This is the pluralistic point of view in general. According to this view, the State is to be reduced to a position of equality with other permanent groups like the family, the church, the trade union, the social club, etc. which cater to our varied interests. We refuse to accept this view because of our conviction that the State is unique in its character. It is the only one of its kind. It is a class by itself. It is an all-inclusive association, an association *par excellence.* By saying all this, we do not mean to suggest that we are prepared to accept the orthodox monistic point of view *in toto,* We realise that the time has come for us to recognise that the various permanent groups within society have a definite and distinct place to fill in the life of man and that, in order to do this satisfactorily, they should have as large a degree of internal autonomy as possible. Nevertheless, we need a superior organisation to adjust relationship and to keep the various subordinate organisations in their proper places. That organisation is the State.

9. The modern totalitarian view of the State regards the whole life of the individual as coming within the jurisdiction of the State. There is no part of a man's life which he can call his own. If he lives, he lives for the State; and if he dies, he dies for the State. Mussolini states the totalitarian view in the words: 'All within the State, none outside the State, none

against the State'. The motto which he placed before the youth of his country was: 'To believe, to obey, to fight'.

It is needless to say that the totalitarian view means regimentation of the life of the individual. It is a wholesale denial of the worth and dignity of human personality. The individual becomes a mere cog in the wheel of the State.

A Positive Statement of the State

1. Priority of the State

The State is the highest form of human association. Without it man's life is incomplete. It provides the environment for the self-realization and self-development of the individual. As Aristotle holds, the State and household differ, not in degree, but in kind. The household exists for satisfying the physical needs of life, the State for the moral and intellectual needs. The notion of a city (for State), says Aristotle, naturally precedes that of a family or an individual for the whole must necessarily be prior to the parts. The state is thus prior to the individual. There is a natural impulse for men to associate with each other. It is by the completion of civil society that man is the most excellent of all living beings. Without law and justice man would be the worst of all beings. Only in the State does the individual really become a man. Without the State he might be potentially a man, but would be actually a brute.

2. The State as Will and Mind

Thus the State, as an idea, is prior to man. This does not mean that the end of the State is some thing apart from, or contrary to, the end of the individual. Properly understood, the end of both is the same, viz. the development of human personality. In view of what has been said earlier, it is clear that this development is impossible in isolation. No man is sufficient to himself. The family, social organisation of one kind or another, and the State testify to this act. As Lord puts it, the State is an essentially necessary aspect of, or element in, the individual's own will. It is partly an external organisation fulfilling the most universal and permanent needs of human personality and partly the individual himself in a different capacity. It is the extension and completion of the moral and rational will of the individual. It is a rational organisation of the various interests and purposes of the individual.

3. The State of Force

In one aspect, then, the State is the individual's mind. In another, 'it is his body and force'. It completes the bodily force of its citizens. Physical coercion is an indispensable element in the constitution of the State. In the last analysis the State must have power to coerce the unsociable and recalcitrant will. The State interprets the individual to himself. Force used by the State is an effective means of freeing the individual from the low level of existence which he tends to reach in his ordinary and unreflecting moments to a higher level of existence where he is enabled to see his individual good as an intrinsic part of the common social good. There is more truth than may appear at first sight in Hegel's contention that the criminal has a right to be punished.

4. The Uniqueness of the State

The State is the one organisation that transcends class and stands for the whole community. None of the other associations—social, religious, political economic, educational, etc. can include the whole of the individual. In the striking words of Miss Follett, 'The State cannot be composed of groups, because no group, nor any number of groups, can contain the whole of me and the ideal State demands the whole of me. Again, the true State must gather up every interest within itself. It must take over many loyalties and find how it can make them one. I have all these different allegiance. I should indeed lead a divided and, therefore, uninteresting life if I could not unify them. The true State has my devotion, because it gathers up into itself the various sides of me, is the symbol of my multiple self, is my multiple self brought to significance, to self realsiation. If you leave me with my plural selves you leave me in desolate places, my should craving its meaning and its home. The home of my soul is in the State'.

5. The State as an Adjuster of Relationships

A corollary which follows from the above view of the State is that we require a supreme organisation, viz. the State to adjust the 'outstanding external relationships of man in society'. Life becomes a chaos without the State. It is the State which reconciles differences and gives unity and meaning to the many-sided life of man. In a complex and complicated world where there is an ever-growing conflict of loyalties, there is an urgent and increasing need for the State as an adjuster of relationships. It is the business of the State to keep the family, the church, the trade union, the social club, etc. in their proper places and to see that nothing is one to disturb the harmony of society.

6. The State and Universal Interest

The State can concern itself only with those interests of man which can reasonably be regarded as universal. It cannot undertake the promotion of the sectional or class interests of its numbers. For this latter purpose, we have such organisation as the family, the church, the trade union and the cultural organisation. As Garner puts it, while the purpose of a voluntary association is limited to the pursuit of one, or at most, a few particular interest's, the State is charged with the care of general rather than particular interests. This explains the reason why trade unions in England are not allowed to exact a political levy. In the words of Laski, 'the State stands above all narrow interests in the society and uses its coercive power on behalf of the permanent and abiding interests for which men live together.

7. The State and Morality

Finally, the State can regulate only the outer aspects of conduct. It cannot take motives into account, since they are altogether of an inner character. The State may consider intentions, but motives fall outside its scope. When we consider intentions, we are concerned with the question whether a given act was purposeful or only accidental. But when we consider motives, we are concerned with the inward and moral nature of the question in hand. Although the State is a moral and spiritual institutions and is an extension of the personality of the individual, the instruments at its disposal are of such an external character (force) that it can deal only with outer conduct and intentions, but not with motives. From this is follows that the State cannot enforce or promote morality directly. It can only make it possible for the individual to earn his own morality. T.H. Green rightly says: 'the only acts which it (the State) ought to *enjoin* or *forbid* are those of which the doing or not doing, *from whatever motive,* is necessary to the moral end of society'. In simple language, it means that the State ought to undertake only those actions which are so absolutely indispensable to the good life of society that in enforcing them it can take the risk that some people will perform, or refrain from them, form a low and unworthy motive. Mechanical action or automatism is the risk which the State at times takes in enforcing its will in the best interests of its members.

To sum up the discussion, the State is not an end in itself. It is a means by which the collective needs of men can best be secured in an orderly and just manner. Without the State, the individual sinks into insignificance. It is the State which holds the social order together. By a judicious use of reason and compulsion, permission and authority, it can promote the true well-being of society, of which the true well-being of every individual is an intrinsic part. The State has no right to crush or hinder the individuality of any single person. Nor has it a justification for existence so long as the minimum conditions necessary for the good life of every individual are absent.

ESSENTIAL ELEMENTS OF THE STATE

The essential elements of the State are population, territory, sovereignty, and government.

1. Population

It is obvious that there can be no State unless people live together an associated life. The question relating to the number of persons necessary to constitute a State is only of theoretical interest, although ancient writers laid much stress on it. Plato in his *Laws* fixed the number of citizens for an ideal State at 5040. Aristotle considered 100,000 too many. In recent times, Rousseau who was an ardent admirer of the Greek city-state life wanted to revive the ancient city-state with a compact population. According to him 10,000 would be an ideal number. Modern states vary in size and population as widely as the British Empire, Russia, and china on the one hand; and Monaco and San Marino on the other, the latter of which has only an area of 38 square miles.

From the legal point of view, population as an element of the State includes both those who rule and those who are ruled. the people of a State possess a dual character. In the capacity of those who have share in framing the will of the State, they are citizens, and in the capacity of those who obey the will thus formed they are subject. The distinction we owe to Rousseau. Even in a non-democratic State, this truth holds good for the absoute monarch, for example, is only an agent for the expression of the will of the State'. As citizens, people possess rights and as subjects they have duties.

2. Territory

There can be little doubt that without fixed territory there can be no State. Yet not all political thinkers are absolutely agreed on it. The modern State undoubtedly requires a definite portion of earth's territory over which it can have undisputed authority. In contrast with the ancient State, the modern State is essentially territorial in character. A nomadic people cannot be said to constitute a State, although they may have some form of political organisation through common subjection to a leader or chief. In the words of Prof. Elliott 'Territorial sovereignty or the superiority of the State over all within its boundaries and complete freedom from external control, has been a fundamental principle of the modern State life'.

A fixed territory is so much an essential factor of the modern State that no two separate and unrelated States can claim jurisdiction over the same area. The only apparent exception is that of the federal State, where two 'States' exercise authority over the same territory. But it should be remembered that 'they are related States' and that 'the spheer of each is carefully determined by the provisions of the written constitution.

3. Sovereignty

Sovereignty and law are the two distinguishing characteristics of the State. By sovereignty we mean ultimate authority, an authority from which there is no appeal. Associations other than the State may have population, territory, and even some from the governmental organisation, but they have no sovereignty. In the last resort, all individuals and groups of individuals within the State have to submit to the will of the State. This fact we express by the term internal sovereignty. In external relation, too, the modern State claims final authority. It may obey international conventions and understandings, but there is no power on earth which can compel such obedience. This attribute of the State we express by the term external sovereignty. By virtue of its sovereign authority the modern State claims supremacy in internal matters and freedom from the control of external governments. To use the language of Laski, 'it is by the possession of sovereignty that the State is distinguished from all other forms of human association.

The orthodox view of sovereignty, as found in Hobbes, Bentham, and Austin is expressed by Lewis when he says: 'The sovereign has the complete disposal of the life, rights and duties of every member of the community. MacIver and many other modern writers dissent from this view. To MacIver, the State is an association, unique in its kind and of invaluable significance but still an association, like the rest. We shall take up a criticism of this view in a later chapter.

4. Government

As seen already, government is the political organisation of the State. It is the instrumentality through which the sovereign will of the State finds concrete expression. If the ultimate sovereign in a democratic country is the people, the legislative sovereign is the government. A State without government is inconceivable, for the State wills and acts through the government. No particular form of government is essential. The form of government depends upon the nature of the State which in turn depends largely upon the political thought and character of the people.

DEFINITIONS OF THE STATE

A great number and variety of definitions of the State have been given. We shall give only some of the most satisfactory Holland defined the State as a 'numerous assemblage of human beings, generally occupying a certain territory among whom the will of the majority or of an ascertainable class of persons is by the strength of such a majority made to prevail against any of their number who oppose it. Philimore, looking at the State from the point of view of international law, defines it as 'a people permanently occupying a fixed territory, bound together by common laws, habits, and customs into one body politic, exercising through the medium of an organized government independent sovereignty and control over all person and things within its boundaries, capable of making war and peace and of entering into all international relations with the communities of the globe.

Burgess defines the State as a particular portion of mankind viewed as an organized unit.' This definition is substantially the same as that given by Bluntschli to whom 'The State is the politically organized people of a definite territory.' Wilson's definition is both short and simple. To him the State 'is a people organized for law within a definite territory.'

Among the definitions given by contemporary writers, those of Garner and MacIver deserve special mention.

Garner says: 'The State as 'a concept of political science and public law, is a community of persons more or less numerous, permanently occupying a definite portion of territory, independent, or nearly so, of external control and possessing an organised government to which the great body of inhabitants render habitual obedience.

MacIvar's definition which carries with it a pluralistic tingle is: 'The State is an association which, acting through law as promulgated by a government endowed to this end with coercive power, maintains within a community territorially demarcated the universal external conditions of social order.' This definition which, in many ways, is the best, emphasises 'law, 'government', coercive power,' 'communal unity' 'clearly marked territory,' and 'the universal external conditions of social order'—of which are elements which should enter into any sound view of the State.

Laski defines the State as 'a territorial society divided into government and subjects claiming, within its allotted physical area, a supremacy over all other institutions.

Definitions like those of Hegel are highly abstract and rather onsided. A recent writer defines the State as 'the organised body of human beings living under one government and in one definite territory.'

The Organic Nature of the State

From the days of Plato down to the present day it has been the common stock-in-trade of political thinkers to compare society and, in turn, the State to a living organism. Some have used the analogy, while some have tried to apply it at every point, with the result that not a few among the most serious-minded writers on political science are inclined to dismiss the conception wholly as being useless, if not mischievous.

Plato compared the State to a magnified human being. He drew an elaborate parallel between the functions of the State and those of the individual. His three-fold classification of society into the rulers, the warriors, and the working classes, Plato bases upon the three faculties of the human soul, *viz.* wisdom, courage, and desire. The State is to him like the capital letter 'A' while the individual is comparable to the small letter 'a'. The State is the macrocosm and the individual, the microcosm. Aristotle drew a comparison between the symmetry of the State and symmetry of the body and held firmly to the belief that the individual is an intrinsic part of society. Cicero, who in many respects depended upon the Greek thinkers for his political ideas, brought out a parallel between the head of the State and the spirit which rules the body. In the early days of the Christian Church, St. Paul regarded the Church as the living body of State. On the basis of this teaching medieval writers based their controversies on the relative claims of the Church and State to the allegiance of man in both spiritual and secular affairs.

Among the early writers of the modern period, Hobbes and Rousseau gave much attention to the organic conception of the State. Hobbes compared the State to a huge, imaginary monster called the Leviathan, 'which is but an artificial man, though of greater strength and stature than the natural'. He even drew a minute parallel between the weaknesses of the State and human ailments. Thus the State could suffer from boils, scabs, pleurisy, etc. This elaborate parallel between the social organism and individual organism is amusing, coming as it does from one who adheres to the social contract theory, according to which the State is a deliberate creation of the human will. According to Rousseau, both the body politic and the human body possess the 'motive powers' of 'force' and 'will'. The legislative power of the State is compared to the heart and the executive power to the brain.

The nineteenth century political thought began with a reaction against the view that the State is an artificial creation of man. It tried to establish the truth that the State was not man-made, but a gradual, unconscious, and inevitable development of human nature. In this endeavour the familiar conception of the organic nature of society was revived and became a fundamental part of the thinking of German idealists especially. Fichte, who belonged to this latter group of theorists, was the first to bring out clearly the interdependence of the individual and society. He held that the individual had no meaning and significance in and by himself, apart from society, but was an essential part of the social whole. In his own words: 'In the organic body each part constantly maintains the whole, and is in maintaining the whole thereby, itself maintained; just so stands the citizen in relation to the State'. Early idealists thus looked upon the State as a moral organism.

Among later German writers, it was Bluntschli who exaggerated the organic doctrine more than any of his predecessors. He went so far as to attribute qualities of sex to the State. The State, he said, was masculine in character, while the Church was feminine and on this ground, Bluntschli vigorously opposed the extension of political rights to women. In spite of this exaggerate description, there are elements of truth in the organic conception of the State as presented by Bluntschli which need to be noted. The State, he says, is a moral and spiritual personality. 'As an oil painting,' he says, 'is something more than a mere aggregation of drops of oil, as a statue is something more than a combination of marble particles, as a man is something more than a mere quantity of cells and blood corpuscles, so the nation is something more than a mere collection of external regulations'. The State is a union of mind and will. It is the community in action.

Herbert Spencer in the nineteenth century is the supreme example of a writer who works out to the munutest possible extent the parallel between an individual organism and a social organism and yet misses the essential points of the comparison. He uses the organic analogy to prove his own preconceived notions of individualism. The analogy is used so very literally in an earlier essay that the up and down lines of a railway are compared to the arteries and veins of an animal. Money is compared to the blood corpuscles and the telegraph wires to the nerves. The text on which Spencer preaches a homily is: 'an organism grows and is not made'. The homily is that since the State is an organism it should be allowed to grow of its own accord, to grow spontaneously, and should not be propped up by artificial aids. Free education, compulsory sanitation, public libraries, public parks, etc., all interfere with the spontaneous growth of the organism, and are, therefore, unjustifiable. Spencer overlooks the fact that since the State is a highly evolved and cultivated organism, the proper comparison is not between it and a simple type of organism like the jelly-fish, but between it and a more evolved and cultivated organism like a plant in the garden or a domesticated animal. An organism of the higher kind grows as well as is made. But Spencer's organic State chooses ever to remain at the jelly-fish stage. Moreover, Spencer does not seem to realise that in the realm of politics, one who uses metaphors as literally as he himself does, can deduce from the analogy of an organism with its central idea of a nervous system, a theory of State socialism with greater ease and logical consistency than he is able to deduce his extreme individualism, with its accompanying doctrine of natural rights. As E. Braker points out, Spencer adopts where it is useful, and rejects where it is not, the organic conception of the State.

Elements of Truth in the Organic Theory

Almost the first thing that needs to be said in the use of this conception is that analogy is not argument. To establish a parallel between two objects is not necessarily to establish a logical connection between them. It is the failure to recognise this simple truth that accounts for the literal way in which the organic conception has been used by writers like Bluntschli, Spencer, and Schaffle. We must remember that what an analogy can do after all is to make difficult things plain and abstruse things clear. It cannot take the place of proof.

Society or the State is not an organism. It is *like* an organism in some respects and *unlike* an organism in other respects.

1. Like a physical organism, it has in it the principle of life, growth and development. We are not prepared to say with some writers that every State passes through youth, manhood, old age, decay, and death. Since the changes that occur in the social organism are more or less imperceptible and incapable of exact measurement, we cannot very well apply to society terms like manhood, old age, decay, and death. Nevertheless, we believe that societies and states have a life, will, and continuity of their own apart from the lives and wills of the individual members living at any one time.

2. In the social organism, just as much as in the individual organism there is present an inter-relation an inter-dependance of parts. The parts depend upon one another and upon the whole; and the whole in turn depends upon the parts. The welfare of each is involved in the welfare of all. Individual good and social good are intimately related. What concerns the individual sooner or later concern the rest of society as well, although the intensity of feeling is not so strong as in the case of the individual organism, society is not a loose collection of isolated or unrelated individuals. It is an organic unity, a living structure. It has a responsibility to the individual even in that sphere of conduct which Mill styles 'self-regarding'. Just as the family is bound to take an interest even in the supposed individual interests of his members, so also is society bound to take such an interest. This does not mean that society should always be meddling in all individual matters.

3. Both the individual organism and the social organism embody the principle of differentiation of part and the related principle

> of the distribution of functions according to fitness. 'Tools to the man who can use them' is the underlying idea. It is impossible that the whole body should be an eye, or ear or stomach. In the striking words of St. Paul: 'The body is not one member, but many. If the foot shall say, because I am not the hand, I am not of the body; is it therefore not of the body? And if the ear shall say, because I am not the eye, I am not of the body; is it therefore not of the body? If the whole body were an eye, where were the hearing? If the whole were hearing, where were the smelling?... Now they are many members, yet but one body. And the eye cannot say unto the hand, I have no need of thee; nor again the head to the feet, I have no need of you... And whether one member suffers, all the members suffer with it; or one member be honoured, all the members rejoice with its'.

To press the analogy beyond the above general truths is sure to lead us to difficulty. The state is not an organism in the sense of being a physical structure. It is a mental structure, a 'union of different minds in a common purpose'. It is a self-determining system of minds which are themselves self-determining. It is not a mechanical unity.

Value and Limitations

To Gettel we owe the following points in summing up the value and limitations of the organic theory:

1. The theory teaches us the importance of the historical and evolutionary points of view.

2. It insists upon the effects of the natural and social environment.

3. It lays stress upon the inter-dependence of citizens and political institutions.

4. It emphasizes the essential unity of social life and the intricate causal inter-relations of all its parts.

5. It teaches that society is something more than an aggregate of individuals loosely thrown together without any unifying

bond. It shows clearly that the members individually are in a peculiar sense dependent upon the whole and the whole in turn is conditioned upon the parts.

6. It believes that men by nature are 'political beings' and that their universal tendency to social organisation creates the State.

At the same time, many of the analogies between the State as an organism and the individual organism, while striking, are often far-fetched and contradictory.

1. The will of the State is not always identical with the wills of its component units.
2. In the individual organism, the laws of evolution are followed intuitionally. The growth of the State, however, is in a large measure capable of conscious direction and control.
3. The organic theory further runs the risk of magnifying the State as an end in itself, and of losing sight of the fact that the purpose of its existence is the well-being of its individual members. In other words, it is in danger of sacrificing the individual to society.
4. The individual in the State does not exist solely to support and perpetuate the life of the whole. Each individual has to a large extent the shaping of his own life. He has a consciousness and will of his own. All this is not true of the cells of the animal organism.
5. A physical organism perishes and ceases to be living matter if the members are cut off. Such is not the case with a State when a member separates himself from it.

In conclusion, it must be said that the organic theory being of a flexible character should be used with great caution. Analogy should not be pressed too far. To apply it at all points is sure to lead to illogical and even absurd results.

Select Readings

Barker, E.—*Political Thought in England from Spencer to Today.* pp. 175-183.

Follett, M.P.—*The New State,* Chs. 23-28.

Garner, J.W.—*Introduction to Political Science,* Ch. II.

Garner, J.W.—*Political Science,* and Government, Chs. IV-VII.

Gettell, R.G.—*Introduction to Political Science,* Chs. II-IV.

Gettell, R.G.—*Readings in Political Science,* Ch. II-IV.

Gettell, R.G.—*Problems in Political Evolution,* Ch. III.

Gettell, R.G.—*History of Political Thought.*

Gilchrist, R.N.—*Principles of Political Science,* Ch. II.

Laski, H.—*The State in Theory and Practice,* Chs. II.

Leacock, S.—*Elements of Political Science,* Ch. I.

MacIver, R.M.—*The Modern State, Introduction.*

Rousseau, J.J.—*The Social Contract,* Ch. II, IX and X.

Seeley, J.—*Introduction to Political Science,* Chs. I-II.

Willoughby, W.W.—*The Nature of the State,* Ch. II.

6

The Origin of The State

In discussing the origin of the State, it is wise to distinguish the primary or pre-historical origin of the State from the evolution of the State in historical time. The first question is more or less of a speculative character. It takes us back to the pre-historical ages and to primitive man. We have no authentic information how the State first began. The modern sciences of sociology, ethnology, and anthropology and the history of law no doubt cast some light upon this dim past, but they are unable to give us an insight into the primary origin of the State. As Gilchrist aptly remarks, 'Of the circumstances surrounding the dawn of political consciousness from history we know little or nothing. In spite of this uncertainty, we are safe in saying that the State has existed in some form or other—rudimentary or somewhat developed—wherever human begins have lived together in large numbers. Lacking positive historical proof concerning primitive political institutions, we are obliged to resort inference and generalisations regarding the dim past on the basis of the slender evidence at our disposal.

The Primary or Pre-Historical Origin of the State

Various theories concerning the primary or pre-historical origin of the State have been propounded by historical and political writers. These theories are:

1. The Divine Origin Theory;
2. The Social Contract Theory;
3. The Force Theory; and

4. The Patriarchal and Matriarchal Theories.

Kranenburg (author of *Political Theory,* 1939) groups these theories under (a) Theocratic, (b) Natural Law, and (c) Power theories.

1. The Theory of Divine Origin

This is the oldest theory concerning the primary origin of the State. According to it, the State is established and governed by God Himself or by some superhuman power. God may rule the State directly or indirectly through some ruler, who is regarded as the agent or vice-gerent or vicar of God. Such a State is known as a theocratic or God-ruled State. The Divine Origin or the theocratic conception is almost as old as the State itself and is found universally among early peoples. It is a well-authenticated fact that early forms of political authority were believed to be connected with the unseen powers. The earliest rulers were a combination of priest and king or the magic man and king.

The chief exponents of the Divine Origin Theory in the early times were the Jews. In the Old Testament we have constant references to the conception that God selects, appoints, dismiss, and even slays rulers. The king is treated as owing responsibility to God alone for his acts. The Greeks and Romans regarded the State as only indirectly divine. Although they did not divorce religious ideas from politics, they regarded the State as a natural manifestation of man's political instincts. 'The Roman legend of foundations of Rome, while not omitting religion, said that people and king created the State. The blessings of the gods followed.

The theory of Divine Origin found some of its most earnest supporters among the early Church Fathers who based their teaching on the exhortation of St. Paul to the Romans. 'Let every soul be subject unto the higher powers. For there is no power but of God: the powers that be are ordained of God.

The teaching of the Old Testament and the Church Fathers profoundly influenced the mediaeval writers in the controversy between the Church and the empire. Some of these writers used the Divine Origin Theory to establish the supremacy of the Church over the State and others to establish the supremacy of the State over the Church.

The Protestant Reformation gave a great impetus to the Divine Origin Theory and to the related doctrine of passive obedience or non-resistance to Government authority, although in religious mattes it stood for in individual liberty and the supremacy of individual conscience. The Divine Origin Theory more and more took the form of the theory of the Divine Right of Kings. This is particularly true of sixteenth and seventeenth century England. The leading exponents of this latter doctrine were James I, the first Stuart King, and Sir Robert Filmer. Bousset in France elaborated this theory in supporting the despotism of Louis XIV.

The Divine Right of Kings

In his work called *The Law of Free Monarchies,* James I gives a clear exposition of this doctrine. He claims that the king has derived his authority directly from God. Therefore, he is above the people as well as above the law. He is subject to God and his conscience alone. He owes no legal obligation to the people. The only obligation that he has is a moral obligation to God to govern the people well. Kings make laws; laws do not make kings. The king 'is master over every person, having power over life and death'. James I assumes throughout his work that kings are wise and good, but that the subjects are weak and ignorant. A king, he declares, is a great school master for the whole land. A 'Free Monarchy' he interprets as a monarchy which is free to do what it pleases.

Even if the king be wicked, the subject has no right to rebel against him. To rebel against the king is to rebel against God Himself, for the king is God's chosen vessel. A wicked king is to be regarded as a plague for people's sins sent by God. Therefore, it is unlawful to shake off such a burden. The only check on a bad king is his far of punishment in the life after death, which is sure to be terrible. To quote the forcible words of James I: 'Kings are justly called gods; for they exercise a manner of resemblance of divine power upon earth'. As it is atheism and blasphemy to dispute what God can do, so it is presumption and high contempt in a subject to dispute what a king can do or to say that a king cannot do this or that'.

The salient features of the doctrine of the Divine Right of Kings are:

1. Monarchy is divinely ordained;
2. Hereditary right is indefeasible;
3. Kings are accountable to God alone; and
4. Resistance to a lawful king is sin.

It is more than likely that even the supporters of this doctrine did not fully believe in all is extravagant claims. The chief reason for advocating it, in the Middle Ages, was that it might serve as a bulwark against the audacious claims of the Pope and that it might strengthen the State against the inroads of the Church. 'Divine Right thus began its career as a defensive weapon against militant Catholicism'. In supporting it, people forgot the danger of the king becoming a tyrant. Later, the theory was used against the growing political consciousness of the people and the rise of democratic ideas, and was made to support royal despotism. It was not until the end of the eighteenth century that it was rejected as unsound in theory and dangerous in practice. In countries like Austria, Germany, and Russia it lasted for a still longer time.

Today both the Divine Origin Theory and the Divine Right of Kings are without supporters among political thinkers. To refute them in great detail is to flog a dead horse. It is sufficient to say that the general consensus of opinion is that although human institutions like the family, the State, etc. are in accordance with a divine plan or purpose, the origin of the State is not due to God's direct intervention in human history. The State is an historical growth. Its laws are created by men and enforced by them. 'To say that God selects this or that man as ruler is contrary to experience and commonsense'. The State is the outcome of the political instinct of men and its authority is exercised through human agencies. The causes of the decline of the theory, as brought out by Gilchrist, are:

1. The rise of the contract theory, with the emphasis it gave to consent;

2. The rise to supremacy of the temporal as distinct from the spiritual power, or, in other words, the separation of church and state;

3. The actual refutation of the absolutism which the theory supported by the growth of democracy'.

As a doctrine of political philosophy, it received its death blow at the hands of Grotius, Hobbes, and Locke.

It was unscientific and could not be proved by any ordinary canons of reasoning. If established authority were a proof of divine approval, what is one to say of a successful usurper who overthrows an ancient dynasty and places himself in power or of a revolution which results in the shifting of authority? Does divine sanction follow victory on the battlefield or success in the realm of diplomacy? Further, what are we to say of divine sanction when political authority is divided between a king and a parliament, and the two come into conflict with each other?

Although the Divine Origin Theory is exploded and scarcely needs any serious consideration, yet it has had certain values, some of which are suggestive:

1. At a time when man was emerging from semi-civilised conditions and was not accustomed to obedience to a secular authority or to a self-imposed law, the doctrine of the Divine origin of the State must have been a powerful factor in preserving order. It was a bulwark against anarchy and did much to strengthen the respect of man for person, property, and government.

2. It may be interpreted to mean that the instinct for order and discipline is deep seated in man and that it reveals itself in political organisation.

3. Its supreme value lies in the fact that it indirectly emphasises the moral basis of the political order. It emphasises the fact that government is for the good of the governed. Even the

absolute ruler owes a moral accountability to God for the way in which he exercises his authority.

2. The Social Contact Theory

1. *Statement of the Theory.*—This theory holds that the State is the result of a deliberate and voluntary agreement on the part of primitive men emerging from a State of nature. It assumes that there was a period in human history when there was no State at all and no political law. This pre-civil or pre-political period is regarded by some writes as pre-social as well. In this state of nature the only law which governed human relations was the law of nature. Advocates of the Social Contract. Theory are not agreed upon what exactly this law of nature was. The state of nature was either too idyllic to last long or too inconvenient and unbearable. Hence men in this primitive state of nature society soon abandoned the state of nature and set up a political society through the instrumentality of a covenant. As a result of the covenant each man lost his natural liberty in part or wholly, but in its place he obtained the security and protection of the State provided by political law.

The contract is interpreted in various ways by its advocates. According to some, it is responsible for the institution of civil society alone, while others regard it, in addition, as a agreement between the rulers and their subjects, resulting in the institution of a particular government. The first type of contract is known as the social contract, and the second as the political or governmental contract. The contracting parties of the original or the social contract are the individuals themselves, emerging from the state of nature agreeing with one another and with all. The parties to the second or the governmental contract are the people in their corporate capacity, on the one hand and an agent or ruler on the other. A further difference which we find among the advocates of the Social Contract Theory is that while some regard it as an actual historical fact, others consider it as a historical fiction which conveys philosophical truth. An example of the former conception is found in Locke while Kant illustrates the later conception. To

Kant the contract is merely an idea of reason. One other difference to be noted among the propounders of the theory is the varied use to which they put it. Hobbes uses it to justify royal absolutism; Locke to support constitutional government or limited monarchy; Rousseau to uphold the doctrine of popular sovereignty. On the whole, the theory has been used to justify the conception that government authority, if it is to be legitimate, must rest ultimately on the consent of the governed. The weight of its influence has been in general in the direction of safeguarding the rights and liberties of the people and of checking the arbitrariness of rulers. It has also engendered a general irreverence towards the States because of its assumption that the State is an artificial creation and that government authority is a restraint upon man's natural freedom.

2. *History of the Theory*—The theory is almost as old as political speculation itself. In the Greek times, it was first found among the Sophists, who were professional teachers of wisdom. They did not belong to a single school of thought. Nevertheless, as a class, they regarded the State as an artificial creation built upon man's self-interest. Political control they considered as essentially selfish in aim. The State, they said, was a hindrance to man's self-realisation and was opposed to the life of nature. It was the result of a contract.

Plato and Aristotle who represented the summit of Greek political philosophy repudiated the Social Contract Theory. To them the State was natural and necessary. The Epicureans who followed revived the Social Contract conception. The key-word of their teaching was self-interest and they based the State upon that. They explained social and legal relations as resting wholly upon individual self-interest. Obedience to law was justified only when it protected the individual against personal injury. Justice to them did not mean anything more than some convention for mutual advantage. Political life, they said, 'was burdensome and incompatible with the repose of spirit necessary for an ideal existence'. In all these views of the Epicureans we see a fore-shadowing of the latter Social Contract Theory. The Stoics, who were the contemporaries of the Epicureans and in many ways represented an opposite type of thinking, contributed to the contract theory, the conception of natural law to be interpreted by man's reason. This conception of the natural law was later incorporated in Roman jurisprudence.

In the Roman law the conception of the contract played a very conspicuous part. The people were regarded as the ultimate repositories of political authority. But the idea of contract taught by the Romans was not the social contract of later writers; it was only a governmental contract. It was a contract between the people and government officials. Once officials were chosen, they had complete power and the people had no right to withdraw it. Thus no revolution was justifiable. In this respect we find that the Roman theory was more like the theory of Hobbes than like that of Locke. The Romans did not develop the idea that the State itself owed its existence to convention or agreement. The State was never viewed as anything so artificial as all that. As recent writer observes: 'In political discussions, the theory of social contract became significant during and after the Middle Ages'.

Among English writers, the first one to give a definite statement of the contract theory is Richard Hooker (1554-1600) in his *Laws of Ecclesiastical Polity* published in 1594. In the tenth section of the first book, Hooker outlines the social contract theory. As regards the law of nature and life of man in the state of nature, he adopts a middle course between the gloomy view taken by Hobbes and the roseate picture drawn by Rousseau in his earlier writings. The central question which the author faces is whether subjects should obey a political authority which they themselves have not set up. His answer is that the original contract obliges people to obedience and that if it is to be revoked, it can be done only by universal agreement. Since universal agreement is practically impossible to attain, disobedience to political authority is nearly always wrong. Thus Hooker's position anticipates that of Hobbes. In spite of his advocacy of the contract theory, Hooker does not consider society to be purely artificial and contractual. The contract is to him a part of man's instinct and not the result of despair. 'From the standpoint of psychology and of historical truth Hooker is here far in advance of Hobbes with his grossly mechanical interpretation of the fact of community'.

The Social Contract theory of Hobbes, Locke, and Rousseau is considered separately in. After Rousseau the theory gradually 'withered away'. Kant and his disciple Fichte used it at some length. Kant used the contractual conception to measure the justness of laws. Fichte's ideas on the subject were not always consistent. In his earlier writings at any rate he advanced the idea that man was subject to the moral law alone and that therefore he could terminate the contract at any time he pleased. In the world of practical affairs the Social Contract theory of Rousseau influenced the French Revolution, and the theory in general had its effect upon the makers of the American constitution.

The nineteenth century marked the decline and downfall of the contract notion. This was brought about largely by the historical and scientific attitude of the period which replaced the former speculative approach. Montesquieu in France gave an impetus to the historical method in politics, and Darwin and his followers helped thinkers to understand and interpret institutions in the light of evolution.

3. *Criticism of the Social Contract theory*—The Social Contract theory has been attacked from three different angles, the historical, the legal, and the philosophical or rational.

In the words of Kranenburg it employs too much deductive and too little inductive reasoning.

(a) Historical

(i) The most obvious criticism that suggests itself to one is that the theory has no basis in fact. To assume that primitive men came together at some particular time and established a political society by means of a contract is to read history backwards. The idea is too advanced for primitive man. It is a mere fiction. No one has yet been able to give a single instance of a State coming into being as the result of a deliberate and voluntary agreement between individuals emerging from a state of nature. It is true that the Mayflower Compact (1620), the Providence Agreement (1636),

etc. are given as instances of the historicity of the social contract. But it must be remembered that the men who formed these contract were not emerging from a state of nature. They had been living in the State elsewhere, were well acquainted with political organisations there, and were simply transplanting to new lands, institutions, and ideas with which they were already familiar.

(ii) There have been historical examples of governmental or political contracts. But such contracts are contracts between people already living in the civil state. They do not by any means explain the historical origin of the State. They only define the rights and duties of the rulers and subjects. Governmental contract is a fact, but social contract is a fiction.

(iii) The theory assumes that primitive man was much of an individualist. It assumes that he was a free man who could enter into voluntary agreements with other free men. This is not what research into early times shows. Early law was more communal than individual. The individual was of little importance. The family was the unit. Property was held in common. Law took the form of customs. The individual had his prescribed place in society. In these circumstances the free contracting of individuals with one another is so important a matter as the institution of the State is an absurdity.

(b) Legal

(i) Even if we assume for the sake of argument that primitive man had advanced far enough in his social consciousness to enter into a contract, the fact remains that such a contract has no legal binding force whatever. A contract, in order to be valid, requires the force or sanction of the State. But for this contract there is no such sanction, for it precedes and does not follow, the establishment of the State. In the words

of T.H. Green, 'the covenant by which a civil power is for the time constituted cannot be a valid covenant. The men making it are not in a position to make a valid covenant at all'. There is no 'imponent' behind it.

(ii) Thus, if the original contract has no legal meaning and is invalid, all subsequent contracts based upon it are equally invalid, and the rights derived from it have no legal foundation.

(iii) Besides, a contract has binding effect only upon those who accept it voluntarily. But the social contract is supposed to bind generations of men who have had no say in the matter at all. If the fathers eat sour grapes, why should their children's teeth be set on edge? In reply to it, it may be argued, as is done by Locke, that residence in a State constitutes tacit assent to the original contract. This is just a patent evasion of the difficulty. Strictly speaking, the State should expire with the death of the original parties and every new generation should enter into a fresh contract. It needs hardly any demonstration to prove that such a state of affairs would undermine political authority and even result in the dissolution of the State itself.

(c) Philosophical

The theory is open to several objections on the philosophical side. These objections are even more important than the historical and legal objections. As said already several of the contract writers admit that the contract notion is only a historical fiction and yet use it in order to convey certain philosophical principles. The objections are:

(i) The theory assumes that the relation between the individual and the State is a voluntary one. This is a position which will not stand careful scrutiny. We are members of a state in the same way in which we are members of a family. Membership of a child in the family and its duty of obedience

to its parents do not rest upon the basis of consent. We are born in the State, and we do not ordinarily choose it; and if later on we change our citizenship we are still in the State. The State is not an artificial creation of man. Membership in it is not voluntary. If the State were a voluntary organization like a company or firm, a person would be at liberty to enter it or leave it at will. The obligations of the citizen to the State are not contractual at all. If the literal consent of every citizen were the justification for State action, State life would become an impossibility, for there is hardly any matter upon which we can get unanimous agreement. An individualist like Spencer who starts out with the idea that literal consent is the only basis of political obligation, virtually admits the futility of such a position. The contract writers try to overcome this difficulty by assuming that a unanimous consent is necessary for the original contract, but that majority vote will suffice after that. This is illogical. If we begin with unanimous consent, should we not adhere to it throughout? The State is not a mere partnership in the ordinary sense of the term. To use the oft-quoted and striking words of Edmund Burke: 'the State ought not to be considered as nothing better than a partnership agreement in a trade of pepper and coffee, calico or tobacco, or some other such low concern, to be taken up for a little temporary interest, and to be dissolved by the fancy of the parties'. If the State is a partnership at all, it is a partnership in a higher and more permanent sense. To quote Burke again: 'It is a partnership in all science, a partnership in all art, a partnership in every virtue, and in all perfection. As the ends of such a partnership cannot be obtained in many generations, it becomes a partnership not only between those who are living, but between those who are to be born'. Thus, the individual is not a member of the State through voluntary association. He is a born member of it. His obligations 'do not rest upon covenant or consent, but rather upon the general interests or necessities of society, or upon grounds of utility'.

(ii) The entire conception of the state of nature and of the laws of nature is unsound. It assumes that whatever preceded the institution of the State is 'natural' and that whatever has

followed it (including the institution of the State) is artificial. There is no warrant for dividing history into two parts with a hatchet, so to speak. Civilisation is as natural today as was barbarism in the past. Man is a part of nature and the State is the highest expression of his nature. The State is a growth and not a manufacture, 'Men do not make a bargain consciously; the agreement exists because of their nature'.

Even if we grant that their was a state of nature governed by laws of nature, meaning thereby laws of inherent morality, the setting up of a State in such a situation is not a progressive step, but the opposite. To exchange laws of inward mortality for the force of the State is a backward step. As Green puts it: A society governed by such a law as a law of nature, i.e. with no imponent but man's consciousness, would have been one from which political society would have been a decline, one is which there could have been no motive to the establishment of civil government'.

Furthermore, if the state of nature is one where a contract could be formed, it must have been a state where there was a consciousness of a common good, implying the ideas of social authority and individual obligation. But such a one, we claim, does not materially differ from a civil or political state. It is virtually, though not in name, a political state. 'The necessary element constituting a political society are already present there.

(iii) The Social Contract theory implies a false notion of rights, T.H. Green aptly remarks: 'The real flaw in the theory of contract is not that it is unhistorical, but that it implies the possibility of rights and obligations independently of society'. According to any sound view of rights, the basis of rights is *social recognition,* i.e. recognition on the part of society of a common good of which the individual good is an intrinsic part. Right can exist only between persons, in the moral sense of persons, i.e. persons possessing a rational will. But the contract theory assumes that we can have rights even in a pre-social state. Such rights, we contend, are not rights at all. They are mere powers. To quote Green again: 'Natural right as a right in a state of nature which is not a state of society, is a contradiction. There can be no right without a consciousness of common interest on the part of members of a society.'

(iv) *Elements of Truth in the Theory*—Although as a theory explaining the origin of the State or the right relations between man and man in society, the Social Contract theory is defective and finds no support today, it contains certain elements of truth. If we are to understand the theory properly, as it was elaborated in the seventeenth and eighteenth centuries specially, we should know the practical aim which impelled its adherents to enunciate it, namely, to give a more satisfactory and human explanation of the fact of political authority and the duty of obedience rather than explanations based upon divine fiat. In the place of the Divine Right theory which called upon subjects to render unquestioning obedience to the 'powers that be', the Social Contract theory laid down the fundamental truth that obedience rested upon the consent of the governed and that the sovereign had no right to act arbitrarily. In working out this truth, the Social Contract theory served as the basis for the modern democracy. It emphasised 'the importance of the individual, the possibility of modifying political institutions by direct human effort, and the fact that ultimate political authority lies, at least potentially, in the people'. Thus it was that 'Advocates of freedom preferred it; for it suggested ways of limiting the claims of arbitrary authority. All who aspired to philosophy preferred it; for a contract can be discussed, criticised, and amended, whilst the fiat of Heaven cannot. And if we set aside its peculiar historical context, it is still attractive, for it appeals to one important aspect of human experience'.

3. The Force Theory

According to this theory the State is the result of superior physical force; it originates in the subjugation of the weaker by the stronger. It is natural to suppose that in primitive times the man of exceptional physical strength was able to overawe his fellow-men and to exercise some kind of authority over them. The same is probably true also of superior tribes and clans in their relation to other tribes and clans. On the basis of this supposition, advocates of the force theory contend that all States have come into being through physical coercion or compulsion.

Oppenheimer, who is a keen advocate of the theory, traces the origin of the State through various stages. Jenks, who is another prominent supporter of the theory, in his *History of Politics,* holds that there is not the slightest difficulty in proving that all political communities of the modern type own their existence to successful warfare. So according to this theory, it is war that begets the State. Advocates of the theory argue that what they regard to be fundamental features of modern political society—military allegiance and territorial character—are based on the relation between the war chief and his followers and on conquest which brings under the authority of a single ruler people of different countries and of different races.

Some writers use the term 'force' so very broadly as to include not only physical prowess but also power derived from intellectual and religious factors.

Like the Divine Origin and the Social Contract theories that we have considered already, this theory is advocated both as an explanation of the historical origin of the State and as a rational justification of the State to be; and like them, also it is defective on both counts. In its practical form, it reduces itself to the position that government is the outcome of human aggression. Such a view is found in earlier works of Herbert Spencer who says, 'Government is the offspring of evil, bearing about it the marks of its parentage'. We admit that force must have been an important factor in the evolution of the State, but to regard it as the one and only one factor is a clear mistake. Several other factors must have entered into the composition of early political societies. The State must have grown as much by voluntary amalgamation as by force and conquest. After conquest the State must have grown more as a result of conciliation and agreement than as a result of coercion. The force theory minimises the element of cooperation and other such peaceful agencies which must have played an important part in the evolution of the State.

Force is an essential element of the State both for internal unity and for security against external attack. Without the element of force, the State would become a prey of disruptive factors and soon cease to be. But force alone cannot account for the historical origin of the State or for its continuance in modern times. 'Might without right can at best be only temporary, might with right as a permanent basis for the State'.

The Force theory like the Social Contract theory, has been used for various purposes. Some have argued that since the State is the outcome of force, people should obey it absolutely. Such a position seems altogether illogical. As Rousseau has pointed out clearly, the right of the strongest is no right at all. Right based upon might hasts only as long as might lasts. 'But what kind of right is that which perishes when force fails? To quote Rousseau again, 'Force is a physical power...... To yield to force is an act of necessity, not of will—at the most, an act of prudence'. Some of the early Church Fathers also used the theory, their purpose being to discredit the State as compared with the Church. They argued that the State was based on brute force, which the Church was the work of the God and hence superior. The individualists, as well as the socialists, have also employed the Force theory to support their respective doctrines. The individualist argument is that just as the State is the result of superior strength, so within society itself the race should be for the swiftest. This means unrestricted competition and unlimited scope for individual efforts. The socialists attack this argument on the ground that individualism means an improper use of force and that the state, by means of its superior force, should check the exploitation of the weaker by the stronger and mete out justice to the workers.

4. The Patriarchal and Matriarchal Theories

While there is general agreement that the origin of the State should be understood in terms of evolution, there is considerable difference of opinion as to the stages in this evolution. It is in this connection that we came across the patriarchal and matriarchal theories.

Sir Henry Maine is a chief advocate of the patriarchal theory. He defines it as 'the theory of the origin of society in separate families, held together by the authority and protection of the eldest male descendant'. He believes that the State is the family writ large.

He assumes that the original group consisted of a man and his wife and children and that this family soon gave rise to several families and that the original father or the eldest male descendant became the protector and ruler of this common patriarchal family. Relationship is traced in such a family through males, and from the same ancestor. The State is simply a further development of the patriarchal family. To state this development in Maine's own words. 'The elementary group is the family connected by common subjection to the highest male ascendant. The aggregation of families forms the Gens or House. The aggregation of Houses makes the Tribe. The aggregation of Tribes constitutes the commonwealth.

The theory rates on three fundamental assumptions:

1. That the patriarchal family was based on permanent marriages and kin relationships.
2. That the State is a collection of persons descended from the progenitor of an original family, and
3. That the ultimate source of all political authority is to be found in the extensive and unlimited power exercised by the head of the patriarchal family, who on his death-bed bequeathed to his successor all the legal rights that he enjoyed.

Evidence in support of the Theory.—In support of the theory, its advocates adduce the family history of the Hebrews of the Greeks and Romans, and of the Aryans of India. Among the Hebrews the eldest male parent was absolutely supreme and exercised almost despotic power over his dependents. He held the possessions of the family in a representative rather than in a proprietary manner. The Athenians had their 'families' and 'brotherhood', and in Rome the 'patria potestas,' the power of the father, 'gave the head of the house-hold almost unlimited authority over its members'. In India, too, where the joint family system prevails, 'large numbers are included in one house-hold' under the headship of the eldest male. 'In certain rude communities today large groups of individuals have been found in one so-called family, each man having large numbers of brothers or sons or cousins. The patriarchal theory, adopting this as the unit and supposing the headship bequeathed from one chief to another, by easy stages transforms the father into the chief or king and the family into a civil community'.

Criticisms of the Theory—(1) Modern research into the history of early man shows that the patriarchal system was by no means universal. There are some who contend that the matriarchal system, where relationship is traced through the mother, was earlier in point of time, McLennan, who is a staunch advocate of the Matriarchal Theory, claims that polyandry and the matriarchal family were the primary social facts and that polyandry later developed into the monogamous family, and the matriarchal family into the patriarchal state.

(2) Jenks, who is another strong supporter of the matriarchal theory, asserts that the process by which families expand into clans and clans into tribes according to Maine's conception is, in fact, the reverse. According to Jenks, the tribe is the earliest and the primary group, then comes the clan, and finally comes the family. In support of his contention, Jenks gives the examples of certain societies among the primitive races of Australia, Malay Archipelago, & C.

(3) The existence of polyandry and transient marriage relations and kinship through females in uncivilized communities shows that the patriarchal family did not continuously exist.

(4) The most serious criticism of the theory is that it does not account for the origin of the State. It is simply a speculation into the beginnings of early society, particularly of the family.

The Matriarchal Theory

This theory is suggested by the institutions of savages still in existence such as the aborigines of Australia and certain communities in India. Savage life disclose a type of society which appears to be more primitive than the patriarchal society. The fundamental features of this savage society are:

1. Transient marriage relations,

2. Female kinship,
3. Maternal authority, and
4. Succession of females only to property and power.

Some writers on the matriarchal theory consider all these four features as essential, while others mean by the theory only 'mother-right' and 'mother-relationship,' and not 'mother rule'. It is the latter of these two views which seems more reasonable.

According to the matriarchal theory, in the above restricted sense, the matriarchal family precedes the patriarchal family. It is natural to suppose that polyandry and transient marriage relations were more common in primitive society than monogamy or polygamy. The Veemah marriage also existed, according to which the husband is incorporated into his wife's family. Under such circumstances descent is traced through the mother; for, as Jenks points out, motherhood in such cases is a fact, while paternity is only an opinion. 'The woman here', says MacIver, 'is regarded as the agent of transmission, not the active wielder or even the participant of power. The system 'gave the woman, the wife and mother, a *social* rather than a *personal* standing.' It was at a later stage that 'mother right' gave place to the patriarchal society 'through the adoption of settled pastoral and agricultural habits in place of the purely wandering or hunting life of primitive man.'

Criticism

1. The examples can be found of the polyandrous type of society in various parts of the world, there is no proof to regard it as universal or as necessary beginning of society.
2. Other forces and elements besides patriarchal and matriarchal relations must have entered into the process of political organisation.
3. Both the patriarchal and matriarchal theories undertake to perform too big a task. They seek too enquire into the beginning of human society. 'The most archaic human society we can picture to ourselves is removed from the actual origin of mankind by a lapse of time demanding geological rather than historical measurement'.

4. Besides, both these theories are more sociological than political.

They seek to explain the origin of the family, rather than that of the State. The assumption that the State is the family writ large is entirely wrong, for the two institutions are quite different 'in essence, organisation, functions, and purpose'.

The conclusion to which we are led with regard to both the patriarchal and matriarchal theories, can best be summed up in the words of Leacock: 'No single form of the primitive family or group can be asserted. Here the matriarchal relationship, and there a patriarchal regime, is found to have been the rule,—either of which may perhaps be displaced by the other. Indeed one has to admit the fact that there is no such thing as a 'beginning' of human society. All that can be asserted is that in the course of time the monogamic family tended to become the dominant form, though even until today it has not altogether supplanted other forms of organisation. Mr. Ruthnaswamy observes that 'there has been a parallel development (of patriarchal and matriarchal society) but the patriarchal line is thinker and longer'.

The Historical or Evolutionary Theory of the State

Over against the above five theories which are more or less speculative in character, is advanced the Historical or Evolutionary theory which furnishes a correct explanation of the origin of the State. According to it, the State is a historical growth or the result of a gradual evolution. It is a continuos development. It cannot be referred back to any single point of time. As Burgess puts it: 'It is the gradual realisation ... of the universal principles of human nature'. It is futile to seek to discover just one cause which will explain the origin of all States. The State must have come into existence owing to a variety of causes, some operating in one place and some others in other places. Whatever it is, the State is not the deliberate creation of man any more than language is a conscious invention. Political consciousness must have taken a very long time to develop and the primitive State must have grown along with the development of this consciousness.

Factors in State Building

More profitable than speculation which seeks to reduce to a single theory the origin of all States, is inquiry into the factors which have gone into building up of the early State. As seen already, the State must have arisen from various causes and under different conditions. Its emergence is almost imperceptible. The chief factors which have influenced the formulation are:

1. Kinship.
2. Religion, and
3. Political Consciousness

1. Kinship

There can be little doubt that social organisation had its origin in kinship., Blood relationship, either real or assumed, was the most important bond of union. It knit together clans and tribes and gave them unity and cohesion. But kin-relationship by itself could not have led to the formation of the State. People had to develop a common consciousness, common interest and common purpose. Kin-relationship must with great difficulty have given place to social relationship. 'Kinship' says, MacIver, 'creates society and society at length creates the State'.

It is natural to suppose that authority and organisation, resembling political authority and political organisation, first came into being with the institution of patriarchal society. Prior to this man must have been a hunter and wanderer; sex relations must have been promiscuous; and polyandry and transient marriage relations must have been common. There was probably no common authority. Whether such a State of affairs should be called the matriarchal society or not is immaterial for our present purpose. Whatever it be, the onward march of mankind meant the abandoning of such a State of affairs, not necessarily consciously, and working towards a type of society which we call patriarchal. The factors which went to the establishment of such a society were domestication of wild animals, increased wealth, control of property, pursuit of pastoral industry, and the institution of slavery. Of these factors, control of wealth was probably the most important. Property had to be possessed securely and disposed of in an orderly manner. This meant the increasing social dominance of the male.

Patriarchal society was organised on the basis of kinship through males. Women came to be regarded more and more as a form of property. Wives had to be sought outside one's own group. Marriage relations became more permanent and polygamy was the order of the day. The patriarch or the House Father had complete control over the lives and persons of his descendants in the male line. When he died authority passed to the eldest male descendant. The practice of adoption in order to continue the male line, was widespread. This patriarchal community did not go on growing and developing till it became a nation. It broke up into several patriarchal groups, all recognising some form of allegiance to the original group. The heads of these groups or clans probably formed a council of elders assisting the Patriarch, who later became the tribal chieftain, and this chieftain combined military, judicial and religious authority. The rulers or chief were more concerned with the privileges and powers of the dominant few than with the welfare of community.

In the patriarchal society custom played a very important part. It took the place of law. As yet there was no conception of morality or a definite sense of legality. 'The customary is both the right and the permitted'. The sense of individual initiating and responsibility was altogether lacking. The patriarchal law was enforced by the Patriarch or the House Father who was both the judge and executioner. Custom governed both him and the accused. Custom was the king of men and was only gradually transformed into law. As yet there was no State in any accepted sense of the term, but some of its constituent elements were present. MacIver aptly says that it is a mistake to think 'that wherever we find a "headman" in a savage tribe we are in the presence of the State. We can not say when or where the State begins. It is implicit in the universal tendency to leadership and subordination, but it only emerges when authority becomes government, and custom is translated into law'.

Patriarchal society differed fundamentally from modern society in the following ways.

1. It was *Personal,* rather than territorial. Membership in the community was based upon kinship—real or fictitious—rather than on locality. The whole group might migrate without disturbing its organisation. Early kings were kings of their people, and not of their land.

2. It was *Exclusive.* It had no lust for numbers. Strangers had to live outside the ancient city walls. They could be admitted into the group only by adoption or as slaves.

3. It was *non-competitive.* Its life was based on custom. It bound all alike and fixed the scale of social duties and rewards. The idea of change or of progress was looked upon with disfavour.

4. It was *Communal,* not necessarily, communistic. It was a series of concentric groups, beginning with the single household, ascending to the village or guild, finally to the tribe or city. Interdependence rather than independence, was the ideal. *'Laissez faire'* was wholly alien to it. It tended to repress individual effort and to restrict the free play of intelligence. The freedom of patriarchal society meant the freedom of the group rather than the freedom of the individual.

The transition from patriarchal society to modern society was marked by feudalism, and patriarchal ideas long existed after the State was well developed.

2. Religion

A second important factor in the creation of social consciousness and, in turn, in the emergence of the State is early religion. As Gettell observes: kinship and religion were simply two aspects of the same thing. Common worship was even more essential than kinship in accustoming early man to authority and discipline and in developing a keen sense of social solidarity and cohesion. Those outside were regarded as stranger and even as enemies.

Patriarchal religion, says Jenks, was almost universally ancestor-worship, i.e., the cult of deceased ancestor. Patriarchal man must have believed in the continual existence of his ancestor, because he continued to see him in his dreams. He offered him sacrifices and worship and adhered to all ancestral precedents lest he should offend the deceased in any way. Thus offering to the dead became a characteristic feature of patriarchal religion. The patriarchal meal gradually became to occupy the place of religious ceremony. Patriarchal religion was rigidly enforced on all the members of the group.

Kinship and religion were so closely inter-twined that the Patriarch, who later became the tribal chief, was also the high priest. He was the head of the family (later of the tribe), the guardian and interpreter of customs, high priest, and often the magic man or the medicine man. Such a ruler was naturally looked upon with awe and reverence. He ruled with a rod of iron, and in this, religion was his powerful ally. Despotism in those early days was not an unmixed evil. It strengthened the tribal organisation and accustomed men to authority and obligation. It was the best friend of progress and liberty in the early stages. All this explains how religion and politics went together for a long time and are not completely separated even today.

When the patriarchal tribe began to expand by incorporation or conquest, patriarchal religion was not quite adequate to meet the new situation, 'in spite of adoption and the fiction of common origin found in early state'. It was at this point that nature worship came to the rescue. Nature worship, in the form of crude animism, was present even in primitive times. But it now appeared in a somewhat advanced form and easily mingled with ancestor-worship and 'served as a sanction for government and law. Religious and political ideas were little differentiated, and obedience to law and to authority rested largely on the belief in the divine power of the ruler and in the sacredness of immemorial institutions'.

3. Political Consciousness

A third factor in the development of the state is the need that man felt at a very early time for order and protection, and along with it went the lust for power on the part of those who were strong and clever.

Once early man gave up his hunting and wandering habits and took to the pastoral and agricultural life, several changes took place. The population began to multiply. Contacts with neighbouring people increased. Wealth was accumulated. The idea of property took root. The economic life advanced. All this necessitated some form of organisation which would ensure internal order and give protection to person and property. Such an organisation received further support from the need that man felt for an authoritative body to regulate their social relations such as the family and marriage, as also from the need for concerted action for purposes of common defence and aggression.

The ambition for power was no doubt a strong motive in the formation of State-institutions. Military activity furnished the best opportunity for the resolution of such an ambition. In some cases at least 'war begat the king'. Earlier family organisations were gradually replaced by more purely political forms. Successful war leaders became kings and nobles, and society was stratified into classes. Power more and more passed into the hands of select classes who were claiming prerogatives and superior rights.

Thus kinship religion, and the need for order and protection 'contributed the organisation from which the state usually emerged'. They necessitated some form of law and a government to enforce that law, and the State was the next step in this political evolution.

Select Readings

Gettell, R.G.—*Introduction to Political Science,* Ch. VI.

Gettell, R.G.—*Readings in Political Science,* Ch. VI.

Jenks, E.—*The Ship of State,* Ch. III.

Kranenburg, R.—*Political Theory,* pp. 3-19.

Lowie, R.H.—*Origin of the State.*

Oppenheimer, F.—*The State.*

Sidgwick, H.—*Development of European Polity,* Lecture III.

Willoughby, W.W.—*The Nature of the State,* Chs. III-IV.

7

The Sphere of The State

Ancient and Medieval Views

One of the most difficult problems which the student of political science has to solve is that of determining (to use the words of Edmud Burke) 'what the state' ought to take upon itself to direct by public wisdom, and what it ought to leave, with as little interference as possible, to individual freedom'. In an earlier section, we pointed out that, in our view, there is a distinction between State and Society; this means that there are limits to State action. This, however, has not always been the view among the peoples of the world. Among the Greeks, for instance, according to Bluntschli, 'the State was all in all. The citizen was nothing except as a member of the State. His whole existence depended on and was subject to the State'. The ancient idea of the State embraced the entire life of man in the community, in religion and law, morals, art, culture and science. Well might Burke's description of the State be applied to it: 'a partnership in all science, a partnership in all art, a partnership in every virtue and in all perfection.' The State's end being the comprehensive one of securing a good life for all citizens, all forms of control calculated to secure that result were considered proper, and no line was drawn between matters political, moral, religious or economic. The State might control trade, prescribe occupations, regulate religion or amusements. To the ancient Greek, the city was at once a State, church and school. In other words, the Greeks made no difference between State and Society.

Sidgwick, however, contests this view. He says that, outside Sparta (and if we put aside the regulation of religious ceremonies and military service), the practical difference between ancient and modern conceptions of the function of government in ordinary civil life and transactions is not very great. He points out that 'when we look through the list of actions, public and private, or the list of officials at Athens, or the offices treated as normal by Aristotle, we find no sign of any excessive *réglementation*. We hear of controllers of markets,... whose business it was to prevent fraud and disorder, of commissioners of the city... who had to prevent private houses from encroaching on the public streets.' But the prevention of fraud, disorder, and encroachment on public streets is one of the elementary functions undertaken by modern Governments. Briefly, ancient Governments were not as omnipotent as they are made out to be.

Perhaps it is better to say, with Barker, that the individual was not regarded as having rights of his own, to be protected as against the State. The mark of the Greek State is rather a desire for the action of the State and an attempt to stretch the lines of its action than any definition or limitation of the scope of its interference.

The Romans adopted the Greek conception of the State with some modifications. They 'left very much to social customs and to the religious nature of man. The Roman family was more free as against the State'. This does not mean that the Roman State was less powerful in theory; no one could resist the State if it uttered its will. Rather, the Roman State limited itself; it restricted its own action.

In the Middle Ages, two new forces, the growth of Christianity and the rise of the Teutonic races, brought into prominence a different conception regarding the sphere of the State. It was held 'that the whole religious life of the community, although not altogether withdrawn from the care and influence of the State, was yet essentially independent,' and should be regulated by the Church:

It took some time for the new idea to prevail; indeed, a struggle had to be waged by the Church against the State to get the idea accepted. The State was now only 'a community of law and politics, no longer also of religion and worship'.

Secondly, only with reluctance does the Teuton submit himself to the sovereignty of the whole body. He 'claims for himself an inborn right which the State must protect, but which it does not create, and for which he is ready to fight against the whole world, even against the authority of his own Government. He rejects strenuously the old idea that the State is all in all. To him individual freedom is all-important. The rights of the State are thus limited by the rights of the individual as well as by those of the Church.

Thirdly, the Middle Ages were pervaded by the feudal conception. Men became sovereigns by virtue of owning land. The functions of government under such a system were simply the functions of proprietorship, of command and obedience. Government was for the most part divided out piecemeal among a thousand petty holders. The dispersal of governmental power among a considerable number of persons gradually gave rise to the idea of the rights of individuals against a central authority.

THE EARLY NINETEENTH CENTURY

In the early nineteenth century, the prevalent view was what is generally known as individualism or *laissez-faire:* the sole duty of the Government is to protect the individual from violence or fraud. The Government is best which governs least. As John Stuart Mill put it in his essay *On Liberty:*

"The sole end for which mankind are warranted, individually or collectively, in interfering with the liberty of action of any of their number, is self protection... The only purpose for which power can be rightfully exercised over any member of a civilized community, against his will, is to prevent harm to others. His own good, either physical or moral, is not a sufficient warrant. . . The only part of the conduct of any one, for which he is amenable to society, is that which concerns others. In the part which merely concerns himself, his independence is, of right, absolute. Over himself, over his own body and mind, the individual is sovereign.'

According to this theory, the following functions of government alone would be proper:—(i) to secure to the individual the right of personal security including security of health and reputation, the right to private property together with the right of freely transferring property by gift, sale or bequest and the right to fulfillment of contracts freely entered into; and (ii) to protect the individual from foreign aggression. Briefly, the State was to be a 'negative' or 'police' State.

Such important functions undertaken by modern States as the provision of education, poor-relief, and unemployment insurance, the regulation of public health, and aid to agriculture and industry, which in fact make the modern State a social service State, were considered improper. The theory was justified on psychological, economic and biological grounds.

'The psychological argument is a simple one: individuals may be expected in the long run to discover and aim at their own interest better than a Government can do it for them. Self-help is the best help.

On economic grounds, it pays to let the individual alone. The individual requires a steady supply of good commodities and services at a cheap price. This requirement is best satisfied under conditions of free competition; for the consumers, seeking their own interest, will create an effective demand for commodities and services; producers, seeking their own interest, will meet this demand. Competition among consumers and producers will keep prices at a reasonable level and ensure quality.

From the biological point of view, the fittest will, and ought alone to survive. That is the natural law. Besides, the health of the social, as of the natural, organism depends on the observance of the law of specific function—that every part should do that function for the performance of which it has been intended by nature. Government 'is a joint-stock company for mutual assurance'; its natural function is to hinder hindrances. Its interference in any other aspect of life is unnatural and socially harmful.

Laisssez-faire was popular in England approximately from 1750 to 1850. This popularity was due partly to the failure of the older policy of mercantilism and partly to the Industrial Revolution. Mercantilism meant well-nigh complete Government control over trade, commerce and industry. By 1780 with the loss of the American Colonies, this policy had become discredited. The tremendous leap forward in industry as a result of the introduction of mechanical power and the factory system did away with the necessity for the subsidies and protective measures of mercantilism. It was now felt that non-interference by Government in industry and trade would enable the leaders of industry to take the maximum advantage of the new inventions, and lead to an enormous increase in national wealth. The Government, by a series of laws, therefore relaxed its control over trade and industry:

1784-6	The reduction of tariff duties.
1796	Relaxation of Navigation Laws in favour of the United States of America.
1813	The trade to India was thrown open.
1846	Repeal of the Corn Laws.
1849	Repeal of the Navigation Laws.

The *immediate* result of *laissez-faire* was that it led to an enormous expansion in trade and industry, and, indeed, seemed to justify its adoption.

The Passing of Laissez-Faire

In the long run, however, *laissez-faire* proved disastrous to the community: its social cost outweighed its economic gains. Long hours of labour, inadequate wages, overcrowded factories, and insanitary arrangements—these were the lot to which the workman had to submit. 'I have worked till 12 p.m., last summer; we began at 6. I told book-keeper I did not like to work so late; he said I must. We took our breakfast and tea as we could, a bite and a run, sometimes not able to eat it from its being so covered with dust.' Such is the recorded evidence of one of the factory workers of those days. Children too were overworked.

'The parent who would endeavour to realize this life of a factory child in 1832', writes Walpole, 'should try to imagine his own little boy or girl—eight or nine years of age—working in a factory. He should try to recollect that it would be his duty to rouse the child on a cold winter's morning at five that it might be at its work at six; that, day after day, week after week, month after month, it would be forced to rise at the same hour; that with two short intervals of half an hour each, it would be kept to its dull employment for thirteen hours every day; that during the whole of that time it would be breathing a dusty, unwholesome atmosphere, rarely able to relieve its limbs by sitting down'.

This social misery was directly due to certain unforeseen but inherent defects in the policy of non-interference. That policy, in Joad's analysis, wrongly assumes that each individual is equally farsighted and has an equal capacity for knowing what he wants, that each individual possesses an equal power of obtaining what he wants and has an equal freedom of choice under free competition, and that the satisfaction of the wants of all individuals is identical with the well-being of the community. Briefly it forgot two elementary propositions:

(i) Free competition can lead to the best social advantage only where there is approximate equality of bargaining power. As it was, 'free competition' was free in name only; the employers with their immense resources could in effect get their terms accepted by the starving wage-earners; for the latter, the freedom to reject the terms offered meant little more than the freedom to perish. It is the duty of society to moralize competition.

(ii) Social organisation can supply a much needed corrective to the ignorance and self-interest of individuals. In Joad's expressive phrase, economic action is 'blind'; that is to say, the economic activities of individuals, concerned as they are with individual

ends, often lead to results which are willed neither by society nor by any individual. To cite an example: if there is a rumour that a bank is in difficulties, depositors are anxious to withdraw their money, there is a run on the bank and the bank fails—a result 'which nobody wants, is nevertheless due to what everybody has individually willed'. Society, through its Government, can regulate economic action in the interest of social good. It can supply knowledge and foresight to mitigate the hardships of blind action and promote social welfare. Two examples in point are: (a) the salutary effect produced by the social organisation of agricultural marketing in India. Government has helped to put the farmer in possession of better value for his goods by timely intervention; (b) the prevention of widespread starvation by enforcement of rationing in many parts of Indian in rice and wheat. Rationing has clearly helped the equitable distribution of these commodities at their prices.

Gradually, every State began to realize the folly inherent in *laissez-faire* and to assume greater responsibilities, particularly in the economic field. Factory Acts, Mines Acts, Trade Board Acts Shop Hours Acts and similar laws were passed. Thus *laissez-faire* passed away.

While *laissez-faire* is clearly a fallacious theory, its merits should not be ignored. It teaches the wholesome lesson, so necessary as a set-off to current totalitarian ideas, that too much Government help (maternalism) and too much State regulation (paternalism) are bad. It teaches the value of self-help and reliance; to kill individual initiative is, as the saying goes, to kill the goose that alone can lay golden eggs. Social action, while achieving social ends, should encourage individual initiative, because it is a great social asset.

THE PRESENT DAY

While there is general agreement in rejecting the conception of *laissez-faire*, such agreement is wanting in deciding on the positive limits of political control. One view is the socialistic one, which is discussed later. Another is the totalitarian conception of the State: 'Nothing beyond the State, nothing against the State, nothing outside the State.' This, however, is an extreme view, which is considered in general to be inimical to liberty.

More generally, it is agreed that it is the State's duty to promote the greatest happiness of the greatest number. The State is an organisation to promote social good on the largest possible scale. And in attempting to achieve this purpose, the tendency is for Governments to make themselves more and conspicuous, especially by the planning of economic life.

(i) *Personal security.* Admittedly Government aims, first, at assuring to the individual personal security, and protecting the whole State from foreign aggression. To achieve this aim, it defines and punishes crime, administers justice, maintains the police and the fighting forces, and conducts dealings with foreign States.

(ii) *Property.* It protects the right to private property, together with the right to the free transference of property by gift, sale or bequest; it also enforces the right to fulfill contracts freely entered into.

(iii) *Political rights and duties.* It determines the political rights and duties of citizens, passes laws to regulate voting and delimits constituencies.

(iv) *Education.* There is a tendency to enforce compulsory elementary education and to supervise and aid secondary and higher education.

(v) *The family.* The family is a natural institution requried by the needs of may. It man well be said to be the nursery of the State, as the moral and intellectual training of society very much depends on it. The modern State exercises a certain control over its exterior aspect, generally insisting on conformity to the prevailing type of marital union, prescribing limits of kinship within which marriage is prohibited, regulating divorce and making rules regarding inheritance.

A few States encourage marriages by providing financial aid; some insist on certain health and age requirements as conditions of marriage; nearly all States have regulations to ensure the protection and care of children and to safeguard wives against non-maintenance and other economic consequences of desertion, and generally provide institutions to meet those cases where the family fails in its task of rearing its young. There is a tendency for the State to take over, by the provision of hospitals, old-age pensions, insurance schemes and by free compulsory education, the obligations which formerly fell upon the kin.

(vi) *Industry*. The tendency towards increased State interference is particularly manifested in industry. This interference is effected with a view to protect (a) the home manufacturer, (b) the worker, (c) the consumer, and (d) the investor.

(a) State help to industry in the form of protective duties is generally advocated and given. First, it is argued, as against the Ricardian theory, that every State should have a certain amount of economic independence or self-sufficiency, especially in times of war. Secondly, there is the infant industry argument: the natural resources and circumstances of a country may be such that while the initial cost of starting and establishing certain industries may, in the face of foreign competition, be great, such industries, once established with State protection, may well be able to stand foreign competition. The story of discriminating protection in India, particularly as applied to the iron and steel industry, is a clear instance of this. Thirdly, it is believed, whatever economists may say, that protection will partly solve the problem of unemployment.

(b) The State's attitude towards industrial labour is no longer one of individualism. The Factory Acts contain provisions for fire escapes, the fencing of machinery, ventilation, etc.; they regulate hours of labour for men,

women and children, besides prescribing rest intervals and holidays and fixing the minimum age for children to enter factories. Similarly, various Acts regulate the conditions of employment in mines. The laws regulating trade unions and trade disputes, the system of compulsory insurance and old-age pensions and Workmen's Compensation Acts, now operative in various countries, further demonstrate the solicitude of Governments for the welfare of labour.

To illustrate: In India the Factories Act of 1948, as at present amended, prescribes a daily limit of 9, and a weekly limit of 48, hours of labour in factories. The maximum hours of work for children are 4½ per day. Rest intervals and a weekly holiday are prescribed. Further, every worker is entitled to leave with wages after twelve months' continuous service at the following rate: adults—one day for every 20 days of work, subject to a minimum of 10 days; children—one day for every 15 days of work, subject to a minimum of 14 days. Necessary conditions with regard to ventilation, light, temperature, sanitation and safety are also insisted on. In some states, e.g. Madras, special Maternity Benefit Acts have been passed to provide leave of absence (with a wage of allowance) to women for some months before and after confinement. The Workmen's Compensation Act (1933), the Payment of Wages Act (1936) and the Industrial Employment Standing Orders Act (1946) are other important laws; the first regulates the compensation to be paid by employers for certain kinds of injury, occupational disease, or death arising from employment; the second defines the periods of wage payment and deductions from wages; and the last requires the larger employers to frame standing orders defining the conditions of employment and get them ratified by the appropriate Government authority.

(c) To protect the consumer, the State interferes with competitive prices. The old idea that prices should be left altogether to the play of free competition among buyers and sellers has been found to be productive of serious injustice to the buyer due to the increasing prevalence of monopoly. The State therefore regulates

trusts and cartels, fixes standards of weights and measures, passes anti-adulteration laws and encourages the consumers' co-operative movement. In war-time, Governments everywhere passed laws to prevent profiteering and the hoarding of essential commodities like rice, and even introduced, where necessary, schemes of rationing in order that the available supply of such commodities should be equitably distributed. A special case of the interference of the modern State in regard to prices, as Leacock points out, is seen in legislation concerning railway rates, which are of course prices charged for transportation of persons and freight. The distinctive position which the railways occupy in the industrial world has induced some modern Governments not only to subject them to special regulations, but also, as in India, to own and operate railways. Indeed, opinion is gaining ground that what are known as key industries and public utilities—for instance, coal-mines, railways, electricity and gas supply—should be nationalized, i.e. owned and worked by the State. The same eagerness to protect the interests of the consumer may be seen in the emphasis on compulsory arbitration in the labour legislation of several countries and particularly India. This rightly stresses the idea that the interests of both capital and labour have to be subordinated to the larger interests of society.

(d) To protect the investor, Governments regulate banks and companies.

(vii) *Agriculture.* As illustrated below with reference to India, Governments everywhere interfere to protect the tenant from exploitation by the landlord, to help the ryot with cheap credit and marketing facilities and to organize agricultural research. They also construct, as in India, large irrigation works to help the ryot.

(viii) *Other functions.* Besides the above-mentioned functions, modern States maintain sanitation and health departments, looking to drainage and hospital relief, aiding the poor and the incapable by maintaining workhouses and institutes for defectives. They also undertake those functions which obviously fall outside the sphere of the individual, such as the control of currency and credit, the postal system, the carrying out of surveys and censuses, and the collection and dissemination of data of various kinds.

(ix) *Distribution*. There is, finally, the social control of distribution. The State endeavours to direct wealth into new channels as it is produced by seeing that the daily result of production goes into the pockets of those who have so far been receiving less than they should. This is done partly by the regulation of profits and wages, and partly by taxation. The progressive principle of taxation, generally adopted by the modern State, enables it to take wealth from those who have it and transfer it to others either by direct payments (old-age pensions, unemployment allowances, etc.) or by the provision of communal enjoyments (such as free education, free libraries, parks, hospitals, etc.).

To summarize: the modern State is a social service State, a positive State as compared with the police or negative State of the *laissez-faire* conception. It properly intervenes to uphold social standards, to prevent exploitation and manifest injustice, to remove the needless hazards of the economic struggle and to assure and advance the general interest against the carelessness or selfishness of particular groups.

Reasons for Increased State Activity

The increased activity of the State in modern times may be explained by the following reasons:

(i) *The nature of economic life since the Industrial Revolution.* The most outstanding social result of the Industrial Revolution has been the introduction of large-scale production in factories. This, in its turn, has brought about a fundamental change in world economy. For mass production has meant a distance between the producer and the consumer, between the employers and the employed, and between the company-promoter and the investor; the human element in all these relationships tends to be ignored. The possibilities of fraud and of exploitation are increased, necessitating increased State intervention to protect the weak and the exploited. Again, mass production necessitates wide and ever-expanding markets abroad; the interdependence between State and State in capital, market, and labour becomes marked, and without the help of the State the industrialist is unable to make the maximum profit. Further, unemployment is implicit in a system where the production is dependent upon the anticipation of a demand which is affected by world factors; frequent crises are the result; the State has to attempt to mitigate the social evils of unemployment.

(ii) *The growth of monopolistic corporations.* The rise of trusts and cartels, which virtually introduces an element of monopoly in trade, increases the necessity for the State to safeguard the interests of the consumer and the worker.

(iii) *The Failure of laissez-faire. Laissez-faire* has been weighed in the balance and found wanting.

(iv) *The political enfranchisement of the working classes.* In the nineteenth century, the vote was extended to larger and larger numbers of people. The political value of the vote was not lost on the enfranchised people; they naturally returned people to Parliament who were pledged to support all measures calculated to achieve a better distribution of wealth. The formation of the Labour Party in Britain, and similar socialistic parties elsewhere, has given a fillip to State action.

Paradoxically, the failure of democracy and the rise of dictatorship in States like Germany (1933-45) and Italy (1922-43) brought about a similar result in those countries.

(v) *The Great Wars.* The wars of 1914-18 and 1939-45 accustomed men to greater State interference in their lives; the habit of acquiescing in such interference has helped such interference to continue.

(vi) *Political theories.* The influence of radical political theories, like socialism and communism, has been pronounced. They point to evils to be remedied and maladjustments in economic life to be adjusted. The Government has necessarily to act to remedy the evils, which are pointed out with obvious sincerity, both within the Legislature and outside, by socialists.

THE STATE AND EDUCATION IN INDIA

Education comes within the sphere of the State because (i) popular education is necessary for the preservation of those conditions of freedom, political and social, which are essential to free individual development. It is necessary to fit the citizen for the tasks of citizenship. Further, the great social problem of our day, the reduction of inequalities, is largely a question of the provision of adequate opportunities, which, again, is largely dependent on education. (ii) No machinery less extensive in its power than Government can secure popular education.

There are three possible ways by which the State may ensure to every child the necessary minimum of education. First, it may leave the education of the child to the care of the family. Second, it may command that every child should receive a certain minimum of education as a legal right and compel the family to provide it out of the family funds. Third, it may order that every child should have shooling up to a certain age, and make education free, providing the necessary funds from its revenues. The tendency in modern states is to adopt the third method, for experience has shown that the first two do not achieve the desired result.

In India, compulsory and free elementary education remains a distant ideal. It is true that even as early as 1904 the Government of India had gone so far as to 'fully accept the proposition that the active extension of primary education is one of the most important duties of the State'. That they have not appreciably succeeded in such extension may be seen from the fact that at present only 24% of the boys and girls of school-going age are under instruction. Finance is the greatest stumbling-block. The memorandum prepared by the Educational Adviser to the Government of India in 1944 estimated the cost of a system of universal, compulsory and free education for all boys and girls between the ages of 6 and 14 in the area then called British India (i.e. excluding Indian Sates) at Rs. 200 crores a year. In view of the fact, however, that education is a great social investment, funds must be found and every effort made to attain the ideal within a measurable period of time. A study of the education budgets of progressive countries is an eye-opener in this regard. The educational expenditure per head in England is Rs. 32-2-0; there is no good reason why in India it must be as low as Rs. 2-3-2.

The first task, then, of the Governments in India is to increase literacy by the gradual application of the principle of compulsory and free elementary education; the second is to see that with lavish expenditure on education is secured an increased return in educational value. Mere quantitative expansion, in other words, is not enough; it must be accompanied by the prescription and enforcement of proper standards in respect of staff, equipment, etc. It is not necessary that the State should directly run all the schools; the system of grants-in-aid and the provision of an efficient inspecting agency will secure the object. Where local bodies run the schools, Governments have a particular duty to see that the schools are properly managed.

Somewhat different considerations apply in secondary and higher education. Secondary education obviously cannot be made compulsory or free; there are far too many practical difficulties for such a task to be attempted. The best that the Governments can do is to make liberal grants-in-aid to schools managed by private agencies and local bodies and to insist that the money be spent properly. Higher education is also important as a preparation for political leadership and for administrative duties. Here the duties of the State in India appear to be to provide financial help, consistent with its more onerous obligations in respect of elementary and secondary education; to lay down the necessary framework of university bodies, and, having done this, to allow the universities the largest possible internal freedom; and to provide facilities to bona-fide students for research in the Government record offices.

Finally, there is the important problem of adult education. Its magnitude can be seen from the fact that in India 800 people out of a thousand are illiterate. Governments could do a lot to wipe out adult illiteracy by, first, realizing the urgency of the problem; second, enlisting the co-operation of non-official agencies; third, making liberal grants-in-aid; and, finally, making available such expert advice as is necessary.

The Central Government in India performs a useful service in maintaining a co-ordinating agency in its Central Advisory Board of Education. This Board serves to bring educational experts from various provinces together to compare notes and consider how best improvements can be effected in the system of education.

PROHIBITION

The issue of prohibition came to the forefront in Indian politics after the Congress party secured majorities in the Legislatures of seven provinces in India in the elections of 1937; for among the first social reforms attempted by the Congress ministries was the introduction of prohibition, i.e. the prevention by law of the manufacture, sale, or use of intoxicants. Madras was the first province to introduce it (1938).

Social legislation of this magnitude naturally met with some opposition. The arguments against prohibition may be summarized thus:

(i) Prohibition is difficult to enforce. The instance of America which introduced prohibition in 1920 and revoked it in 1933 is a warning. That instance shows indeed not only that it is difficult to enforce, but that it creates a widespread habit of disobedience to law, which offsets any advantage it might otherwise have.

(ii) It involves great financial loss, and that in a double sense. Its enforcement is costly, needing as it does an extra police force; it also means the loss of considerable revenue. The revenue from excise is, next to land revenue, the biggest item in state revenues, and, in view of the urgent need for funds for the nation-building departments, should not be forgone, especially at the present stage of Indian economic development.

(iii) It is an unwarranted interference with the freedom of the individual. Man cannot be made moral by Act of Parliament.

(iv) It creates unemployment among that section of the population which lives by supplying 'drink', such as tappers, toddy-sellers, etc.

But in favour of prohibition, it is rightly argued:

(i) Drink is an evil both from the individual and social points of view. Alcohol is bad for the health of the individual. Socially it is undesirable because it results in a larger number of crimes and increases the poverty and misery of the masses. Family life is often unhappy not only because womenfolk are beaten by drunken husbands, but the money which ought to be spent in supplying the needs of the family is spent on drink.

(ii) In India, prohibition is not difficult to enforce, because the religious sentiment of the country is against drink. The lesson of America does not apply *in toto* to India; in western countries, unlike India, drink is an integral part of ritual and food.

(iii) To make up the loss of revenue resulting from the introduction of prohibition, alternative sources of revenue, such as the sales tax, can be found. Retrenchment also can be resorted to.

The experience of the working of prohibition so far does not help the student to arrive at a final judgement. The reports issued by the Madras Government in the early years of its introduction (1938-40) as well as by impartial investigators sent out by universities, showed that prohibition was a great boon to the masses: it resulted in great economic and social improvement. Family life was happier and there was less crime. People ate better and more food; women and children had better clothing. But from 1940 onwards reports were less optimistic. Cases of breaches of the law were on the increase. The Government in power, therefore, felt that it was difficult to enforce the law and suspended it from 1 January 1944. It is too early to conclude from this experiment that prohibition cannot succeed in India. The lesson rather is that prohibition, to be successful, requires enforcement for a long time, at least two generations, and demands incessant vigilance on the part of the administration as well as the enthusiastic co-operation of the general public, particularly in detecting law-breakers. The Congress Government in Madras, who are enthusiastic supporters of prohibition, reintroduced it in 1946 in eight districts. It is now universal throughout the state, as also in Bombay and elsewhere.

THE STATE AND AGRICULTURE IN INDIA

The general principles of State interference which we have laid down earlier apply to agriculture as well, i.e. the State properly intervenes to prevent exploitation and manifest injustice, and by placing the resources of the State at the disposal of the individual helps to remove the needless hazards of the economic struggle. As the Royal Commission on Agriculture put it concisely, the aim of the Government's agricultural policy must be to help to establish a smiling and happy countryside.

Four main lines of government activity are noticeable in regard to agriculture:

(i) *The promotion of scientific agriculture.* This is mainly the function of the Departments of Agriculture, acting in co-operation with the Indian Agricultural Research Institute at New Delhi (maintained by the Union Government), the Indian Council of Agricultural Research, and the Veterinary Departments. Their methods are: (a) Research, with the object of introducing new crops, manures, implements and methods of cultivation and of improving indigenous types, destroying insects that are a pest to crops, and breeding superior types of live stock. (b) Propaganda, with the object of inducing the cultivator to adopt the results of research. This takes several forms: demonstrations at experimental farms, or on the cultivators' own land, lectures, pamphlets, and the distribution of the new varieties of seeds, manures and implements. (c) Agricultural education through the establishment of agricultural schools and colleges.

(ii) *The organization of rural finance.* In India, as in other countries where small-scale cultivation is practiced, the problem or rural indebtedness is a vital one: those who help the agriculturist to get cheap credit for necessary purposes help him to get a better net return from his land. Action is being taken to deal with the problem of rural indebtedness as well as to increase the supply of finance to cultivators. Relief from indebtedness is being provided to the cultivator by (a) scaling down old debts either by amicable settlement or compulsorily; (b) by exempting lands and homesteads from attachment; (c) by controlling the nefarious practices of moneylenders; and (d) by fixing the maximum rates of interest that can be charged. The supply of rural finance is being increased (a) through the provision of takkavi loans and (b) by the organization of Co-operative Credit Societies and Land Mortgage Banks. The Co-operative Credit Societies supply short-term credit while Land Mortgage Banks provide long-term credit.

The history of the co-operative movement in India starts with the passing of the Co-operative Credit Societies Act of 1904; the Act has since been amended in several respects; several defects have been discovered in the working of the societies and attempts have been made to remove them. In this context it is sufficient to say that the Government in India, in the early stages of the movement, supplied not only the much needed initiative, but also provided an official inspecting agency to direct the movement on right lines and to audit the accounts of societies.

(iii) *The protection of the tenant.* A series of Acts have been passed since 1859 in order to protect the tenants against exploitation by the landlord. The general features of this legislation are: (a) There is a limit to the enhancement of the rent both as regards the amount and the period which must elapse before rent can be increased. Thus, in Bengal enhancement can occur only as a result of agreement and cannot be more than two annas in the rupee. (b) The tenant cannot be ejected at the will of the landlord for frivolous reasons. (c) The occupancy right is hereditary and can only be alienated on certain conditions.(d) The payment of rent can be demanded only by instalments. (e) Remissions and suspensions of land revenue granted by the Government to landlord must be followed by corresponding concessions to tenants from landlords. (f) The right to make improvements on land without enhancement of rent is protected within certain limits.

Moreover, far-reaching agrarian reforms have recently been undertaken in Uttar Pradesh, Bihar and a number of other states. These aim at eliminating intermediaries—zamindars, jagirdars, etc.—between the State and the cultivator. Such reform are also accompanied by schemes for the transference of ownership rights to cultivators at reasonable process.

(iv) *Stepping-up agricultural production.* During the last few years the problem of increasing agricultural production, particularly food crops, has assumed very great importance. A number of Central and State Committees (e.g. the Famine Inquiry Commission, the Sub-Committee of Policy Committee on Forests, Fisheries and Agriculture) have studied the various aspects of the agricultural problem and have made comprehensive recommendations for the reorganization of agriculture on more efficient lines. The immediate problem of stepping-up production is being tackled in three ways. Firstly, the Government are giving financial assistance either by way of loans or by way of grants for the construction of such works as will increase the production of food crops as well as cotton and jute. An idea of the effort being made can be gauged from the fact that for the two years 1949-50 and 1950-1, Rs. 34 crores have been placed at the disposal of the Ministry of Food and Agriculture for the Grow More Food schemes. Secondly, the Government are arranging to supply the means of production (seeds, fertilisers, iron and steel, cement, etc.) to cultivators either on a concessional basis or on a no-profit-no-loss basis. Thirdly, legislative action is being taken to increase the area under cultivation, conserve farmyard manure and to prepare compost, develop irrigation channels and to regulate production of non-food crops, etc.

(v) *The organization of marketing.* On account of his chronic indebtedness and need for money, coupled with the lack of storage facilities, the Indian cultivator is normally compelled to sell his produce to middlemen at a time when prices are low. The Sates have recently begun to encourage the formation of regulated markets and co-operative sale societies with the object of enabling the farmer to realize a better price for his goods. The Government of India have appointed a marketing expert of the staff of the Indian Council of Agricultural Research. Marketing officers have been appointed by state Governments to conduct marketing surveys of the principal crops in the different states. To secure the proper grading of agricultural produce, an Agricultural Produce (Grading and Marketing) Act has been in operation since 1937.

Many other improvements are necessary if the object of promoting a smiling countryside is to be achieved. *The Report of the Royal Commission on Agriculture in India* (1928) is a mine of valuable suggestions in regard to legislation designed to promote the consolidation of holdings, measures to prevent the spread of contagious cattle diseases and for protection against insects and pests, and the re-examination and readjustment of railway freights on fodder, fuel, timber and agricultural implements. *The Report of the Famine Enquiry Commission* (1945) also deals with the improvement of food production, nutrition and the agricultural economy in general. Special aspects of the agricultural economy are dealt with in the reports of the various sub-committees of the policy committees on Agriculture, Forestry and Fisheries. For detailed information the interested student is referred to these documents.

Select Bibliography

V. Anstey, *The Economic Development of India,* chs. VII & VIII, Longmans, 1931.

J.K. Bluntschli, *The Theory of the State,* Bk. I, 3rd ed., chs. III to VI, Oxford, 1901.

T.H. Green, *Lectures on the Principles of Political Obligation,* pp. 154-247, Longmans, 1921.

C.E.M. Joad, *Introduction of Modern Political Theory,* pp. 24-32, Oxford, 1924.

S. Leacock, *Elements of Political Science,* Part III, ch. I, Constable, 1933.

J.S. Mill, *On Liberty,* 'World's Classics' No. 170, Oxford H. Sidgwick, *The Development of European Polity,* lecture XII, Macmillan, 1903.

———, *The Elements of Politics,* chs. III & IV, Macmillan, 1908 R.H. Soltau, *The Economic Functions of the State,* Pitman, 1931.

F.G. Wilson, *The Elements of Modern Politics,* ch. XXI, McGraw-Hill, 1936.

W.W. Wilson, *The State,* chs. XV & XVI, Heath, 1899.

8

The Justification and End of The State

Even more important than investigation into the origin and evolution of the State is the question relating to the justification and end of the State. Merely to show that the State has come into being due to one reason or another is not enough. What we are most concerned with is, why should there be a state at all? Has the State a rational basis? Can we not get on without the State? At a very early time, Aristotle saw the force of these queries when he claimed that the State first came into being in order that we might live, but was continued in order that we might live happily. Aristotle thus justified the State as being essential to man's good life. In spite of the reasoning, we cannot but feel that even in the best among Greek writers we do not find an adequate justification of froce exercised by the State. They show us convincingly that the full and free development of man is impossible in isolation and that man requires society for the attainment of this end. But the problem of force wielded by the State hardly engages their attention, largely because it is a modern problem.

The State is a way of regulating human conduct, by compulsion if necessary. The will of the State is in many ways superior to all other wills. The State has the power to take away the individual's life, liberty, and property. It commands him to surrender his property by means of taxes and his life upon the battlefield or in punishment for crime. Can all this be justified? Many attempts have been made to justify, and even condemn, the existence of the State in all ages. We shall sum them up under the following heads:

1. The Anarchist View

The anarchists have frankly no use for the State. They believe that the State has no rational purpose to serve and that the sooner we get rid of it the better it will be for man's growth and development. The revolutionary anarchists want to subvert the present social order by violent methods. With these anarchists we are not much concerned in a serious study of political science. The type who demand our attention are the philosophical anarchists such as Tolstoy. Their objection is not so much to the State as such, but to force used by the State. They claim that the truly moral life is realised by one's own effort and that the authority of the State is a hindrance to the development of such morality. They see in this authority a destruction of all moral values. The State is to them red rag to a mad bull. Instead of making a moral, it really makes him immortal by the force that it wields. Instead of trusting the individual to do the right thing, it distrusts him and threatens him with punishment. Government, they argue, are therefore not only useless, but also mischievous. According to them, voluntary organisation can very well undertake the work of society and, if the State is to be retrained at all, it should become a voluntary organisation. Laws should take the form of suggestion and advance, and taxes the form of voluntary contribution. The philosophical anarchists believe that society should be governed by love and not by the 'irrational' principle of force. Man should be so educated that he will voluntarily and almost instinctively do that which is true, good, beautiful, and noble. The perfect society they conceive in terms of a love-knit family, untouched by authority. The only kind of government that they are prepared to support is the perfect and unfetered self-government of the individual.

Criticism

Several lines of criticism suggest themselves to us in considering philosophical anarchism.

1. We are prepared to concede to the anarchists that true morality is largely self-earned. But this is not to admit that State action means a complete destruction of moral values. The State cannot *directly* promote or enforce morality. Yet

it can so order external conditions as to make it possible for the individual to live the good life. Therefore, our contention is that State action does not destroy moral values; it only diminishes them. Even in the case of the best of us, the policeman's club is at times an aid to living the good life. The requirement of good action does not prevent the growth of morality. We can do right by conformity.

2. The anarchist is mistaken in thinking that liberty is the greatest of all political goods. Liberty, we need to remind ourselves, is not an end in itself. It is simply a means to an end. Liberty and authority are not opposed to one another, as the anarchist conceives them to be. They are supplementary and complementary to each other. No human association leaves the individual completely free. Every group implies some restraint upon individual freedom.

3. The anarchist gives us a faulty picture of human nature. His assumption is that organised political society has debased human character and that once it is removed, man will once again become a noble being. This is very much like the assumption of Rousseau in his essay on *Inequality* that man in the state of nature lived an idyllic life and that the development of civilisation has brought about all our present ills. However, Rousseau himself considerably modified the view in the latter *Social Contract* and came to the conclusion that the balance of advantage was on the side of the civil state. It is easy enough to become poetic regarding the virtues of the 'noble savage', but what we know of human nature and the history of primitive man gives the lie to such a roseate picture. We are safe in saying that man has reached his present level of development in and through organised political society.

The anarchist assumes that we can effect tremendous improvement in human nature by education, persuasion, and moral teaching and that, in some far-off day at least, we can entirely get rid of the State. While we do not want to deny that human nature can be greatly improved by the means suggested and that the scope within which it is possible to improve human nature has not yet been fully discovered, we fear that the destruction of the State at present or in any conceivable future will lead to general disorder and chaos. The brute in man cannot be easily destroyed and it is the coercive authority of the State which keeps it in check.

4. The anarchist assumes that there is nothing but love in the perfect household. This is a false assumption. Authority, law, and restraint are not evident on the surface in an ideal family. Nevertheless, they are there. As Hearnshaw observes, in order to curb criminal tendencies in the natures of all, it is necessary to have the might of the State in reserve. Therefore, at least for the present, we cannot dispenase with the tutelage of Government and the sanity of law.

5. The anarchist wants to do away with the authority of the State and substitute for it the authority of the individual conscience. But the individual conscience, as has been aptly remarked, is an extremely tricky and capricious sovereign.

2. The Religious View

From very early times people have justified the existence of the State on the supposed ground that it is the creation of God and that obedience to the State is in accordance with the Divine purpose. Oriental monarchies were for the most part theocracies. Membership in the state was at the same time membership in the religious body. Since the head of the State was also the head of the religious organisation, the State and the religious community were identical. The conception of theocracy was most highly developed among the Hebrews who regarded themselves as God's chosen people. The Jewish State was the direct result of the Divine will and was justified wholly on religious grounds.

The Greeks, too, justified the State in the religious terms, although they did not carry the theocratic conception so far. Among the Greeks the worship of common gods lay at the foundation of State life. The institution of the State was attributed to the interposition of some god or other, and each city had its special deities who presided over it. Plato and Aristotle, the best among Greek political thinkers, advanced a different view. They looked upon the State as natural and necessary. But they did not solve the problem of the reconciliation of political authority with individual freedom. They contended themselves with the view that the State had come into existence owing to natural causes and that the life of the man apart from the State was incomplete and even meaningless.

Like the Greek city-state, the Roman State had a religious origin. The Romans, too, had their special divinities and the Roman tribes were knit together by a common religious worship. Later on when Rome became an empire divine attributes were assigned to the Emperor.

Criticism

In this age of scientific inquiry the argument that we should obey the State merely because it is supposed to have been created by God does not carry any conviction. There is no positive proof to show that any State is the direct creation of God. The most that even religious-minded writers are prepared to admit is that State-life is in accordance with the divine purpose. Even if we assume for the sake of argument that the State is divinely created, such theory does not help us to distinguish right forms of political authority from wrong forms.

3. Physical Force

From the very early days of political speculation an attempt has been made to justify the existence of the State on the ground that it possesses superior physical force. The Sophists held that the State was either the rule of the strong for the oppression of the weak or the combination of the weak, who formed the majority, against the physically strong but less numerous. The early Fathers of the Christian Church and the theologians of the Middle Ages emphasised the mere physical strength of the State in their enthusiasm to exalt the authority of the Church over the State. Thus Pope Gregory VII wrote in 1030; 'Which of us is ignorant that kings and lords have had their origin in those, who, ignorant of God, by annoyance, rapine, perfidy, slaughter, by every crime, with the devil agitating as the prince of the world, have continued to rule over their fellow-men with blind cupidity and intolerable presumption? To Machiavelli the State is only a power-organism. Yet towards the close of his celebrated book, he admits that the power of the State is not for its own sake, but for the sake of the prestige, honour, and well-being of the people.

In modern times, Spinoza, Marx, Engels, Nietzsche, and Spencer have given currency to the view that the State is the embodiment of force. Spinoza held that the state expressed superior physical strength and that its right was only limits by its power. Marx and Engels regarded the State as an organisation of the classes for the exploitation of the masses. Nietzsche built his theory of the 'Superman, on the basis of physical strength'. Spencer held that the State was an expression of mere brute force and that its power should be curbed in the interest of individual liberty.

Criticism

To say that we must obey the State because it is the rule of the strongest seems absurd. This absurdity is clearly brought out by Rousseau when he says: 'A brigand surprises me at the edge of a wood: must I not merely surrender my purse on compulsion; but even if I could withhold it, am I in conscience bound to give it up? For certainly the pistol he holds is also a power'. To yield to force is, at best, an act of prudence. It is not a moral duty. 'Force in itself', as Laski says, is void of moral content'. Political subjection, if it is to be justified, calls for the *will* of the subjects. Without such a will in the State, we have a mass of slaves and not a body of citizens. Force is justifiable only in so far as it maintains and furthers human rights. In the striking words of T.H. Green, 'It is not supreme coercive power, simply as such, but supreme coercive power exercised in a certain way and for certain ends, that makes a State; viz., exercised according to law, written or customary, and for the maintenance of rights'.

This theory is in essence a revolutionary theory. For, if it is fully worked out, it will mean that any group is justified in asserting itself and securing control of the government as soon as it is physically able to do so. The force of the State is justifiable only as long as it is able to repel other forces. But the moment one of these forces is able to establish itself successfully, it becomes right and original force ceases to be right. We may, therefore, ask with Rousseau, 'What kind of right is that which perishes when force fails'? To quote Rousseau again, 'If force creates right, the effect changes with the cause: every force that is greater than the first succeeds to its right. As soon as it is possible to disobey with impunity, disobedience is legitimate; and the strongest being always in the right, the only thing that matters is to act so as to become the strongest... If we must obey perforce, there is no need to obey because we ought; and if we are not forced to obey, we are under no obligation to do so. Clearly, the word 'right' adds nothing to force: in this connection it means absolutely nothing'.

At best, this view justifies the existence of government but not the existence of the State. It justifies the governance of a particular ruler, but not the authority of organised political society.

The Contract View

In the 17th and 18th centuries in Western Europe, this view was the most popular in justifying the existence of the State. According to it the authority of the State is justifiable because we have set it up ourselves by free choice. At first sight, it would appear that there was no better way of justifying the existence of the State than this. The State, it might be argued, is the product of the will of the individual and, therefore, obedience to it is thoroughly reasonable.

Criticism

A moment's reflection is enough to show that to base political authority upon a contract is to base it upon shifting sand:

1. History knows of no State which came into being as the result of a deliberate agreement between men. The State has not been made by any body but has evolved gradually.

2. If subjection to the State is justified on the ground of free consent, it is reasonable to demand unanimous consent for every law of the State before it can become operative. Majority opinion is not enough. There is no reasonable

ground for the coercion of a dissenting minority by the majority. The force of this criticism is clearly brought out in the political theory of Herbert Spencer. Like a true individualist, Spencer argues that the State should undertake only those functions which the people are likely to hand over to the State because they are unable to undertake them themselves. According to him, these functions are (a) protection against external enemies; (b) protection against internal enemies; (c) nationalization of land. (In his latter works, Spencer gives up the last mentioned function and substitutes for it the enforcement of contracts.) No sooner has Spencer assigned these functions than he proceeds, illogically enough, to introduce certain qualifications. He realizes that even on these three vital matters we cannot get unanimous consent in any society. Thus he says that Quakers and conscientious objectors to war will be opposed even to a defensive warfare, criminals to the State undertaking defence against internal enemies, and landlords to the nationalization of land, and that the principle of absolute unanimity will have to be disregarded in these cases. The question that we naturally ask ourselves is that if the principle of unanimity is to be set aside in these cases, why should it not be ignored in other cases as well? Spencer is opposed to popular education, factory legislation, etc. Yet there are many people to-day who think that compulsory conscription is worse than factory legislation and that, if coercion is to be employed, it is much more justifiable to employ it in the latter case than in the former. The conclusion, then to which we are inevitably driven is that the principle of literal consent is of no avail in solving the problem of political authority and individual obligation.

3. Even if literal consent is possible in any matter, it is ruled out in the modern State by the fact that representative government in some form or other is the only way by which the will of the State can find expression. Direct democracy is impossible under modern conditions. To say that tacit consent is enough in these cases, according to the argument of the contractualists, is not justifiable. 'Because consent

involves the notion of a deliberate act of will, something more positive than this (viz., tacit consent) is requried'.

4. If consent is freely given, it is logical to argue that it might be freely withdrawn and that those so withdrawing might freely unite again to form another State. Hobbes realised this difficulty and attempted to solve it by declaring that it was a law of nature that men should keep their covenants when made. It is obvious that such an argument carries with it no conviction whatever. It is a pure assumption on the part of Hobbes driving no support from experience or reason. Other contractualists have argued that people who want to withdraw their consent from the law of the State may be regarded as 'strangers within the State'. This is sheer nonsense. We cannot agree with Spencer when he claims that the individual has a right to make an 'outlaw' of himself and yet remain within the State. A 'right' of this description would make administration impossible and eventually lead to anarchy.

5. David Hum advanced the most damaging criticism of the contract theory when he claimed that it was in essence revolutionary as it provided no power which could hold the individual to his agreement. T.H. Green reiterates this criticism when he claims that the contract which people in the State of nature are supposed to make is no valid contract at all, for there is no 'impotent' to enforce such a contract. The sovereign authority succeeds the contract and does not precede it, as it should.

3. The Unity Theory

Many thinkers have tried to justify the existence of the State on utilitarian grounds. They argue that the rationale of the State lies in the fact that it provides law and order, protects the individual against internal and external enemies, enforces contracts, adjusts relationships between individuals and group, fosters literature, art and science, and provides, in short, the frame-work within which the life of society can be carried on with the least possible friction and the maximum advantage possible. Thus Laski in his *Introduction to Politics* (p. 32) says: 'The power of the state can be justified only in terms of what it seeks to do. Its law must be capable of justification in terms of the demands it seeks to satisfy. The state presides over a vast welter of interests, personal and corporate, competing and co-operating. Its claim to allegiance must obviously be built upon its power to make the response to social demand maximal in character. It must strike such a balance of interest that what emerges as satisfied is greater than can be secured on any alternative programme.

Criticism

There is no doubt that the above justification of the State is much more satisfactory than those what we have previously considered. Nevertheless, it is open to criticism.

1. Theories based upon utility are apt to take too narrow and materialistic view of the State and to regard the State as 'a mere public utilities company'. We have considered this point of view in an earlier chapter and have said that the State is not a mere partnership for the attainment of certain material ends. The State should undoubtedly secure the material well-being of its members. But at the same time it has a moral and spiritual function to fulfil. It is 'a partnership in all virtue'. One of its ends, and, perhaps, the most important is the promotion of the 'excellence of souls'. The State is one of the primary ethical institutions of society. To justify the State purely on the ground of utility is like saying that the family exists solely for conjugal happiness, the procreation of children, and the rearing of human race. Both the family and the state have a moral purpose to fulfil. Both provide a life of fellowship and make the self-realization of the individual possible.

2. The utility theory is apt to regard the State as a mere means to the welfare of the individual, while as a matter of fact, it is both a means and an end. The State considers the welfare not only of existing generations but also that of generations yet to be. In this latter respect it may be regarded as an end in itself.

In spite of these defects, we may agree with Dr. Appadorai when he says that the theory supplies a slogan which gets implanted in the popular mind and which can serve as a touchstone in judging State action.

Necessity of Organisation

A particular form of the utilitarian justification of the State is expressed by some who emphasize the need for organisation. Primitive man did not know the value of organisation. What organisation he had was of an elementary character, and more or less instinctive in origin. But civilised times have witnessed the establishment of organisation for every conceivable purpose. Experience has taught us that the group can do certain things more successfully than the individual. We organise ourselves for the conducting of business, for the promotion of pleasure, of art, science, and religion, and for purpose of war and peace. We even organise to secure peace by force. The number of organisation in our modern society is innumerable, and the state is the most important and the most comprehensive of all of them. It is the one organisation which underlies all others and the one from which all others derive their necessary support. Such an organisation requires a set of rules and regulations for the realization of its purposes, as well as an adequate physical force to make its will effective.

Criticism

While there is no objection to this justification of the State, it must be said that the criticism mentioned above in connection with the utilitarian theory hold good here as well.

7. The Psychological View

Attempts have been made since the days of Aristotle to show that man has a political instinct and that it is a part of man's nature to be ruled. Man, it is said, is a 'political animal'.

Criticism

1. If this be so, how do we account for the fact that there are those who deny that they have an instinctive sociability or political sentiment? Basing our argument on the history of the Eskimoes, who constitute a society, but do not have a state, it would seem that the State was not a universal

necessity, (2) Besides, merely to assert that the State is rooted in human instincts is not enough. Not everything that is instinctive is necessarily good and worth preserving. As Willoughby has aptly pointed out, our problem in political theory is to justify political authority as humanly exercised, and to harmonise it with man's personal freedom. The psychological view does not help us in this task, for it does not show how, or by whom, political authority is to be exercised and how it is to be reconciled with individual freedom.

8. The Idealistic View

From the point of view of idealism which seems on the whole the most satisfactory theory, obedience to the State is justifiable because the State expresses the best in us. It is not an enemy of man, not even a disinterested observer, but the true friend of the individual. In obeying the will of the State we are obeying our own wills, purged and purified of their selfishness. In their true being, the State and the individual are identical. To use the language of Hegel, the State is the 'actualization of freedom' or 'the embodiment of concrete freedom'.

From the idealistic point of view the State is an ethical institution. It makes possible free social life, without which man cannot realize himself fully. It is we ourselves in a different capacity. It is the natural expansion and development of the individual. It enables the will and reason of man to express itself. It furnishes the external conditions of the moral life. It gives 'unity', stability, and increasing self-consciousness to society as a whole'. It is 'the organiser of rights and the guardian of social justice'. Hence obedience to the State becomes a moral duty.

It is in this manner that T.H. Green justifies obedience to the State. He controverts the popular belief that the root of morality is man's conscience and that of political subjection is force. He rightly holds that both mortality and political subjection have a common source, viz., 'the rational recognition by certain human beings... of a common well-being which is their well-being, and which they conceive as their well-being whether at any moment any one of them is inclined to it or not, and the embodiment of that recognition in rules by which the inclinations of the individuals are restrained, and a corresponding freedom of action for the attainment of well-being on the whole is secured'. 'Both morality and political subjection imply the two-fold conception, (a) 'I *must,* though I do not like' (b) 'I must *because* it is for the common good which is also my good'. Green goes on to say that simple fear can never constitute true obedience to the State. To represent simple fear as the basis of civil subjection is to confound the citizen with the slave. A habit of subjection founded upon fear cannot be a basis of political or free society.

Criticism

1. It will no doubt be said that the view presented here is fanciful inasmuch as there is no actual State which answers to the picture painted. It may be asked, as Green has pointed out, 'Is it not trifling with words to speak of political subjection in modern State as based on the *will* of the subjects'? But as Green himself says, it is only to the extent to which the individual realizes that the State serves a common interest of which his interest is an intrinsic part, that he is likely to become a loyal subject. If his patriotism is to be true and abiding, he needs to have a feeling for the State analogous to the feeling which he has for the family and home. We admit that such a feeling is very partially realised even in the best State. We do not argue, as Hegel did, that the ideal State is identical with the Prussian State of Hegel's day or with any other State. Nevertheless we contend that the State embodies, however imperfectly, the conception of a common good, and it is this conception which is the true source of political subjection.

2. Those who are opposed to the idealistic justification of the State will probably argue that force creates the State and habit perpetuates it or that political subjection is in the interest of social expediency. There is no doubt whatever that self-interest, force, and fear have played a considerable part in the creation and perpetuation of the State, but they have produced good results only so far as they have been 'fused with and guided by some unselfish element'. "The fact that

the State implies a supreme coercive power gives colour to the view that it is based on coercion, whereas the coercive power is only supreme *because* it is exercised in a State, i.e., according to some system of law, written or customary'.

3. It may be further said that even if it be granted for the sake of argument that will is the basis of the State, it can be the basis only of the democratic State; how can people have a feeling for the State and an appreciation for the common good unless they 'actively participate in the legislative and administrative functions of the State? This is a forcible criticism, and we are bound to accept it as generally valid. Nevertheless we believe that even in a country which is not democratically governed, we may assume that general will is indirectly present so long as there is peace and order in the country and there is no general upheaval.

In the light of all that we have said, we come back to the conclusion that obedience to the State is obedience to the citizen's own better self and that even if it be not so in any particular case, it should be our constant endeavour to make it so.

The End of the State

The justification of the State is incomplete without a consideration of the end or purpose for which the State exists. In discussing this theme it is usual to distinguish between the immediate or proximate end, and the final or ultimate end. While it is easy to determine the former, the latter is more a matter of faith than of knowledge.

To the Greeks the purpose of the State was self-sufficiency. The State, they said, should provide for its citizens all that was necessary for their highest development and happiness. Plato regarded the State as a macrocosm in which the individual could find his proper place and perform the duties for which he has best fitted. The rulers and warriors should give their undivided attention to the highest well-being of the state, and to this end Plato laid down a communistic way of life for them. To the mind of Plato the State was a well-developed organism in which each individual and each class had a particular place to fill and was happy in so doing.

Aristotle believed that the purpose of the State was to secure the development of virtue in the citizens; but he too, believed in the self-sufficiency of the Greek city-state, which was to produce the greatest happiness in the individual. Thus in his *Politics* Aristotle devotes a whole chapter to this theme. A free paraphrase of the chapter is as follows:

The State exists not for the sake of wealth or security or society, but for the sake of a *good life.* If life were the only object of the State, slaves and brute animals might form a State, but they cannot, for they have no share in happiness or in life of free choice. If alliance and security from injustice or exchange and mutual intercourse were the only objects, all who have formed commercial treaties, would be citizens of the State. They do not have common magistracies, are not concerned with the wrong and wickedness of the other States, and do not endeavour to make the citizens what they ought to be. The State also takes into consideration *virtue* and *vice.* It is more than a mere alliance designed for the protection of life and property.

The State implies not only inner-marriage, intercourse, exchange, and a common locality, but much more than these—*a community of well-being.* It is not a mere society, having a common place, established for the prevention of crime and for the sake of exchange. It is a community of well-being in families and aggregations of families for the sake of a perfect and self-sufficing life. Such a community is possible only among those who live in the same place and inter-marry. The end is good life and the means are family connection, brotherhoods, common sacrifices, amusements, etc., that is friendship. The State is made up of families and villages having for end a perfect and self-sufficing life.

Political society therefore exists for the sake of noble actions, and not for mere companionship, and those who contribute most to such a society, have the greatest claim to power.

The Romans did not speculate much on the end of the State. Most of their energies were absorbed in the building up of the Roman Empire. Rome came to be the centre of the Western World and of Western Civilization, so much so that even after the fall of the Empire, here name and fame lasted for many centuries.

During the Middle ages, too, there was not much speculation regarding the end of the State. Ecclesiastical writers generally regarded the State as an instrument with which to defend Christianity against the attacks of infidels. Aquinas thought that the State existed in order to establish peace and unity and promote right living among the subjects. The state was valued as doing service to an end conceived in religious, and more particularly in theological terms.

Serious discussion regarding the end of the State began only with the modern times, with the rise of liberalism and the overthrow of the idea that the State was the patrimony of the Prince. When men began to realise that the State belonged to the people, there developed theories regarding the end of the State.

According to Hobbes, the purpose of the State was to maintain order and the right of property. Hobbes took such a gloomy view of the state of nature preceding the establishment of civil society that he held that any State was better than no State. Tyranny was to him preferable to anarchy. Locke, likewise, claimed that the purpose of the State was to maintain life, liberty, and property, by means of a known law and a common judge. When we come to Rousseau, we find a revival of the idea that the State exists in order to make good life possible for the individual, although he does not state it in this particular form. He is convinced that the State is not a mere matter of convenience for the gaining of utilitarian ends, but the highest expression of the best in man.

1. The End and General Happiness

Jeremy Bentham in the early part of the 19th century popularized the idea that the purpose of the State was the promotion of the greatest happiness of the greatest number. This utilitarian view is strongly held even today. It was largely responsible for a great number of reforms in the social and political life of 19th century England. In particular it brought about reforms in the poor law, land law, prison management, divorce law, franchise, popular education, etc. To remove the odium which attaches itself to 'happiness' in the sense of 'pleasure', some writers have substituted 'greatest good' or 'general welfare' for 'greatest happiness'. In spite of this improvement, the theory is in danger of sacrificing the minority to the majority. 'The excellence of the few may be made subservient to the incompetence of the many'. The theory tends to develop mediocrity in society and to crush individual excellence. Besides, the term happiness in the sense of pleasure is difficult to define. No two individuals are agreed on what happiness means. Therefore, to assign to the State the task of measuring pleasures and of promoting general happiness seems an impossible task. A knows what gives him pleasure and B knows what gives him pleasure, but neither A nor B knows what general pleasure would be like. Furthermore, the Utilitarian theory is individualistic in its outlook and does not take into account the organic nature of society. In spite of these serious defects by using terms like happiness in a very loose way, the theory has helped to bring about much humanitarian legislation. As Gilchrist observes, it is 'a commonsense expression of the ends of legislation but as a complete expression of the end of the state it breaks down on close examination'.

2. The End as Maintenance of Order

In the 19th century many other views were proclaimed regarding the end of the state. One of the most popular of these was the individualistic view that the state existed merely to maintain law. Some writers extended it to include order and security. It was argued that each individual should be left to work out his own salvation free from the activity of the state and that the State should simply provide external and internal protection so that men might live together peaceably. This theory presents too narrow a view of the end of the State. Undoubtedly it is the business of the State to provide security of person and property, but it is not the complete end. In its practical working, the theory tends to justify *in toto* things as they are and to discourage progress.

It is in danger of perpetuating the *status quo* whether the *status quo* is worth perpetuation or not.

3. The End as Progress

Some have defined the end of the State as progress. This theory does not say much. It does not state clearly what the end is. The term progress is meaningless apart from the end or goal towards which progress is made. 'We must determine the end in order to make progress possible'.

4. The End as Social Service

Those with a socialistic turn of mind claim that the State exists in order to promote 'certain social services, which have nothing to do with protecting the individuals from external attacks, nor the maintenance of law as between the individuals in the State, but which have to do primarily with the social interests of the community'. Such an end, we find, is coming more and more to the forefront in the practice of modern states, which undertake the care of public health and public morals and the promotion of the economic interests of the people. A large group of these writers want to extend the power of the State so as to include the ownership and management of the means of production and distribution. The chief criticism of this view is that it is a theory of the limits of State action rather than of the final end of the State.

5. The End as Justice

A great many modern writers regard justice as the end of the State. These are usually idealists, but not all idealists accept justice as the political end.

Hetherington and Muirhead in *Social Purpose* claim that the organisation of justice has always been the main function of the state. They interpret justice in the sense of 'an order of life in which human personality and its ideals can be realised'. They further say that 'at bottom, the state is the expression of a view of the good life for men... In this larger sense, then, we may still hold that the end of the state is the organisation of justice, and that therefore it is pre-eminently a moral institution'.

While we are prepared to accept the general statement that the end of the State is ethical, we cannot help feeling that justice as apolitical end is too narrow a view. Hetherington and Muirhead use justice in a very wide sense embracing the whole field of morality, but this is not the ordinary usage of the term. Further, as Gilchrist observes, 'Justice is more a condition dependent on the realisation of the true end. Complete justice, too, involves absolute knowledge, which belongs only to God.

Is the State an End or a Means?—Many other theories have been advanced regarding the end of the State. It is not necessary that we should examine all of them. A question which has engaged the special attention of modern writers is this: 'is the state as end in itself or is it only a means?' The ancients, particularly the Greeks, regarded the State as the highest fulfillment of human life and as an end in itself. The present-day distinction between the individual and the State was altogether foreign to them, because the conditions under which they lived were totally different from ours.

The view that the State is an end in itself was received in recent times by Hegel, who identified the will of the individual with the will of the State. This view has been carried to its logical conclusion by modern Fascism. Article I of the Italian Labour Charter reads: 'The Italian Nation is an organism having ends, a life and means superior in power and duration to the single individuals or groups of individuals composing it. It is a moral, political and economic unit which finds its integral realisation in its Fascist Stage'.

Over against such absolutism is the view of individualist, to many of whom the State is only a means for the promotion of the welfare of the greatest number of individuals. The chief objection to such a view is that the State does not concern itself entirely with the welfare of any one generation. It takes into account the welfare of generations yet to be, and in ensuring this distant end it imposes heavy burdens upon its citizens. Individual welfare, it is clear, is not the only end of the State.

The general consensus of opinion today is that the State is both an end and a means. Thus Willoughby, in *The Nature of the State,* argues that, if we look at the state purely from the individualistic point of view, 'it is only a means, an instrumentality, or an expedient through which the highest possible development of humanity is obtained. But if the state is considered as an institution distinct and apart from the citizens who compose it, it is, of course,...an end in itself'. Bluntschli explains the double nature of the State by a striking analogy. 'A picture is often means of obtaining a livelihood for the artist. Yet a true work of art is to the artist the aim of his higher effort, he sees in it the expression of his most vivid feeling, the embodiment of his ideal. In this way it has an end in itself'. Similarly the State is means to the well-being of the individual as well as an end in itself, for it looks far beyond the well-being of any particular group of individuals or any one generation.

In considering the end of the State, it is profitable to distinguish between its general or fundamental end and its particular ends, as also between its ultimate or remote end and its immediate or proximate ends. Adopting such a classification, Holtzendorff distinguishes between the actual ends of the State and the ideal ends. The State, he says, should fienst of all develop its national power against other States as well as against individuals and groups of individuals within the state. In the second place, it should secure individual liberty by marking off a sphere within which the individual could develop himself without any interference on the part of the government or other individuals. Finally, it should promote general welfare by maintaining peace and order and by aiding and educating its subject.

Bluntschli states the proper end of the State is 'the development of the national capacities, the perfecting of the national life, and finally its completion, provided, of course, that the process of moral and political development shall not be opposed to the destiny of humanity'. According to this view, it would appear that the immediate end of the State is the maintenance of national power, and its development, and the final end, 'the destiny of humanity'. It is interesting to note that during the Great War when one would have expected the nationalist view to receive the greatest attention it was the wider end of humanity which made the most powerful appeal. The nationalist view, pure and simple as contained in the early part of Bluntschli's definition raises the same objections as those to which pure and simple individualism is open. Both of these may develop interests detrimental to the welfare of society as a whole. As Gilchrist observes: 'In the modern world we are more and more tending to look beyond the (national) boundaries for an ideal. Internationalism is gradually replacing nationalism'.

A recent American writer, Burges, speaks of the primary, secondary, and ultimate end of the State and regards each of these as being in turn a means to the accomplishment of the succeeding ends. The proximate end, says Burgess, is government and liberty. The State should first and foremost preserve itself and its individual members. But as soon as this end is attained and the law-abiding habit becomes fixed, the State should mark off a sphere of individual liberty and protect it against all encroachments and increase it from time to time. The secondary end, growing out of the proximate end, is the perfecting of the principle of nationality of the development of the national genius. For the accomplishment of this end, nation-states, resting on natural, physical and ethnic foundations, are the best instruments. The final end is the perfecting of humanity or the advancement of the civilisation of the world at large.

Criticising this point of view, Garner remarks: '.......here again we have what seems to be a confusion of ends with means. It is difficult to see, for example, why the establishment of the government should be considered as an end to be realised rather than the means through which ends are sought'. According to Garner, the triple end of the State is, firstly the advancement of the good of the individuals, secondly, the promotion of the collective interests of individuals in their associated capacity and finally, the furthering of the civilisation and progress of the world.

Select Readings

Garner, J.W.—*Introduction to Political Science,* Ch. IX & X.

Garner, J.W.—*Political Science and Government,* pp. 69-74.

Gettell, R.G.—*Introduction to Political Science,* pp. 377-379.

Gilchrist, R.N.—*Principles of Political Science,* pp. 424-431.

Wilde, N.—*The Ethical Basis of the State,* Ch. VII.

Wilson, W.—*The State,* Ch. 15 & 16.

Willoughby, W.W.—*Nature of the State, Ch. 12.*

9

The Historical Development of The State

The Evolution of the State

We have so far concerned ourselves with the speculative theories regarding the origin of the State and the factors which have gone into the building of the early State. We now turn our attention to evolution of the State in historical times. Here wc are on more solid ground.

1. The Early Empire in the Orient

Almost the first type of State which emerged from primitive and patriarchal conditions was the Imperial State, particularly of the Orient. Patriarchal society did not have a large enough area or population to enable it to become a State. There probably existed loose alliance and confederacies of various tribes knit together by ties of blood, real or assumed. But these could not have produced the extended State. Conquest and domination were necessary before tribal man could accustom himself to larger loyalties and the political authority and obligation.

The warm and fertile plains of the Orient, watered by great rivers, and the plateaus of Maxico and Peru produced the earliest forms of civilisation and the earliest State. There were regions where production was plentiful with the least amount of exertion. People multiplied rapidly and soon passed from the earlier family and religious systems to the newer political order. The rapid growth of population and the enervating climate of these warm regions led to the existence of a large servile class. Those who possessed surplus wealth, leisure, and power could easily domineer over the rest and establish despotisms. Social differences and caste distinctions came into vogue. From this state of affairs there soon arose vast empires—such as the Sumerian, the Assyrian, the Persian, the Egyptian, and the Chinese—all centering round cities. The different parts of the empire, were not closely knit together, except in the Persian empire, which attained a certain degree of unity and stability. These early empires were loosely organised, and their authority rested on fear and despotism. For the most part they were merely tax-collecting and recruit-raising agencies. There was no common purpose and no common loyalty. As soon as the ruling dynasty became weak, powerful rivals contested for rule and authority. No individual liberty or true political progress was possible. The early empire was thus an unstable institution. It was at best 'a loose congeries of semi-independent States' and the imperial sceptre shifted 'not only from dynasty to dynasty, but also from city to city'. In spite of these shortcomings, the early empire performed a great service to political evolution in accustoming man to obedience and authority.

2. The Greek City-State

The second important stage in the evolution of the State was reached in Greece. Although civilisation arose later in Greece than in the orient, it developed much faster. The country is peculiarly fitted by its physical environment for political growth and experimentation. It is a country broken up into numerous valleys and islands by the mountains and the sea. Its natural features are varied and moderate. There are no great mountains or rivers or other natural phenomena to paralyse human activity. The Greek religion and outlook were naturalistic and the people had no awe for their gods. Since nature was not so profuse as in the tropical countries, people looked to colonisation and trade. The patriarchal clans took possession of small areas and built their village communities around hills which could be easily defended. Some of these clans were fused together by conquest, peaceful union, or ties of kinships. But they never developed a national unity. Local patriotism continued to the end.

In their self-governing and self-sufficient city states, or rather city communities (the phrase used by MacIver), the Greeks developed a variety of political organisations. These communities contained the principle of growth. Sparta alone remained conservative and maintained 'a steady tradition of unbroken continuity in its government. In the other States the normal political evolution was from monarchy to aristocracy, from aristocracy to tyranny, and from tyranny to democracy'.

The Greek was passionately devoted to his city-state. The only life which mattered to him was a life of partnership in the city. 'Citizenship was a function, almost a profession'. The Greeks looked upon the city as an ethical institution. It performed multifarious functions. In fact, it was identical with the whole life of society. It was an all inclusive partnership. The Greeks believed that man could not attain the highest life apart from the State. The Greek outlook was social through and through.

While the Greek city state reached a very high level of political development and individual liberty, it had many serious drawbacks. It rested upon a foundation of slavery. Further, the Greeks could not unite and form a common whole. They never realised a common political consciousness. The city-states formed loose confederations, but nothing more. Frequent wars destroyed in turn the power of the leading cities. An all-inclusive partnership within the city meant an attitude of bitter exclusiveness towards other cities and the outside world. Greece, thus weakened, fell an easy prey to Macedon and then to Rome.

3. The World Empire of Rome

Rome began her political career as a city-state, very much like the city-states of Greece. The city-state of Rome was formed by a union of several tribes or curiae occupying seven easily defensible hills on the fertile plain of the Tiber. At first this city-state was not of much consequence. But her central position and her location at the head of the only important navigable river soon led to her pre-eminence. Community of religious worship was a strong bond of union between the various tribes living within her borders. In early days, her government was monarchic. The king was magistrate, monarch, and high priest all in one. The nobility known as the Patricians had a share in political authority. The landless, propertyless common people known as the Plebeians had no share at the beginning but acquired the privilege later on.

In early Rome as in the Greek cities, tendency was towards a more democratic form of government. About 500 B.C., monarchy fell and a republic was established with two chief magistrates, who later came to be called consuls. For two centuries following the change, the patricians and the plebeians were engaged in a struggle for political control. The economic consequences of many wars intensified the struggle. Finally, the two fighting classes fused into one citizen body, having equal political and civil rights. In this process the government too underwent a change. A plebeian had to be chosen as one of the two consuls.

At this stage Rome began to look outside her own borders, with a view to annexing territories. In the realisation of this ambition, the geographical conditions of Italy favoured her, since Italy was better adapted for conquest and expansion than Greece. Rome began her development with the incorporation of the neighbouring Italian States, which had a greater or less degree of local independence. By 90 B.C., after the 'Social War', which was a serious revolt of eight Italian tribes against Rome, practically all the peoples south of the Po were granted full citizenship. This citizenship of Rome was a much more flexible and adaptable system of rights than that of Greece. As Maclver notes, 'from early times the Romans had the wit to distinguish between civil right—rights of equality before the law—and political right—rights of membership in the sovereign body. Some cities of Italy were given civil rights, but no political rights.

Soon after the conquest of Italy Rome destroyed Carthade, her only rival in the West, and became a great naval power. A large part of the fragments of Alexander's empire came under her control. By the close of the first century B.C., practically the whole of the entire civilized western world was united in a single political system.

An effective system of centralised administrative control and worked out to hold the empire together. The conquered territory was divided into provinces and over each province was set up a

Roman official known as the proconsul, who had full powers in civil and political affairs. The only check which restrained him was the possibility of impeachment at home on his retirement from office. In Rome itself the republican form of government was replaced by military despotism. The emperor became all in all. Popular assemblies ceased to have any important functions. The Senate still had a prominent position, but the emperor got control over it by having a dominant influence in determining its position. The emperor's decrees finally came to be recognised as law.

By the end of the second century Roman citizenship was extended to the provinces. All the members of the State were equal subject to the rule of the emperor. During this period the old theory that the ruler received his power from the people gave place to the divine origin theory. Imperial authority came to be viewed as the divine origin. The emperor himself was worshipped as god for a time. Later, with the acceptance of Christianity as the State religion, the divine origin theory was interpreted to mean that the emperor was the agent of God's will on earth. Thus the ancient democratic city-State became the autocratic world-empire. Emphasis was shifted from the Greek ideals of liberty, democracy, and local independence to the Roman ideals of unity, order, universal law, and cosmopolitanism.

It is to the lasting credit of Rome that she gave to the world the first well-organised and well-governed State. Her rule lasted from five centuries in the West and for fifteen centuries in the East. The Catholic Church modelled her organisation after the pattern of the Roman imperial system. The idea of a universal empire haunted the minds of people throughout the Middle Ages. Roman law and Roman methods of colonial and municipal administration have come down to modern times. Rome's well-worked out ideals of sovereignty and citizenship and her methods in welding diverse peoples into political unity are some of her monumental achievements.

In spite of these great achievements, Rome could not make her empire permanent and enduring. Among the causes that led to her decline; and downfall were the sacrifice of individual liberty for the sake of securing unity, the soulless efficiency which characterised her administration, the moral depravity of the upper classes devastating pestilences, the unsound economic basis of the empire, failure to make rules for the succession of emperors, religious disintegration' and the invasion of barbarian hordes. Though Rome fell on account of these and other causes, her influence (her name and memory) have been more powerful in death than in life. Comparing the relative contributions and limitations of Greece and Rome, Gettell aptly remarks, 'Greece developed democracy without unity; Rome secured unity without democracy'.

4. The Feudal State

The downfall of Rome meant the death of the 'State' in Western Europe. A long period of confusion followed. The Teutonic barbarians who invaded Rome from the north were still living in the tribal stage. They had no idea of a strong central authority. They were lovers of local independence and individual liberty. Their kings were simply successful war chiefs. The freemen had a voice in all public affairs.

When such people came into contact with the Roman political system which was characterised by order, unity, and centralisation, conflict was the inevitable result. Out of this conflict feudalism-arose as a compromise. It was a compromise between the clan type of society represented by the Teutonic barbarians and the imperial State type represented by Romans. It is easy enough to decry feudalism and belittle its importance in the evolution of the State. It has been rightly said that it was not a system at all. But in the anarchic state into which society had fallen following the decline of Rome, it was feudalism which gave the people of Europe comparative peace and protection and preserved the machinery of the State. It marked the transition from the imperialism of the Roman world to the nationalism of the modern world.

How Feudalism arose and what it meant

On the decline of the Roman empire, the vast territories of Rome fell into the hands of powerful nobles. Each of these nobles became an authority unto himself and created a community of his own around him by a process of 'sub-infeudation' of land. The supreme lord parcelled out his land among the tenants-in-chief, and the tenants-in-chief among the tenants, and the tenants in turn among the vassals and serfs. Thus a hierarchy was built up on the basis of ownership of land. A rigid system of classes was established and the 'State' was swallowed up in the community. Services of various kinds, particularly military, were rendered to the immediate overlord, and the control of the supreme lord or king at the top of the social and economic ladder over the vassals and serfs at the bottom of the ladder was indirect and remote. The loyalty of each class was in the first instance to the class immediately above it. As a result of such limited loyalty, the idea of a sovereign power reigning supreme in a given territory remained foreign to the feudal period. In the place of a system of uniform and impartial law which the Romans had done so much to build up, there was a reversion to custom as law. Real political progress was impossible as long as feudal ideas prevailed. Yet feudalism was not synonymous with anarchy. It justified its existence by providing peace and protection to the people of Europe. It was based upon personal loyalty and contract. In its later stage, particularly in England where allegiance to the king took precedence of allegiance to the immediate lord, it helped the growth of the national State.

Another institution which survived the confusion following the downfall of the Roman Empire was the Christian Church. Christianity began as a humble faith among the lower classes of society. But in the course of a few centuries it reached the ranks of the high and mighty, and about the year 337 A.D. the Roman Emperor Constantine was converted to Christianity. By the end of the fourth century it was the only recognised religion in the Roman world. It built its organisation on the Roman imperial model and when the Empire fell to pieces, it was able to step in its place and give Europe order in place. During long periods of the Middle Ages, it was able to control the State and itself became a powerful temporal authority, holding in its possession considerable wealth, especially landed property. As Figgis remarks: 'In the Middle Ages the Church was not a State: it was the State; the State or rather the civil authority (for a separate society was not recognised) was merely the police department of the Church'.

In feudalism the Church found a valuable ally, for it was in the interest of the political aspirations of the Church that Western Europe should be kept divided with no common political superior to offer resistance to its extravagant claims. So long as there were able Popes and weak kings and emperors, and so long as the superstitious reverence of the people for ecclesiastical authority continued, authority prevailed. But from the beginning of the fourteenth century papacy fell on evil days, and never regained the position of pride and authority which she occupied during the pontificates of Gregory VII (1073-85), and Innocent III (1198-1216). The Babylonish Captivity (1303-1373), during which time the Pope was kept as a captive in Avignon by the French king, and the Great Schism (1378-1415) which followed when there were two, and sometimes even three, rival Popes, greatly weakened the authority of the Church and diminished its prestige. The Protestant Reformation which came soon after, practically ended the secular supremacy of the Church, and the way was prepared for national monarchies.

5. The National State of Modern Times

The Renaissance and the Reformation are generally regarded as marking the beginning of the modern period. These movements quickened the life of Western Europe, which now entered upon a period of unparalleled expansion and conspicuous achievement. In the very nature of the case, feudalism could not have lasted long. It had a useful role to play so long as conditions were unsettled and there was general disorder and confusion everywhere. But once conditions became settled and the ethnic, linguistic, religious, and territorial bonds gave people a new sense of unity, feudalism had to give way to a superior order of society.

Even before the close of the Middle Ages several factors conspired to bring in the new day. The Holy Roman Empire, even in the palmiest of its days, was little more than a ghost. It had no real authority behind it. National States were coming into existence in England, France, and Spain in spite of the so-called Empire and the sway of the Pope. Cities grew and commerce was developed. The pride of kings, mortified by the arrogant demands of the Popes, led to their breaking more and more away from Papal authority and making themselves master in their own houses. In this endeavour the people gave them their loyal support, as they desired peace and security. They looked upon the king as the visible symbol of the national spirit which was beginning to capture their imagination. The use of gunpowder, the rise of national taxation, and the setting up of standing armies freed the national monarchs to a great extent from their dependence upon the feudal nobility. The Hundred Year's War and the Wars of the Roses further weakened the authority of the feudal lords and diminished their political importance. By the close of the fifteenth century much of the feudal power was destroyed.

Thus on the eve of the Protestant Reformation the stage was well set for epoch-making political changes. The Reformers were primarily religious teachers. They waged a relentless war against the corruption of the Church, its false teachings, its secular authority, and its enormous wealth. They taught doctrines which had a profound effect not only upon man's religious life, but also upon his political relations—such doctrines as the value and dignity of every human being, the importance of the individual conscience and individual liberty, and the right of the individual to have direct access to God without the intervention of the priest. Out of such teaching there arose in the political field the modern movements of individualism and nationalism. The two powerful conceptions of the Middle Ages—the universal empire and the universal church—received a death-blow.

The immediate effect of the teaching of the Reformers was to strengthen the hands of national monarchs. All the great Reformers enjoined on their followers passive obedience to the State, and taught 'that the powers that be are ordained of God'. They held that political authority came ultimately from the will of God, and that the rulers to whom obedience was due ruled by divine right. Their teaching took root in England and in France and led to the Tudor and Stuart despotism in the former country and the Capetian absolutism in the latter. Louis XIV of France went so far as to say 'I am the State'. The general tendency of the Reformation teaching was to strengthen the hold of the monarchic principle in monarchic lands and the principle of aristocracy in aristocratic lands. 'In both the effect was to strengthen absolutism in the political sovereign'. (Dunning)

Such absolutism, however, did not remain unchallenged very long. With the growth of enlightenment and understanding and realisation of their power and importance, the common people began to question the duty of passive obedience to governmental authorities and to demand more and more political rights and privileges. This meant a prolonged conflict between the king and the people for political control. In the transition from royal absolutism to democracy the Reformation idea of personal worth played a very important part. The common man acquired a new confidence in himself and realised the fact that government existed not for its own sake, but for the good of the governed. Thus, the ultimate effect of the Reformation teaching was to further the cause of individual liberty and democracy.

Royal absolutism was no doubt necessary to weld people together and to bring order and unity out of feudal disorder and disunity. But once that object was fulfilled, there was no reason for its continuance. The democratic movement started very early in England and its progress was on the whole gradual and peaceful. In France it meant a vislent revolution. In other countries, the monarchs generally yielded to the popular will and were content to remain as historic figureheads under a democratic government. The movement had taken such deep root and worked so satisfactorily that, till recently, the democratic national State came to be regarded as the final stage in the evolution of the State. Bentham, for instance, hoped to better 'this wicked world by covering it over with Republics'.

6. The World Federation

Undoubtedly a great deal can be said in favour of the Democratic National State. It would seem reasonable to suppose that every country with a well-defined natural boundary having a homogenous and united people should be allowed to govern itself and claim all the rights of a sovereign State, and that the foundation of such self-governing and self-determining national State was the only way to international peace and good-will. But the history of the last century has shown that such a policy inevitably leads to rivalry, competition, and even war. Colonial empires have well-nigh destroyed the geographic and ethnic unity on which the national State is based. Scientific discoveries of recent years, greater facilities for travel and greater intercourse between people of the different parts of the world, international trade on a gigantic scale, and the world magnitude of present-day problems, all of which are causing 'the shrinkage of the world', tend to break down narrow ideas of patriotism and national sovereignty and point the way to some form of world federation. Just what form this world federation will take, the future alone can show. However, a world government of some sort seem inevitable. H. J. Laski; an ardent champion of World Federation, believes that outside purely domestic concerns, settlement in terms of common rules for all the states is becoming an increasing necessity. He further holds that the sovereignty of the State is in the process of disappearance in international affairs because it has served its purpose there. 'What the individual to-day requires is not the concept of Imperialism, but the concept of Federalism'.

In a recent book, *'Union Now'* Clarence A. Streit visualises a federal union of the existing democracies. He argues that the League of Nations has failed because it was a league of governments and not of peoples. Holding that the doctrine of absolute sovereignty is altogether unsuited to modern conditions, he argues for a world government of the federal type. This new organisation will regulate all the external relations of its members, leaving only matters of domestic concern to the members. The doors will not be closed against the non-democratic countries of the world but they will be admitted into the fellowship as soon as they declare themselves to be in favour of democracy and express their willingness to live in peace with all. In the Federal Union there are to be common citizenship, common currency, common postage, common tariff, and common defence. The colonial possessions of the members will be administered by the new federal government, the sincere aim being to fit them for self-government at the earliest date possible. The broad outlines of the scheme have received the approval of Lionel Curtis and a group of people in England who have organised themselves into a union to explore practical ways of giving effect to the scheme and to bring it to notice of responsible statesmen.

General Features of State Development

From a study of the evolution of the State, we are able to make certain broad generalisations. Gettell sums them up as follows:-

1. 'As in the evolution of all organisations, the process has been from the simple to the complex'. Government has become more complex and complicated than in earlier times. But at the same time there has been an increasing unity and inter-dependence of governmental organs. Different organs of the government perform different functions; but there is a fundamental unity underlying them all. The authority of the State which was uncertain and irregular at the beginning has now become more definite and regular, so that the chances of despotic or capricious rule are steadily decreasing.

2. 'The Development of the State has been accompanied by the growth of political consciousness and purposeful action'. The first State came into being not through the deliberate action of man, but largely through natural causes. Man being a social animal, the organisation of some form of governmental authority to hold society together was almost natural with him. But with the evolution of the State and increasing intelligence, man was able to discover reasons for the existence of the State and mould the State according to his ideals. State authority came to be based on a more rational and stable foundation. The spread of political consciousness to the people led to the formation of democracies.

3. 'In general an increase in the area and population over which the sovereignty of the State extends, characterises the evolution of the State'. 'The advance in political ability,

making possible the successful working of governmental organisation in large areas, the development of communication and transportation, and the improvements in economic conditions, enabling a given area to support a dense population,—all tend to increase the size of the State and the number of its citizens'.

4. 'State development has been marked by the separation of politics from some institutions and by increasing governmental interference in others'. Religion and the State evolved together in the early stages. But, at the present time, in all civilised countries, the Church and State tend to be entirely separate, although the Nazi Germany the Church has become the ecclesiastical department of the State. There is an increasing realisation of the fact that since religion and morality are primarily of an inward character, they should be subjected to the least possible amount of direct State control. At the same time the State should do all that it can to make the religious and moral life possible for the individual. Similarly, the personal life of the individual is becoming more and more free from state supervision. It is generally admitted that the State ought not to interfere with such matters as domestic life and personal likes and dislikes in such matters as food, clothing, fashion, etc., so long as such freedom is not contrary to public order and safety or laws of decency.

On the other hand, there is an increasing demand for State action in the sphere of public welfare, where individuals cannot or will not help themselves. Thus education, sanitation, the care of defectives, the punishment and prevention of crime are justified by all modern States. The general tendency to-day seems to be in the direction of extending State action, so long as it is not the fiat of the executive, but has behind it the united support of the people. 'However dangerous in the future the zeal for making laws may become, men have not yet wholly lost their traditional hatred of executive power or their trust in representative assemblies'.

5. 'In many ways the most significant general feature of development is the method by which the compromise between State sovereignty and individual liberty has been worked out'.

Rigid enforcement of customs and despotic rule were necessary in the early days to make primitive man understand the importance of law and authority. But after this purpose was accomplished, they became rather a hindrance to individual liberty and the unity of the State. The Oriental Empires kept up a despotic rule even after it had served its purpose. The Greek city-states developed individual liberty, but sacrificed unity. Rome perfected her organisation, but crushed freedom. It fell to the lot of the Teutons to work out a compromise between individual liberty and State sovereignty in the form of the modern democratic national State. By the principles of local self-government and representation, an organisation which secures unity in common affairs without sacrificing individual liberty is made possible, and democracy over large areas is at last-secured'. The problem of the future is to keep under changing conditions the balance between sovereignty and liberty, 'and no two modern States are agreed as to what is the proper adjustment, or how best to secure it'.

Select Readings

Dealey, J.A.—*The Development of the States,* Ch.II.

Fowler, W.W.—*The City-State of the Greeks and Romans,* Chs. IV-VI.

Gettell, R.G.—*Introduction to Political Science,* Ch.VI.

Gettell, R.G.—*Readings in Political Science,* Ch.VI.

Jenks, E.—*History of Politics,* Chs. VIII-XII.

Jenks, E.—*Law of Politics in the Middle Ages.*

MacIver, R.M.—*The Modern State,* Chs.I-IV.

Sidgwick, H.—*The Development of European Polity.*

Streit, C.A.—*Union Now.*

10

Modern Theories of The State

Socialism

Socialism may be defined as a theory and a movement aiming at the collective organisation of the community in the interests of the mass of the people through the common ownership and collective control of the means of production and exchange. Its essentials, according to Morrison, are that all the great industries and the land should be publicly or collectively owned, and that they should be conducted (in conformity with a national economic plan) for the common good instead of for private benefit. These points need some explanation.

It is important to observe that socialism, as an economic and political theory, originated as a protest against the evils of capitalism. Capitalism may be defined as an economic system in which private persons are permitted (under regulations laid down by the State), to undertake enterprises, providing for borrowing the necessary capital, and taking the profits, if any, after all the costs of the enterprise have been met. Its essentials are the private ownership of the means of production, private enterprise and private profit or unlimited acquisitiveness as a motive in individual life. Experience has shown that capitalism has several defects: (i) It results in an unjust distribution of the national wealth, i.e. in *inequality* of wealth, income and opportunity. (ii) It results in *insecurity* also. This is a direct consequence of the wage system, which is implicit in capitalism. The wage system, according to G.D.H. Cole, abstracts labour from the labourer, so that the one can be bought and sold without the other. Consequently wages are paid to the wage workers only when it is profitable to the capitalist to employ his labour. The periodical breakdown of the economic system, with its inevitable consequences of unemployment and misery, is the result. (iii) The wage system results not only in insecurity, but it makes of the worker a 'wage-slave'; for in return for the wage, he surrenders all control over the organisation of production, and all claim upon the product of his labour; the feeling that he is able to express himself in his work is absent. (iv) The price system in a capitalist economy responds not to the real needs of the community but to the demands of those who have money to spend. Therefore production is for profit, not for use. (v) Finally, those who ought to be partners in production, viz. the employers and the employed, are, or tend to be, antagonists.

Socialists suggest that all these defects of social organisation arise from one root cause, viz. the private ownership of the means of production and the desire for private profit. Therefore they would abolish all forms of private capital—private property in land, natural resources, factories—and with it the incentive to private profit. In place of private capital they would substitute common ownership and control. Twenty years ago, as A.C. Pigou points out, socialism was held to include only these two requirements; but recently, as is evident from the definition by Morrison cited at the beginning of this section, there has been an emphasis on central planning as a third requirement of socialism. It is increasingly felt that the efficient organisation of economic life under a system of public ownership of capital demands a central planning machinery to divert the productive activities of society into the most useful channels, and to increase social good to the utmost. There is no doubt that the example of the Soviet Union has had its share of influence in modifying socialist theory in this direction.

Socialists agree on the outline given above; but they are not all agreed on the ideal society they desire to see realised, or on the method of attaining it. Broadly speaking, there may be said to be two schools of socialist thought, the revolutionary and the evolutionary. The former (communists and syndicalists) hold that revolution or direct action is the only effective method of bringing into existence the new society; the latter (collectivists and guild socialists) believe that evolutionary, constitutional methods are not only possible but have more lasting effects. We shall describe these schools of thought in some detail.

Communism

Karl Marx (1818-83) is generally known as the father of socialism. A German by birth, he early displayed signs of intellectual brilliance and took a keen interest in history, jurisprudence, and philosophy. He became a severe critic of the existing economic and political order and soon had to leave the land of his birth for France, and later, in 1849, for England. There he remained for the remaining thirty-four years of his life, studying and writing. He took part in forming a socialist association called the 'International' in 1864, and 'remained thereafter in every way the dominant personality of the socialist movement'. His main writings are the *Communist Manifesto* (1848), drafted in co-operation with his friend and collaborator Friedrich Engels, the *Critique of Political Economy* (1859), and *Capital* (1867-94). The theory of socialism which he developed is known as communism.

The essential principles of communism are all found in the *Communist Manifesto* issued in 1848.

(i) *The materialistic interpretation of history.* The foundation of communism is the belief that the mode of production in material life determines the general character of the social, political, and spiritual processes of life.

'In the social production which men carry on they enter into definite relations that are indispensable and independent of their will; these relations of production correspond to a definite stage of development of their material powers of production. The sum total of these relations of production constitutes the economic structure of society—the real foundation, on which rise legal and political superstructures and to which correspond definite forms of social consciousness.'

(ii) *The class war.* 'Since the establishment of private property, society has been divided into two hostile economic classes. Just as in the ancient world the interest of slave-owners was

opposed to that of the slaves, and in medieval Europe the interest of the feudal lords was opposed to that of the serfs, so in our own times, the interest of the capitalist class, which derives its income mainly from the ownership of property, is antagonistic to the interest of the proletariat class, which depends for its livelihood chiefly upon the sale of its labour power.'

(iii) *The theory of surplus value.* The primary reason for this antagonism is that the capitalist class, through its ownership and control of the means of production, is able to appropriate the 'surplus value' which is created by labour and, therefore, ought to go to labour. The surplus value arises because labour power produces values above the cost of tools, raw materials and the cost of its own subsistence. The modern State is but a tool in the hands of the capitalist class to protect it from rebellion by the workers who suffer from this process of exploitation.

(iv) *A social revolution* is inevitable because the future development of capitalism will take the form of the concentration of capital in fewer and fewer hands, while, at the same time, there will be 'the ever closer and more elaborate organisation of the proletariat'. 'At its climax, the proletariat will arise, overthrow the capitalist class and expropriate them of the means of production.'

(v) *The dictatorship of the proletariat.* The dominant class will not, however, give up comfort and power without a severe struggle. 'The Red Terror', wrote Trotsky, 'is a weapon utilised against a class, doomed to destruction, which does not wish to perish.' This animal, in other words, is naughty; 'when it is attacked, it defends itself without realising that its skeleton is needed for a museum of specimens.' To stabilise the results of the revolution, therefore, a dictatorship of the dominant class, viz. the proletariat, will confiscate all private capital, organise labour, compel all to work, centralise credit and finance, establish State factories, concentrate means of transport and speed up production. 'The road to socialism lies through a period of the highest possible intensification of the State.'

(vi) Ultimately, the State will wither away. After capitalism is completely destroyed, the State is unnecessary, for there will no longer be any capitalists, for whose protection it now exists. Therefore it will 'wither away'.

'When organising production anew on the basis of a free and equal association of the producers,' wrote Engels, 'society will banish the whole State-machine to a place which will then be the most proper one for it—the museum of antiquities—side by side with the spinning wheel and the bronze axe.'

(vii) The new society will then be organised on the principle, 'from each according to his capacity, to each according to his needs'. Each man will contribute to the social wealth by his labour as much as he can, and will take from it what he needs.

Every one of these fundamental principles of communism has been subjected to vigorous criticism by students of economics and politics. The materialistic interpretation on history is a partial view; accident, great men, religion and geography have all played some part in history. The idea of a class war, denying as it does the possibility of a common civic consciousness, is unduly pessimistic. The labour theory of value, on which is based the notion of surplus value, is an inadequate explanation: other factors, such as the relation of supply to demand and the existence of competition or monopoly, must be taken into account. A social revolution of the kind predicted is not inevitable: recent economic history shows that social thought and foresight have brought about a gradual, and can bring a further, amelioration of social ills. As a matter of fact, the first socialist revolution did not, as Marx predicted, arise out of the culmination of capitalist development in the West but out of the pre-capitalist system in the East. Indeed, the very idea that a revolution is inevitable acts as a stimulus to prevent its coming.

Further, the dictatorship of the proletariat envisaged during the transition period is clearly undesirable. Any form of dictatorship is defective because we have no assurance that the interests of the dictators will always coincide with the interests of the community.

Communists constantly emphasise the evils of the concentration of wealth; but they are blind to the evils of the concentration of power. Even if the first dictators are high-minded, we have no assurance that their successors will be. Dictatorship is incapable of voluntary abdication; the State will not wither away. And finally the communist goal is not possible of realisation, for it demands a revolution in human nature. A social ideal which assumes such a fundamental change in human nature and habits is by the nature of things incapable of realisation.

SYNDICALISM

'Syndicalism' is derived from *syndicat*, the ordinary French term for labour union, and may be defined as 'that form of social theory which regards the trade union organisations as at once the foundation of the new society and the instrument whereby it is to be brought into being' (Joad). Its home is France; its main exponents are Sorel (1847-1922) and Pelloutier (1867-1901).

The syndicalists accept the general socialist position that society is divided into two classes, the capitalist and the proletariat, whose claims are irreconcilable; that the modern State is a class State dominated by the few capitalists; that the institution of private capital is the root of all social evils and that the only remedy for them is to substitute collective capital in place of private capital.

Syndicalism differs from communism primarily in the method it advocates for achieving the socialist objective. That method is direct economic action. In contrast to other socialist schools, it stresses the idea that

'The social transformation to be sought by the proletariat must be a self-transformation and that the institutions through which existing society is to be displaced by a new society are institutions that grow out of, and are built up by, the working class through its unaided efforts and in defiance of political authority'.

The efficient organisation of labour unions, by crafts or industries, and of local labour councils is the first step towards syndicalism. The boycott (the refusal to take employment with or purchase articles made by a firm regarded as unfair in its dealings with workers), the label (to indicate work done under union conditions), 'ca'canny' (the practice of doing a minute quantity of work with scrupulous care), sabotage (e.g. the damaging of plant by workmen), strikes, and, on top, the general strike, are the tactics adopted by syndicalists to achieve their ends. The general strike does not necessarily mean, contrary to what the term appears to denote, a strike of *all* the workers in a country. It is sufficient to have a strike of the workers in the key industries (e.g. electricity, gas, and transport) in order to paralyse economic life and to end capitalism.

Regarding the structure of syndicalist society, the syndicalist writers are not clear; they do not, indeed, consider it worth their while to work out the details of a future organisation of society. There will be no political State, as we understand it, which presupposes an organisation in which a delegated minority centralises in its own hands the power of legislation over all matters. Syndicates of workers will control the means of production; they will only use (not own) such property with the consent of society. They will be connected with the rest of society through local unions of workers and a general confederation of labour. This last will control such national services as railways and the post office. This picture is necessarily incomplete and hazy; only two features stand out clearly: there will be the producers' control of industry; the State will disappear.

No criticism of the ideal of syndicalist society is called for, as that ideal has not been clearly stated by the syndicalists themselves. Of their method, the most cogent criticism is that 'a general strike is unnecessary, because a general election is never far off'—for, given the discipline and the unity which are necessary for a successful general strike, the desired end can be achieved gradually, through constitutional methods. Indeed, the chances of success are greater, and the results more lasting, if syndicalists adopt constitutional methods, educate the voters, return representatives to Parliament on the socialist ticket and pass the necessary laws. In a general strike, the working classes are likely to starve before achieving their object; and failure of a strike may produce reaction against the workers. Further, methods like ca'canny and sabotage are sure to have a vicious effect on the morale of the workers.

COLLECTIVISM

Communism and syndicalism agree in being revolutionary. They advocate 'direct' action, rejecting the use of indirect parliamentary methods for achieving the socialist objective. Collectivism believes in the efficacy of the democratic method for this purpose. It is defined as that policy or theory which aims at securing *by the action of the central democratic authority* a better distribution, and in due subordination thereto a better production, of wealth than now prevails. Its principles are best explained by reference to the ideals of the English school of collectivism, known as Fabian socialism.

The Fabian society was established in January 1884. It has counted among its members many distinguished men and women including Bernard Shaw, Sidney and Beatrice Webb, Graham Wallas, H.G. Wells, and Annie Besant. The name of the society is explained by its motto:

'For the right moment you must wait as Fabius did when warring against Hannibal, though many censured his delays; but when the time comes you must strike hard, as Fabius did, or your waiting will be in vain and fruitless.'

The present social organisation discloses several defects; it assures the happiness and comfort of the few at the expense of the suffering many; it secures political freedom but maintains economic insecurity and slavery; there is 'poverty in plenty'. The Fabians therefore aim at the establishment of a society in which equality of opportunity will be assured, and the economic power and privileges of individuals and classes abolished, through the collective ownership and democratic control of the economic resources of the community. But it is no use attempting a sudden and radical transformation. Society must be 'permeated' with socialistic ideas through lectures, books and pamphlets; men who believe in them must be returned to Parliament; and public opinion must urge the adoption of legislative and administrative measures embodying socialistic ideas. To start with, the national minimum of work, leisure, wages, security against unemployment and sickness, provision for old age, self-government in industry, and education must be guaranteed to all. This of course means an extension of the progressive principle in taxation already at work, and the further taxation of inheritances, investment incomes and of unearned increment. The public ownership (national and municipal) of public utilities and natural monopolies must be pressed forward, and ultimately the land and all forms of industrial capital must be nationalised.

'The transfer must be effected gradually, applied at any given time only to such industries as can then be successfully administered by the community, and, though without full compensation, yet with such relief to the expropriated individuals as may seem fair to the representatives of the community in the political department.'

Briefly, the democratic State is the instrument through which the social transformation is accomplished; the democratic State is also retained in the socialist society in order to be the agent of the community to own capital and regulate production and distribution. Socialism, indeed, is viewed as the next step in democracy.

The distinction between communism and collectivism must now be clear. The former is revolutionary, the latter evolutionary. The former considers that the State being dominated by the capitalist is useless as an instrument to abolish capitalism; the latter, that if the citizens of a democracy will simply make adequate use of the political power they have, they can bring about the social millennium through the State. The former envisages a dictatorship during the transition period; the latter, a continuous use of democratic methods. The former suggests that the State will finally disappear; the latter, that the State will have added functions.

GUILD SOCIALISM

Guild socialism has been popularized as a theory by some English writers, particularly S.G. Hobson and G.D.H. Cole. It aims at the achievement of socialism with the guild as its foundation.

The guild is a trade union modified in two ways: it will be inclusive of all workers in an industry, including the unskilled workers as well as the clerical, technical, and managerial workers who are now largely excluded from trade union membership; and it will be organised to control industry, not merely to secure better conditions of work. The trade unions are the key to the situation in two respects: they will become the guilds of tomorrow, and they are the organisations by means of which the actual transition to socialism is to be accomplished.

The guild socialists recognise with other socialists the evils of the present social organisation—poverty, inequality and insecurity. In particular, they stress two defects, the one political, the other economic. From the political point of view, that a Parliament elected from territorial constituencies should exercise a general power of law-making is wrong; no man can represent another; an agriculturist may represent agriculturists; a lawyer, lawyers; and a coalminer, coalminers. Functional representation is clearly indicated. Further, the State, being but one association among several associations, can exercise power only in a limited field, i.e. the political; it should have no concern with other functions which should be left to other organised, functional bodies. From the economic point of view, the most important single defect of the present social organisation is the wage system, for, under present conditions, the wage worker in return for his wage surrenders all control over the organisation of production and all claim upon the product of his labour. This is clearly inadequate. Economic freedom demands that industry should be administered by all the workers, both manual and intellectual, who carry on the industry.

The structure of the guild socialist society is somewhat as follows: (i) There will be a guild for each industry which will be administered by the guild on behalf of society. (ii) consumers' councils will co-operate with the bodies of producers to determine costs and prices. (iii) A common Parliament will (according to some authorities) look to the affairs common to all, such as defence and taxation. On this point, however, there is some difference of opinion, some thinkers suggesting a body representing the essential functional associations to regulate such matters. (iv) There will be local regional bodies to look after matters of common interest in the locality.

The methods to be used to achieve this social order are partly the political method of the collectivist, and partly the economic method of the syndicalist.

Guild Socialism as a political theory has this value: it stresses the desirability of producers' participation in the management of the workshop. Its defects are that (i) as a socialistic system, it asks too much of human nature; (ii) the functional representation which the theory stresses is open to the objection that it underestimates the unity of society; territorial representation with all its defects is a rough device for the expression of the common interest; (iii) it may be unworkable in practice. 'The constitution of the State contemplated, especially in its latest elaboration by Mr. Cole, is a complicated nightmare of committees and joint-committees which reminds one of the machinery made by boys out to Meccano' (Hearnshaw).

An Estimate of Socialism

We have described the various schools of socialist thought and are in a position to form an estimate of socialism. Is socialism practicable? Is it desirable? How far is it likely to remove the defects of the existing social organisation? It is obviously difficult to give definite answers to these questions. Socialism is still largely theoretical and the only big experiment on which a judgement can be based is not only incomplete, but the available accounts of it vary far too much to be made the basis of correct conclusions.

On one thing, there is general agreement: socialism is strong in its critical, if not in its constructive, aspect. It points out clearly the evils of an acquisitive, capitalist society: its inequality, poverty, and insecurity; the agitation it stirs up reveals mal-adjustment, and presents a plea for the needy and the weak. It emphasises the economic foundations of the good life: 'that while civilisation may be everything above mere subsistence, the base cannot be neglected'. It exposes the fallacies of unbridled individualism, and suggests that social action can very largely overcome the hazards of a competitive society. It is a significant challenge to our generation to produce an acceptable alternative, if its thesis is considered erroneous.

It is on its constructive side that socialism has had its severest critics. (i) It is asked whether socialism is at all practicable as a permanent way of social life. It goes contrary to the well-established facts of human nature. Man puts forth his best effort because he knows that the reward of his effort can, in the main, be enjoyed by himself and his family. It is doubtful if he will work for society with the same enthusiasm that he now displays in working for himself. (ii) Socialism is another name for slavery. As Spencer put it: 'Each member of the community as an individual would be a slave of the community as a whole.' If all industry and commerce must be managed from a central authority which has to calculate and regulate everything, it follows that all deviations from the appointed and expected routine on which these calculations are based must be strenuously put down. The order of things established by the State must be maintained at all costs, and all opposing individual interests, wishes or aspirations must be remorselessly brushed aside. (iii) Socialism must mean the regulation of the laws of supply and demand, a task impossible of fulfilment. No central authority can ever regulate production so as to meet the constantly varying demands of every part of a great nation. (iv) State management may be less efficient than private management.

It is significant that academic economists of the standing of Professor Pigou (not a professed socialist) have refused to accept these rather 'old-fashioned' arguments at their face value. They point out, for instance, that the problem of incentive to work is not so simple as stated above: all work is not unpleasant; it is possible by the application of science to reduce the number of unpleasant jobs in society; the latent forces of professional pride, joy in work, and the sport *motif* can be enlisted in the service of society. Again, socialism is not rigid system: it is possible to manage State-owned industries efficiently and maintain the freedom of the individual through the development of new socialistic techniques, as, for instance, their management through public boards or commissions on a semi-public, semi-commercial basis.

Nevertheless, there is an element of uncertainty and of risk when one leaves well-tried paths of economic and social organisation for new ones. Pigou himself therefore prefers accepting for the time being the general structure of capitalism and modifying it with a view to reduce economic inequalities and promote social welfare. There is considerable truth in a remark of M'Kechnie that a true theory of the State must be socialistic and individualistic at once; and it is a false science which finds place for only one of these. What we need is capitalism transformed so as to combine safeguards for public interest with scope for private ownership and initiative, public supervision to be proportionate to public interest. Economic practice and theory are slowly discovering the outlines of such a system: a central planning machinery with the object of increasing efficiency in production all round; the nationalisation of public utilities and their direction for public ends with adaptable commercial business management through public corporations; the encouragement of consumers' and producers' co-operation to eliminate middlemen; the organisation of marketing; the avoidance of large fluctuations in the demand for capital goods through the control of the rate of interest and a wise public works policy; the development of the Investment Trust for the rational direction of the flow of investment; the limitation of profits; minimum and maximum wages; the organisation of the industrial unit in such a way as to secure efficiency as well as freedom; the collaborations of capital and labour in joint councils and corporations; income and inheritance taxes. Details apart, the economic basis of a free society should be a basic equality, the differences to be the outcome of genuine variations and explicable in terms of the common good. This will naturally lead to the predominance of the middle class in society, which Aristotle considered the greatest bulwark of stability in the State.

Fascism

The word 'fascism' is derived from Italian *fascio*, = 'a group or cluster'; it is used of a cluster of plants or branches which grow stronger by being thus bound together. A *fascio* of sticks with an axe in their midst was carried by the Roman lictors before the Roman consuls and represented the authority of the State; it was from the lictors' *fasces* that the Italian fascists derived their emblem.

The theory of fascism is primarily an Italian product, evolved to justify the fascist movement. The creation of a State of truly sovereign authority which dominates all the forces in the country and which at the same time is in constant contact with the masses, guiding their sentiments, educating them and looking after their interests—this is the central political idea of fascism.

In the words of Mussolini, fascism repudiates (i) pacifism, (ii) socialism, (iii) democracy and (iv) individualism.

(i) It repudiates pacifism, because that is born of a renunciation of struggle, and is an act of cowardice. Perpetual peace is neither possible nor desirable. 'War is to man what maternity is to woman.'

(ii) It repudiates socialism, because it believes that the institution of private property strengthens family ties and, if properly regulated, is generally in the interests of the community.

(iii) It does not believe in democracy. The majority, simply because it is a majority, has no power to direct human society; the sum of wills is not the same thing as the general will. The majority is not necessarily more reasonable than the minority. The democratic notion of the equality of man is wrong. Democracy indeed gives power to the masses to decide innumerable issues, about which they cannot possibly have the knowledge required to exercise a sound judgement; the masses are led by clever, unscrupulous demagogues, who have the gift of the gab. Further, popular government does not tend to throw up an aristocracy of intelligence and character.

In contrast to democracy, fascism believes in the principle that authority is exercised for the sake of the community, but is not derived from the community. The specific sanction of a government is its power; its ultimate sanction, its reasonableness. The fascist would wholeheartedly subscribe to Carlyle's idea:

Find in any country the ablest man that exists there, raise him to the supreme place and loyalty, reverence him; you have a perfect government for that country; no ballot-box, parliamentary eloquence, voting constitution building or other machinery whatsoever can improve it a whit. It is the perfect State, the ideal country.'

(iv) It repudiates individualism. The business of the State is to govern. The conduct of life cannot be left to the individual choice of the people; it must be, instead, determined for them by a power which is above them and comprehends them, viz. the State. The State must preside over and direct national activity in every field, and no organisation whether political, moral or economic can remain outside it. 'All within the State; none outside the State; none against the State.' The State is totalitarian. Individuals are transitory elements; they are born, grow up, die and are replaced by others, while society must be considered an imperishable organism, which always retains its identity and its patrimony of ideas and sentiments which each generation receives from the past and transmits to the future. As the fascist Charter of Labour in Italy put it: 'The Italian nation is an organism having ends, life, and means of action superior to those of the separate individuals or groups of individuals which compose it. It is a moral, political, and economic unity that is integrally realised in the fascist State.' The State may, therefore, in principle 'control every act and every interest of every individual or group, in so far as the good of the nation requires it, and of this the State is itself the sole judge. Except by the permission of the State, there may be neither political parties, trade unions, industrial or commercial associations; except under the regulation of the State, there may be neither manufacture, business, nor labour; both work and leisure are within the control of the State; except under the direction of the State, there may be neither publication nor public meeting; education, indeed all the ethical, intellectual, and even religious interests of its members are theoretically within the keeping of the nation and the supervision of the State.'

By way of criticism, it is sufficient to say that fascism represents in political theory a view diametrically opposite to the one developed in the foregoing pages. That view, which may be called liberal, is that the ultimate purpose of man is man himself; the State is a means to the development of individual personality and is not an end in itself. Our aim is, according to the liberal view, to enable the individual to think and express what he likes to plan his way of life in his own way and to grow to his natural height without dictation from outside, provided he does not interfere with the equal freedom of others and does not exploit the weakness of others for his private advantage. The liberal view stresses freedom; the fascist view, authority.

Select Bibliography

F.W. Coker, *Recent Political Thought,* Appleton, 1934.

G.D.H. Cole, *Guild Socialism Re-stated,* Allen & Unwin, 1921

———, *Fabian Socialism,* Allen & Unwin, 1943.

W. Gurian, Bolshevism: *Theory and Practice,* Sheed & Ward, 1932.

C.E.M. Joad, *Introduction to Modern Political Theory,* Oxford, 1924.

H.W. Laidler, *Social-Economic Movements,* Routledge & Kegan Paul, 1949.

H.J. Laski, *Communism,* 'Home University Library', Oxford, 1928.

J.R. Macdonald, *Socialism: Critical and Constructive,* Cassell, 1928.

W.S. M'Kechnie, *The State and the Individual.* Ch. XIII, James MacLehose, Glasgow, 1896.

A.C. Pigou, *Socialism versus Capitalism,* Macmillan, 1937.

G.H. Sabine, *A History of Political Theory,* Ch. XXXIV, Harrap, 1938.

State and Society

A General View of their Relations

The Distinction Between Society and the State

Turning from this historical retrospect back to the ideas of today, as they were summarily described in the beginning of the argument, we may now proceed to develop and amplify that description, with a special reference to English conditions and the general structure of English life. We start from the primary fact of the existence of national society. The nation, one in itself and always retaining the same identical body of members, confronts us, none the less, in a double aspect. This double aspect may be seen from three different points of view.

The first point of view is that of purpose or function. On the one hand, the nation, legally organised and assuming the aspect of a single legal association, acts in the terms and under the 'articles' by which that association is constituted (that is to say, in the terms and under the rules of the 'constitution') for the single legal purpose of making and enforcing a permanent system of law and order. On the other hand, the nation, socially organised (within the framework, but not by the act, of the legal association), and assuming the aspect of a plurality of associations (owing to the number and variety of the different social impulses), acts for a variety of purposes other than the legal purpose; purposes religious, moral, intellectual, aesthetic, economic, and recreational. (The Football Association and the Marylebone Cricket Club must also be counted among 'associations'). In personal composition the legal association and the social organisation—or in other words the State and Society—are one: they both include the same body of persons. In purpose they are different: the State exists for one great, but single, purpose; Society exists for a number of purposes, some great and some small, but all, in their aggregate, deep as well as broad.

The second point of view from which the nation may be seen in its double aspect is that of organisation or structure. Function determines structure; and the difference of purpose or function just noted necessarily involves (as indeed the argument has already implied) a difference of organisation or structure. As organised legally, in the terms and under the rules of the one legal purpose, the members of a nation belong to one organisation only, the State; though that one organisation, if it be federal, may be a State composed of sub-states, and even if it be unitary may still (at any rate where local self-government is practised) be a State composed of units cherishing and practising some measure of 'autonomy' and thus, as that term implies, 'making laws on their own account'. As organised socially, in the terms and under the impulse of their many social purposes, the members of a nation belong to many organisations; though these all combine and coalesce in the general complex of Society. Yet the multiplicity of Society still remains in spite of such combination; and it shows itself twice over. In the first place, there is not only economic society, as the radical economist too readily assumes: there is also the society of religion, the society of moral conscience and of the virtue of charity, the society of art and aesthetic taste, the society of education and culture, and still other forms of society as numerous and as various as the needs of the human mind. Man belongs to some form of society for every purpose he can conceive, since every purpose can be advanced by social action, and none can be far or fully advanced without such action. In the second place, it is well to remember that even economic society itself is various, plural, and even multiple. There is no one economic society, unless or until we attain an undifferentiated workers' society. There is a wide-flung range of economic groups, from the simplest partnership or shop to the greatest of federations or the largest of amalgamations; and in all this wide-flung range, so long as there are still two sides to the economic process (a side of the employers and a side of the employed), the groups are 'two and two, one against another'.

The third point of view from which we may see the double aspect of the nation is that of method. The State employs the method of coercion or compulsion: its purpose of declaring and enforcing a scheme of law and order makes the method necessary; and the unity of its organisation makes the method possible. Society uses the method of voluntary action and the process of persuasion: the nature of its purposes can be satisfied, and is best satisfied, by that method; and the multiplicity of its organisation, which enables men to choose and relinquish freely their membership of its various and alternative groups, enables them also to escape coercion by any group if coercion should be attempted. But we have to admit that this distinction between the method of the State and the method of Society, if true in the main, is not always true. Economic forms of association begin to acquire a power of coercion when trade unions become organisations which a man must enter, and cannot relinquish, if he wishes to get or to keep employment. Distinctions of thought are always clearer than differences of fact. In fact, and in actual life, there is always a 'margin of imprecision'. The State, if it is coercive, has also a voluntary aspect, at any rate under a democratic system of government by virtue of which each citizen lays his mind alongside of other minds in a voluntary process of common debate and mutual persuasion. Conversely, social groups, though voluntary in their nature, may assume coercive power, as churches no less than trade unions have done in the course of history.

The State as a Legal Association, and the Scope of its Legal Purpose

It has just been said that the State exists for the great, but single, purpose of law. The question may be asked, 'But what of the idea, as old as the age of Aristotle, that the State exists for the sake of the general good life of its members?' The further question may also be asked, "Does not the State, apart from ideas, and as a plain matter of fact, actually regulate issues other than legal issues?' A review of history is sufficient to show that the State in its time has touched many issues and played many parts; and it still continues today to be multifarious in its activity. It has acted in the religious field, by measures ranging from the establishment of a State-Church to the regulation of the trust deeds under which free churches own their property and manage their daily concerns. It has acted, and it acts increasingly, in the economic field: in our own history the long line of its acts runs from the Elizabethan Statute of Artificers (and even earlier statutes) to the contemporary statutes which 'nationalise' some of the staple industries. It has acted in the field of the intellect, by a succession of Education Acts: it has acted in the field of conscience, and in the name of social justice, by the institution of a system of public social services: it has acted in matters of the body, as well as in matters of the intellect and of conscience, and what it has done for public health and physical fitness is not the least of its doings. Can all these labours be comprehended under the rubric of law, or ascribed to a single 'legal purpose'?

The answer is that the term 'legal' does not denote a set of things in a separate compartment, comparable to but separable from other sets of things (religious or economic or intellectual or moral) in other similar compartments. Life is not only a matter of compartments: it is also a matter of modes. The term 'legal' connotes a mode, if it also serves to denote a compartment; and what it connotes is of more importance than what it denotes. Considered as a mode, the term 'legal' means a method or process of action, irrespective of the field of action or the content of the field. Legal action—we may also call it 'political', for, as it will be argued later, the political is also the legal, since the State is essentially law—legal action is a mode of treating things in general, things of all sorts and descriptions, religious or moral or educational or economic or whatever they may be, *so far as they can be brought under a rule of law and thus made a matter of compulsory uniformity.* Law touches and treats *all* acts—so far as acts are amenable to its touch and treatment.

But it is only external acts which are amenable to such treatment. A rule of law is an order (ultimately issued, as we shall see later, by the community itself, but immediately issued by some organ which declares and enforces the sense of the community), to do, or to abstain from doing, a defined and definite external act: an order enforced, in the last resort, by another external act of physical coercion. From this point of view the State may order its members, as it did in 1559 by the Elizabethan Act of Uniformity, 'all and every ...to resort to their parish church...upon every Sunday and other ...holy days...upon pain that every person so offending shall forfeit for every such offence twelvepence'. This is a legal order to perform an external act of physical attendance at public worship: an order enforced, in the event of contravention, by another external act of physical coercion which takes twelve pence from the pocket of the offender. In a sense this is not a regulation of the religious life, which is a matter of the inward mind: it is a regulation of external acts performed in connection with religious life. But the crux of the matter lies in the word 'connection'; and the enforcement by the authority of the State of an act so intimately connected with religious life as to be a symbol of inward conviction, and to be regarded in that light by the agent and enjoined with that intention by the authority, is something which is *ultra vires* and beyond the power of law. The long struggle and the ultimate triumph of English Nonconformity, vindicating the principle that 'in matters of the mind there is no compulsion', has recalled the State to its bounds. We recognise today that true religion is a matter of the mind, to be sought and found in voluntary co-operation with others of like mind, and therefore to be sought and found in the area of Society. But we also recognise that the State cannot be excluded wholly from the field of religion. Religion means organisation as well as inward conviction. Organisation involves financial and other external consequences; and those consequences come within the ambit of law, and therefore of the State. Wherever the legal mode is needed, that mode must necessarily enter. Wherever it cannot act—wherever, that is to say, compulsory uniformity is impossible—the mode is necessarily precluded.

The argument which applies to the religious field applies equally to the moral and the intellectual; it applies even to the economic. The economic process is indeed particularly immeshed in financial and other consequences of a legal order which bring it particularly and peculiarly within the ambit of law and the supervision of the State. But so far as it is a process which requires for its operation factors that cannot be 'reduced to the one'—the irreducible inward factors of spontaneity of individual initiative and free variety of individual experiment—so far, and to that extent, it escapes, and will always escape, the net of legal regulation. Here, as in every other field, the argument brings us to two conclusions. The first is that there is no set of things, and no compartment of issues, about which you can say to law and the State, 'You shall not enter; you have nothing to do with it: this is a reserved compartment'. The second is that for every set, and in every compartment, all that law and the State can do is to secure external acts of obedience under the sanction of otherwise applying external acts of coercion.

The first conclusion will lead us to say that the State and its law exist for the sake of the general good life. The second will lead us to say that all they can do for the general good life is to secure, by the ultimate sanction of force, the uniform doing of external acts, and to erect thereby an external framework for the inward movement of a good life which proceeds by its own proper motion. There is no salvation in the State: there is only a sovereign safeguard. Salvation lies in ourselves, and we have to win it ourselves—in the shelter of the sovereign safeguard. We may dream of a State which itself is an institute of salvation. We only dream; and our dream is one which denatures the State and unspheres law. The State of reality is by its nature a sovereign safeguard—no more, but also no less; and the sphere of law is obligatory rules of external action—no more, but also no less. Even if we ourselves, as members of the legal association, are makers and motors of the safeguard, it is only a safeguard, and not an institute of salvation, that we make and move, *in that capacity of ourselves.* Even if we ourselves, acting directly or through an organ appointed by us for the purpose, are the declarers and enforcers of law, it is only law—a set of compulsory uniform rules of external action—which we declare and enforce.

There remains a large sphere of activity which lies outside the State. It is the sphere, in a word, of the inward movement of the good life. That movement is not only a matter of the 'individual', acting as an individual. It *is* a matter of 'individuals'; but how much, and how often, do individuals act *in* groups, or *as* groups—in families (the innermost cells of our life), in schools (which are free societies of the mind in their inward operation, whatever their external framework may be), in churches and chapels, in professions and occupations, in 'clubs', 'societies', and 'associations' of every sort and description? The inward movement of the good life is at least as much social as individual; and voluntary social co-operation is one of its greatest channels. Nor is such co-operation limited to the inward life. It has also helped, and it still helps, in making the external framework, the securing the external conditions, necessary for a good life. The State is indeed the sovereign maker of the external framework; but it is not the only maker. There has always been, and there still remains, a space for social activity in the provision of the framework. In the first place, the State will always be, as it were, behind in the provision which it makes. There will be external conditions which it has not, as yet, secured, because there is not, as yet, a general conviction of their necessity; and the laboratory of social invention, engaged in pioneer's work, has to go ahead in planning and contriving voluntary expedients, and even systems, which at a later stage may be generally adopted and incorporated in the general framework. Secondly, even when the State has itself secured external conditions in this or in that field, it has only secured them (it can do no more by its very nature) in the shape of a uniform rule, which is the same for all indifferently and without respect of persons. But persons are different; and some of them will need their special conditions, over and above, or diverging from, the conditions secured by a uniform rule. Here social activity enters once more, not as a pioneer going on ahead, but as a 'mate' or collaborator standing by the side of the State to make some necessary adjustment or to add some necessary complement. The State, for example, may give unemployment benefit, and even add to it public assistance, by uniform rule; but there will still be special cases, and there will still be room for social action to meet such cases.

The Place and Function of Society in the Course of English Development

If we consider the relation of the State and Society in point of time, we shall find it hard to assign any priority or to say which precedes the other. On the one hand, it may be argued, there must have been society of some sort—some voluntary habit of living together and 'sticking together'—before men could develop a system of conscious self-organisation in terms of law. From this point of view Society is anterior to the State: the naturally given fact of Society precedes, if it does not produce, the consciously created fact of the State. From this point of view, and on this assumption that Society is a naturally given fact, we may also say that it is wrong to speak of a 'social' contract, as if a conscious contract had created Society—though it may well be right to speak of a 'political' contract, wherever at any rate we can detect a conscious agreement creating (or recreating) the State, as we can, for instance, in North America in 1787. (There is a note of Lord Acton, among his manuscripts, 'Rousseau's error was in affirming that society comes from contract: Burke denied that the State itself comes from it—also wrong.' The antithesis is hardly fair, either to Rousseau or to Burke; but the idea behind the antithesis is just.) On the other hand, it may also be argued that there is a sense in which the State precedes Society. When the State is once there, with its scheme of law and order, it provides a general security in whose shelter social formations can easily grow. From this point of view it is possible to regard Society as growing round the State—surrounding it, indeed, with growths—and yet leaving it always as the core. From this point of view, too, we may even say that the State is anterior to Society, or at any rate prior to the great bulk of the voluntary social formations which constitute Society.

It is perhaps idle to discuss priorities, and it is simplest to say that, at any rate in historic times, the State and Society have been concomitants, either acting in turn on the other. In England, at any rate, the interaction has been mutually beneficial; and in particular the presence of a settled State, which we have enjoyed since the Revolution of 1688 (and even that was an agreed transaction rather than a 'revolution'), has been favourable. on the whole. to the existence and action of voluntary social formations, ranging from voluntary hospitals, voluntary educational societies, and voluntary companies (whether or no they are called companies) such as Lloyd's and the Stock Exchange, to free churches, trade unions, and even political parties, which, as has already been noticed and must be noticed again at a later stage of the argument, are really 'social' rather than political in their nature... Indeed it was sometimes suggested in a phase of opinion current at the beginning of this century, that we English were progressing, and ought to progress still further, by way of a regression back to the epoch of the Middle Ages—that paradise of voluntary groups and Eden of pure society. But there is a great difference, in this respect, between the Middle Ages and our own age. Groups flourished in the Middle Ages in the absence of an effective State and an operative scheme of law and order; but the price paid for their flourishing was so heavy that men turned by preference to an effective State and sacrificed groups on its altar. Groups flourish today, if with less luxuriance, in the presence and under the shelter of an effective State; and for us to go back to the Middle Ages, in the sense of abandoning an effective State, might mean a sacrifice of the groups we have for groups we should hardly like to have—on such conditions and at such a price.

It we take a just view of our actual mercies, we shall recognise that the development of England since 1688, and not least in the course of the nineteenth century, has been marked by two characteristics. One of them has been the parallel growth of Society and the State, of voluntary co-operation and political regulation, with one of them sometimes gaining on the other (as at present, and under conditions of emergency, the State would seem to be gaining), but with both still moving and both still active. The other characteristic has been the interconnexion of the two growths—not divided into compartments, but mutually interfused and reciprocally interacting. The latter of these characteristics is particularly notable. On the one hand, as Bosanquet remarked, voluntary social groups, acting first in lieu of the State and then acting upon the State, can do an initial work of social experimentation which will afterwards, if it is successful enough to merit general adoption, be 'endorsed' or 'taken over' by the legislation of the State, as an 'adopted' road is incorporated into the road system of a town. Here Society serves as a laboratory for the State; and here we may cite the history of primary education, which was first conducted by two voluntary societies (one Anglican and one Nonconformist, but both founded about 1810), and then 'endorsed' and 'adopted' by the State in 1870 and afterwards. Here, too, it is to be noted that the State, in endorsing and adopting the results of voluntary initiative, may still respect and preserve the original initiative, as it has done, for example, by the retention of 'voluntary schools' in the general framework of its own system. Again, and on the other hand, just as social action aids the State, so the State in turn may aid social action. It may subsidize approved societies in the conduct of their voluntary work, as it did when a grant of £20,000 (afterwards made annual) was voted in 1833 for the building of school houses and distributed for that purpose between the two voluntary educational societies. In one way or the other—whether through the stimulus applied to the State by social action, or through the aid given to social action by the State—it may be said (as it was said by Mr. Sidney Webb, some forty years ago) that in the course of the nineteenth century 'voluntary association and government action have always gone on side by side, the one apparently always inspiring, facilitating, and procuring successive developments of the other'.

Two factors in English life have contributed to the ready germination of voluntary societies and to easy relations between these societies and the State. One of them may be called, in a term coined by Dr. Johnson, the 'clubable' character of the English genius: its taste for founding and managing clubs and companies, from the East India Company, which governed an empire, to the village cricket club. The club and the committee are part of the general grain. They proliferate equally on allotments and in Pall Mall: in the 'combination' rooms of colleges and in 'combinations' of employers or workers: in 'an assembly of good fellows meeting under certain conditions' (Dr. Johnson's definition of a club), and in the assembly of national representatives, meeting as a Parliament at West-minster, but becoming in process of time a club as well as a Parliament. By itself this proliferation of societies and combinations might have embarrassed the State: indeed at times it has done so; and the State has occasionally stretched out a hand against 'corresponding societies' and against 'conspiracies' in restraint of trade. But a second factor in English life has come to the rescue, and relieved or removed the embarrassment. This second factor is the peculiar character of the English State and of English law. The English State itself has had some of the qualities of a club, and it has thus had a fellow feeling for clubs which has made it generally kind. Not only is the House of Commons something in the nature of a club: political parties, as has already been noticed, have long combined the character of social formations with the activity of political forces; and in the area of local self-government, during the two centuries which followed the Revolution of 1688, the Quarter Sessions of the Justices of the Peace were a sort of county club, which might meet in a county hotel (as the Berkshire justices did when they passed 'the Speenhamland Act' of 1795) to settle issues of county policy. Similarly, English law may be regarded as largely the product of a club, or rather of a group of clubs, the Inns of Court with their barrister members from whom the judges are drawn; and it is certain that in one of its elements, its peculiar law of trusts, English law has provided a shelter and shield for voluntary society. Under the law of trusts a society need not confront the State directly as a property-owning body vested with a corporate capacity which makes it amenable to visitation and liable to dissolution. The property of the society may be vested in trustees—individual persons who hold it for the benefit of the society: who alone are recognised by the State as the holders of the property, so that the society remains in the background; but whom none the less, in case of need, the State will compel to discharge the trust incumbent on the property, with the result that the society in the background has a charmed and protected existence. Free churches, trade unions, and all sorts of societies have flourished under the shelter of the trust, 'so wide', as Maitland has said, 'was that blessed back stair', and so great was the latitude which it gave to 'social experimentation'.

National Society and the National State

The argument may now proceed to a statement of some conclusions involved or implied in its previous course.

(a) Under modern conditions, and as a result of the historic process by which they have been created, the basic form of human community, which we may call the community *par excellence,* is the nation—an inclusive all-purposes body of persons, covering a territorial area or *patria,* and containing within itself a variety of particular-purpose societies. More fully defined, the nation may be said to be a body of persons, inhabiting a definite territory and thus united by the primary fact of contiguity, who physiologically, and in respect of the blood in their veins, are generally drawn from a number of different races or breeds brought by time and their own wanderings into the territory, but who psychologically, and in respect of the content of their minds, have been led by a life of contiguity to develop two forms of mental sympathy. The first is a common capital of thoughts and feelings acquired and transmitted in the course of a common past history: a common capital, or tradition, which includes as a rule a common language, a common religion (which may, however, assume a number of different forms), and a common culture variously expressed in art and architecture, in literature, in social habits, and otherwise. The second is a common will to live together for the future, freely and independently increasing the common capital of thoughts and feelings, and thus exercising a right at the very least of social, but possibly also of political self-determination.

A reflection may be added to this definition of the nature of a nation. When nations became self-conscious, as they did in the nineteenth century and have progressively done in the twentieth, they seek to express and interpret—but they may only succeed in distorting—what may be called the 'idea of the Nation'. The term 'nation' may thus acquire different senses among different nations, and even at different periods of the history of the same nation. In Germany under the National Socialists the nation became, in an interpretation which was also a distortion of its nature, a racial structure built on the basis of an assumed consanguinity or common Aryan blood which was supposed to carry in its corpuscles a psychological treasure (as if time and tradition were not the main makers of such treasure), and which was to be kept pure from any admixture in order that the treasure might also be pure. In Italy, again, the nation became, in another interpretation which was also a visionary distortion, a metaphysical super-person: not a body of persons united by the psychological bonds of a common tradition and purpose, but a person above that body of persons, 'with a being, ends, and means of action' (so it was expressed in a document curiously entitled the *Charter of Labour)* 'superior to those of the individuals, separate or grouped, of whom it is composed'. It is a relief to turn from such interpretations to the simplicity of France, even if France may be said to have exaggerated the *moi* and the sovereignty of the nation. The French conception, based, in its present form, on the Revolution of 1789, is neither racial nor metaphysical. The sovereign nation is simply the population of the territory of France, one and indivisible in the strength of the natural frontiers by which it is enclosed, and united together internally by the bond of a common *amour du pays natal.* In a word, the nation is something rooted in the soil of France—in its sun, its wine, its speech, its social habits, its general culture and way of life...But however the nation may be conceived, and however its unity may be interpreted, the fact of the unity of the national community is the primary fact—except in the philosophy of Communist Russia, which is, or was (for even here the nation will recur), based on the cohesion of an international proletariate rather than on the unity of national community.

(b) The territorial nation provides the space-area and the human material over and upon which the form of the State is generally stamped; and when that form is so stamped, the national community—or, as it may also be called, the society of the nation—while still remaining a national society, and continuing to act as such, becomes also a national State, and acts henceforth as a State by legal methods for legal purposes. The reason why the nation is generally the basis of a State is simple. There must be a general social cohesion which serves

as it were, as a matrix, before the seal of legal association can be effectively imposed on a population. If the seal of the State is stamped on a population which is not held together in the matrix of a common tradition and sentiment, there is likely to be a cracking and splitting, as there was in Austria-Hungary. This is not to say that a single cohesive national society is always, even today, the 'matter' on which the 'form' of the State is impressed: on the contrary, as we shall have reason to notice, there are still heterogeneous States. It is only to say that such a society is the basis of harmonious and viable States.

(c) The stamping of the form of the State on a territorial nation has a triple significance. It means that the natural national society, which is simply there, becomes also a covenanted legal association, which is *put* there. It means, again, that the society achieves this transformation by creating and adopting a legal memorandum of association—or in other words a 'constitution'—which henceforth serves as its primary law; which always contains a scheme (though that scheme is not necessarily written) of the organs and the methods by which the association is to act, or in other words a 'frame of government'; and which may also contain a scheme of the purposes for which it is to act, or in other words a 'declaration of rights'. Finally, it means that the association will henceforth act through these organs, by these methods, and for these purposes, in the way of declaring and enforcing a body of rules of secondary or ordinary law which regulate the external actions of all its members. We may accordingly define a State as 'a juridically organised nation, or a nation organised for action under legal rules'. In greater detail, and in order to elucidate the ideas implied in that definition, we may say that 'a modern State is generally a territorial nation organised as a legal association by its own action in creating a primary body of constitutional law (such action often being a process along a line of time rather than an act at a point of time), and functioning in that capacity under that primary body of law for the purpose of declaring and enforcing a secondary body of ordinary law'.

The fuller definition which has just been given itself requires some measure of addition or amplification. In the first place, it must be repeated that the nation continues to be a nation, and to act as a nation in other than legal ways, even after it has adopted the form of a State for action in legal ways. 'Just because the State is so intimately bound up with law, it is unable to satisfy the pressure of the varied currents of economic, religious, cultural aspirations by its exclusive action.' Accordingly, as a whole and as one, the national society still remains active in the formation and expression of public opinion, social manners, and national character; while as a society of societies, and therefore diverse and manifold, it also continues to act in a variety of channels, and for a variety of purposes, in order to satisfy and express the set of the various currents and the trend of the different aspirations.

There is a second addition, more serious in its nature, which must also be made. The modern State is not always a unitary national Society. It may contain national minorities, of a different temper and separate tradition from that of the majority nation. In that case it is possible that a national minority may be content to exist simply as a *social group,* cherishing its own social manners and customs, its own particular language or dialect, and its own particular form of religious worship. Scotland may be said to be such a group, with its social form of national unity particularly and peculiarly expressed in the Presbyterian Church of Scotland (claiming in any case, as of right, its own inherent independence, but formally recognised by the State in its independence 'as a national church representative of the Christian faith of the Scottish people') and also with the added legal right of separate Scottish courts and some measure, though a diminishing measure, of separate Scottish rules of law. But it is seldom easy for a national minority to be content to exist simply as a *social group.* On the one hand the State, mainly based on the national majority, may seek to insist that the right of a national minority to use its own language does not extend into the area of State institutions, such as the schools and courts of the State; and it may thus raise legal issues which carry the national minority out of the social sphere into that of the legal association and its compulsory rules. On the other hand a national minority may itself raise legal issues, and challenge the legal rights of the State: it may, for example, claim a separate legal position (some form of autonomy or 'home rule') within the legal association; or it may even claim that it ought to be a separate and independent legal association and is therefore entitled to secede and assume the position of a sovereign State. To distinguish between the 'social' and the 'legal' sphere is no solution to the problem of national minorities, unless they on their side are willing to recognise and observe the distinction, and unless the majority nation on which the State is predominantly based is equally willing to recognise and observe the same distinction.

A third and last addition to the argument is necessary in order to explain the place of the constitution in the structure of the modern State. By the terms of the definition suggested, a modern State is a territorial nation organised as a legal association by its own action in creating a constitution. On this showing the constitution is a bridge, made by a nation, which spans the interval and maintains the connexion between the nation and the State. Such a view may readily be challenged. Do all nations, as a matter of fact, create a constitution by their own act, in order thereby to constitute themselves States? It may be argued that constitutions generally are not made, but grow: *nascuntur, non fiunt.* Hegel may be cited in evidence: 'What is called making a constitution is a thing that has never happened in history: a constitution only develops from the national spirit identically with that spirit's own development.' Short of that, it may well be argued that there are at any rate *some* constitutions, such as the English, which have not been made, but have grown historically; and it may thus be contended that the English nation has never created a constitution—but is nevertheless a State.

Two answers may be made to this contention. The first is that almost every modern State (alike in Europe, in America, and in Asia) has come into existence in its present form, and as what it now is, through the creation of a constitution which is the constituent charter of its being. Either there has been a break in the national life, a revolution, followed by a national act reorganising the nation as a new legal association under a new constitution (this happened in France in 1789, and has happened again and again in different countries since); or there has been some act of separation from a larger whole and some consequent reconstruction of the separated unit or units (as the North American colonies separated from Great Britain in 1776 and then proceeded to reconstruct their life under new constitutions of their own making); or, conversely, there has been some union of parts hitherto separate in a new federal body, and this union has been accompanied, and indeed made, by the creation of a federal constitution, such as the American constitution of 1787, or the Canadian of 1867, or the Australian of 1900. In one or another of these ways, or in some way similar to these, almost every State of the modern world has been organised in its present form, and as what it now actually is, by an act creating a constitution; and this act has generally been the overt act of a nation, expressing itself in and through an assembly of national representatives, though sometimes the form of the act may have been that of a royal grant (or *octroi*) in deference to the national will, or again of a parliamentary grant made to a dominion or colony in pursuance of its desires. These are the facts of the modern world; and when we are constructing a theory of the nature of the modern State, we have to adjust our theory to those facts.

But there is also a second answer to the argument that constitutions are historical growths, and not acts of creation. Even when a constitution has not been created at a point of time, but has been developed through the centuries along a line of time: even where a nation, during those centuries, may seem, at any rate in form, to have had little or nothing to do with constitution-making: even then, and even there, the formation of the constitution has been at each step an act of will and creation, and the whole of the constitution, as it now stands, is a nationally endorsed scheme of rules (not necessarily written, but none the less effective) which makes the State what it is today, controlling its operation and constituting its character. From this point of view the distinction between written and unwritten constitutions—or, more exactly, the distinction between constitutions created *uno ictu* and constitutions developed by a long and continuous process (both containing unwritten as well as written elements, though the proportion of the written to the unwritten may be larger in the former than it is in the latter)—is more a distinction of form than a distinction of substance. Both are alike memoranda of the association of the State; and both constitute it equally as the legal association which it is.

A Preliminary View of Sovereignty

In this connexion we may attempt a preliminary account of the notion of sovereignty. There *must* exist in the State, as a legal association, a power of final legal adjustment of all legal issues which arise in its ambit. The legal association will not be a single unit, and law will not be a unity, unless there is somewhere *one* authority to which crucial differences ultimately come, and which gives, as the authority of last resort, the ultimate and final decision. Different social groups may press different views of what is, or ought to be, law; it is even possible that different departments of the State may hold, and seek to enforce, different notions of what is legally right; there *must* be a final adjustment-centre. That final adjustment-centre is the *sovereign,* the topmost rung of the ladder, the *superanus* or sovrano, the 'authority of the last word'. Sovereignty is not the same as general State-authority, or *puissance publique:* it is the particular sort of State-authority which is the power, and the right, of ultimate decision.

In one sense sovereignty is unlimited—unlimited and illimitable. There is no question arising in the legal association, and belonging to the sphere of its operation, which may not come up to the sovereign, and which will not be finally decided by the sovereign if it so comes up to the topmost rung. The adjustment-centre must be competent to adjust *every* issue, without exception, which may stand in need of adjustment. But there are other considerations also to be noticed; and these will show us that sovereignty, if it is not limited to particular questions and definite objects (limited, that is to say, in regard to the *things* which it handles), is none the less limited and defined by its own *nature* and its own *mode of action.*

In the first place, and as regards its *nature,* sovereignty is the authority of the last word. Only questions of the last resort will therefore be brought to the sovereign. Much will be settled in the lower ranges and in the ordinary courses of the action of general State-authority. In the second place, and as regards its *mode of action,* the sovereign is a part and an organ of the legal association. Nothing will therefore come to the sovereign which does not belong to the nature and operation of the legal association, *as such.* Sovereignty moves within the circle of the legal association, and only within that circle; it decides upon questions of a legal order, and only upon those questions. Moving within that circle, and deciding upon those questions, sovereignty will only make legal pronouncements, and it will make them according to regular rules of legal procedure. It is not a capricious power of doing anything in any way: it is a legal power of settling finally legal questions in a legal way. Upon this it follows that sovereignty, confined by its nature to the sphere of the legal association, will not enter or seek to control the sphere of society, unless questions arise in that sphere (such as the interpretation of a trust deed or of the articles of association of some form of voluntary society) which invite a legal decision and are amenable to such a decision. There are areas of social action which cannot be entered by law or brought under legal control. Sovereignty, being by its nature legal, does not impinge on these areas.

Who, then, or what, is the sovereign, in the sense of being the final adjustment-centre of the legal association?

(a) Ultimately, and in the very last resort, the sovereign is the constitution itself—the constitution which is the efficient and formal cause of the association; which brings it into being; which forms and defines the organs and methods of its operation, and may also form and define (if the constitution either contains or is accompanied by a 'declaration of rights') the purposes of its operation. It may be objected to this view that the sovereign is a body of living persons, and not an impersonal scheme; and that ultimate sovereignty must accordingly be ascribed, not to the constitution, but to the constitution-making body behind it which can alter and amend its provisions. But there is an answer to that objection. The impersonal scheme of the constitution is permanently present, day by day, and year by year; it acts continuously, and without interruption, as the permanent control of the whole operation of the State. The body of persons which can alter and amend the constitution (and which, by the way, can act only under the constitution, and in virtue of the constitution) is a body which acts only at moments of interruption, and therefore at rate intervals. The continuous control may more properly be termed sovereign than the occasional interruption; and we may accordingly say that the constitution itself, in virtue of being such a control, is the ultimate sovereign.

(b) Secondarily, however, and subject to the *ultimate* sovereignty of the constitution, we may say that the body which makes ordinary law, in the sense of issuing the day-to-day and the year-by-year rules of legal conduct, is the *immediate* sovereign. That body may be differently composed in different political systems. In the United States, for example, it is composed of Congress and President acting independently (though with mutual checks and reciprocal powers of overriding one another's authority) on a system of co-ordination. In the United Kingdom it is composed of Parliament and His Majesty's Ministers acting interdependently, and with a mutual give and take (though here too there are mutual checks, and Parliament can dismiss the Ministers by an adverse vote as vice versa they can dismiss Parliament by advising His Majesty to use his power of dissolution), on a system which is one of connexion rather than co-ordination. However composed, the body which makes the ordinary law of the land is the immediate sovereign, which issues final legal pronouncements on ordinary current questions to the extent and by the methods authorised under the constitution. The immediate sovereign which makes the ordinary law in the United Kingdom is authorised by the constitution to a greater extent of action, and to action by easier and speedier methods, than the immediate sovereign which makes the ordinary law in the United States; but in either case the immediate sovereign is a body authorised by the constitution, acting and able to act because it is so authorised.

On the argument which is here advanced the constitution is the *ultimate* sovereign, in virtue of being the permanent scheme, or standing expression, of what may be called the primary law of the political association; and the law- and rule-making body is the *immediate* sovereign, in virtue of being the constant source and perennially active fountain of what may be called the secondary law of the land. Two difficulties confront the argument, one of them largely formal, but the other more substantial. The first and largely formal difficulty is that it would appear to be inconsistent to begin by ascribing ultimate sovereignty to the constitution rather than to the constitution-making body, and then to proceed to ascribe immediate sovereignty to the law- and rule-making body rather than to the law. Does not consistency demand either that both sovereigns should be impersonal systems, or that both should be personal bodies; either that the ultimate sovereign should be 'the rule of the constitution' and the immediate sovereign 'the rule of law', or that the ultimate sovereign should be the constitution-making body and the immediate the law- and rule-making body? We may answer that inconsistency is inherent in the nature of the case. The position of the primary law of the State is different from that of the secondary law. In the sphere of the primary law, which is in its nature permanent, it is the law itself, as a constant control, which matters more than the body of persons who occasionally vary and change the control. In the sphere of secondary law, which is in its nature constantly changing with the change of circumstances and situations, it is the body of men constantly making the changes, and always at the helm, that matters most in the eyes of men and is accordingly felt and acknowledged to be the immediate sovereign.

The second and more substantial difficulty raises deeper considerations. It has been said, in the argument here advanced, that the law- and rule-making body acts and is able to act because it is authorised by the constitution. But may it not also be said, and should it not rather be said, that the law- and rule-making body acts, and is able to act, because it is authorised by the nation, or short of that by national opinion, or, simpler still, by the electorate and its vote? And if that may be said, is it possible to ascribe any immediate sovereignty to that body, and should not such sovereignty be rather ascribed either (1) to the nation, or alternatively (2) to the thought of the nation, as expressed in the form of public opinion, or even (3) to the action of the electorate (as the organ *par excellence* of the nation), in electing—and thereby, in some sense, also authorising and even 'instructing'—the body which makes the laws and issues the rules of legal conduct?

Three ideas are involved in the considerations which have just been raised—the idea of the sovereignty of the nation, or 'national sovereignty' (in the sense in which the term is current among French thinkers): the idea (which some English and American thinkers have cherished) of 'the sovereignty of public opinion'; and the idea of 'the sovereignty of the electorate', which in practice, in a number of continental countries, has been often interpreted to mean the sovereignty of the party or combination of parties which has secured a majority of electoral votes. The most serious of these three ideas—all akin to one another, but rivals as well as kin—is the idea of the sovereignty of public opinion. We may therefore begin with that idea: we may then proceed to the idea of the sovereignty of the electorate; and we may end by examining the idea of 'national sovereignty' in the French sense of that term.

(a) By the side of the State—so our argument has run—national Society continues to exist; to pursue a process of general thought in the form of national discussion; and to act for a variety of social purposes through a variety of social organs also engaged in a process of thought (they could not otherwise act) which pours itself into the general pool of the thought of the whole society. By the exercise of this process of thought in the form of discussion national Society precipitates a body of opinion, which we may call indifferently by the name of national or public opinion. This body of opinion will affect and qualify the action of the law-making body. *Legally,* that body still remains the immediate sovereign, and it therefore remains unlimited and illimitable, except by the constitution: *actually,* it has its ear to the ground

of public opinion, and although it may do *de jure* whatever it wills to do within the limits of the constitution, it moves *de facto* within the limits (necessarily, by their nature, elastic) of an encompassing body of opinion precipitated by the nation. Some have made this fact of the relation of public opinion to the law-making body the ground of a distinction between two kinds of sovereignty—political sovereignty, regarded as resident in public opinion, and legal sovereignty, regarded as resident in the law-making body. But the difficulty of this distinction is that all sovereignty is essentially legal, and you cannot divide what is essentially legal into the legal and the other-than-legal. (It is a different matter to make a distinction between two *grades* of legal sovereignty, the higher and ultimate grade of the sovereignty of the constitution, and the lower and immediate grade of the sovereignty of the law-making body: the difference there is a difference of hierarchy and degree in one and the same kind of sovereignty, and not a difference of two kinds.) We shall do well to cling to the idea of the one immediate legal sovereignty of the law-making body, admitting (or rather contending), as we do so, that in operation and practice this sovereignty acts with regard and respect—though not in legal subjection or any legal relation—to the general body of national thought and the weight of its opinion. That, however, is true not only of the law-making body and of the immediate legal sovereignty which it exercises, but also of the whole of government and of State-authority in all its range. Executive officials are particularly bound to act on the ground of law; and yet even they will be wise to remember in the course of their executive action that opinion must count as well as law. The law-making body is particularly able, in virtue of its representative character, and therefore particularly bound (though never legally bound), to remember and regard the existence of public opinion.

(b) The idea of the sovereignty of the electorate is one of a different order from that of the sovereignty of public opinion. The electorate is not the national society, however great its numbers may be; and the verdict it passes, at a given time,

on the programmes and candidates submitted to its choice is something different from the constant play of national thought. The electorate is a legal organ of the legal association: it is part and parcel of the State. Normally, as its name suggests, it exists and acts for the single purpose of choosing the law-making body. It may, however, be authorised by the terms of the constitution to act on occasion for the further purpose of concurring in the passage of law, through the institution of the referendum: it may even be authorised by the constitution to act for the still further purpose of joining, upon occasion, in the first motion of law, through the institution of the initiative. In either of these events, or both, the law-making body is not the legislature only, but the legislature and the electorate acting in conjunction; or rather it is the latter on the occasions when the institutions of the initiative and the referendum are employed, and it is the former, and only the former, on the occasions when they are not. (The oscillation is somewhat perplexing; and that is one of the reasons why the referendum and the initiative have never attained a general vogue.) But it is one thing to hold that the electorate may, in certain circumstances—that is to say, on some particular occasion—become a part of the immediate sovereign: it is another thing to hold that the electorate should, in all circumstances, be regarded as the whole of the immediate sovereign. To profess a belief in the sovereignty of the electorate is to subscribe to this latter view.

But it is difficult, and indeed impossible, to subscribe to the view that the electorate, in and by itself, can ever be regarded as the immediate sovereign. There are, indeed, arguments which may be advanced in support of the view. One of them is the argument that the electorate, merely by the fact, and in virtue of the act, of electing the law-making body is super-sovereign over that body. In itself that argument carries no weight: the electorate which chooses the immediate sovereign does not become an authority over it by virtue of its choice, any more than the electors who choose a professor become an authority over him by virtue of their choice. Another argument may seem to carry more weight. This is the argument that the electorate not only elects the law-making body, but also 'instructs' it at the time of election, and that therefore the body so instructed must act, during its term of office, according to its instructions. There *is* a sense in which the result of a general election is a sort of general instruction to the law-making body. But this general instruction is, at the most, a general expectation that the majority of the persons elected will seek to carry into effect the programme on which they have been elected—subject, however, to the march of events and new conjunctures of circumstance, and subject, above all, to free discussion with the minority (who have also been elected and have also their rights and functions) and to the achievement of some compromise based upon such discussion. Such a general expectation, so qualified and so circumscribed, imposes no legal obligation upon the persons elected: it does not make the electorate a legal adjustment-centre: it does not diminish—it even increases—the duty of the body of elected persons to act as such a centre, and to make the actual adjustments to the best of their ability and by the use of their discretion.

There is a further remark to be added. The idea of the sovereignty of the electorate, when we pursue it to its inmost recesses, is really a cover or outwork for the idea of the sovereignty of party. The name of the electorate may grace the measure, but party is the real flame. The majority party pleads the verdict and instruction of the electorate—that is to say, of the majority of the electorate, for there is also a minority which has also given a verdict and instruction—in order to cover its partisan claim to make adjustments in its own sense and on its own motion. Party has a great and legitimate function in a democratic system of government; the function of formulating choices for the electorate, the function of arraying sides in the legislature, the function of cementing the Cabinet (and also the anti-cabinet, or Leaders of the Opposition) in the sympathy of a common loyalty. But if it is ubiquitous, it is never sovereign; and if it contributes to adjustments, it is not their maker. The hidden notion of the sovereignty of party is something more dangerous than the open idea of the sovereignty of the electorate. The electorate is intermittent: party is always there. The electorate is a legal organ, acting in public and by methods publicly prescribed. Party is partly public, but it is partly also private; it is partly a matter of the State, but it is partly also a matter of Society and voluntary social arrangements. The sovereignty of party, however it might be veiled under the name of the electorate, would be a sovereignty always acting but often acting obscurely and sometimes deviously. There is all the more reason for refusing to accept the idea of the sovereignty of the electorate when we reflect on the nature of the actual sovereign which that idea might be used to veil.

(c) The idea of the sovereignty of the nation (*souveraineté nationale*) is an idea which has had a large vogue in France. It is already indicated in one of the articles of the Declaration of the Rights of Men and Citizens of the year 1791: 'le principe de toute souveraineté réside essentiellement dans la nation.' If, however, we analyse the term 'nation', in so far as it bears on the idea of sovereignty, we shall see that it must mean one of two things. It may mean, in the first place, the whole population of a national territory, considered as the source of public opinion; and in that case what has already been said of the idea of the sovereignty of public opinion must also be said of the idea of national sovereignty. It may mean, in the second place, that part of the population which constitutes the electorate; and in that case what has already been said of the sovereignty of the electorate must also be said of the idea of national sovereignty.

We may therefore conclude that immediate sovereignty cannot be ascribed to the nation, any more than it can be ascribed to the electorate or to public opinion, but must be ascribed to the law-making body, and to that body only. It is that body, and only that body, which makes the actual adjustments of questions under debate; and it is the adjustments made by that body, and only those adjustments, which are binding and obligatory on the members of the State. It is true that the sovereignty of the law-making body is limited: indeed it is doubly limited—legally limited, by the need of keeping within the constitution and acting under the constitution; practically limited, by the need of keeping in harmony with the opinion of national society and acting in conformity with its general trend. The fact that the constitution is a legal limit on the immediate sovereign makes the constitution super-sovereign; the final sovereign; the ultimate sovereign. But the fact that the public opinion of Society is a practical limit on the immediate sovereignty of the law-making body does not make that opinion in any sense sovereign. The term sovereign belongs to the legal sphere, and to that sphere only. The constitution belongs to that sphere: public opinion does not. To vest sovereignty in the public opinion of national Society is both illogical and dangerous. It is illogical, because sovereignty does not belong to the social sphere in which opinion moves, but only to the legal sphere in which the State moves and has its being. Again it is dangerous, for the simple reason that it magnifies unduly the nature and scope of sovereignty. If we say that public opinion, and the nation which forms that opinion, is sovereign, we tie ourselves to an undefined and unlimited sovereign, which can do what it will and will do what it can. The pure legal sovereignty of a law-making body which confines itself to adjusting legal issues, by legal methods, in legal subjection to the constitution, and also, at the same time, in some degree of practical subjection to the trend of national opinion—such sovereignty, so confined, is a definite and limited thing.

The Social Area and the Nature of Social Groups

If we hold fast to the conception of the State as a legal association, acting under an ultimately sovereign constitution, through an immediately sovereign law-making body, we shall recognise that there is a large area of social life which the State will not touch, or, rather, will touch only at those points where the 'social' spills, as it were, over into the 'legal', and thus trends to legal consequences. The State, for instance, will not touch religion, so far as religion is a matter of internal and spiritual activity, though it may be compelled to touch it at points where the existence and action of religious bodies raises legal issues such as the interpretation and the administration of trusts; and the reason why it will not touch religion is the fact that law, through which by its nature the State always acts, is essentially a matter of uniform rules, for the control of external actions, which are irrelevant and inapplicable to the inner nature of religious activity. Similarly, the State will not touch economics, so far as economics is a matter of the internal and mental activities of original decision at the point where a problem arises and original experiment for its solution by the method of trial and error; though it may, and will, be compelled to touch economics where the existence and action of economic bodies and groups raises legal issues of the rights and duties of persons who are immediately concerned or indirectly affected. It is impossible to convert the general operation of economic activity, with its multitudinous problems of particular decision and its manifold requirements of particular adaptation, into a system of uniform legal rules. But it is also impossible not to create a system of such rules, in a field of action which may be called one of 'supervision', rather than 'operation', for the mass of similar problems, involving general issues of the rights and duties of persons, which the activity of economics always presents and which become increasingly pressing as public opinion becomes increasingly aware of their presence.

There is a difference in this matter, as we shall have occasion to notice later, between religion and economics; and the cause of religious liberty is a different cause, at any rate in degree, from that of economic liberty. Economic activity raises legal issues, and is therefore drawn into the area of the State, to a vastly greater degree than the activity of religious life. But the two liberties, even if they differ, have been, and may be, defended together by the same general argument. There are two possible lines on which they may thus be defended. One line of defence, which has just been suggested, is directed to the nature or quality of the subject-matter involved; the other is directed to the nature or quality of the agents which handle the subject-matter. On the first line of defence, the argument advanced in favour of religious and economic liberty is that the subject-matter involved, or in other words the activity in question, is an internal activity, a motion of the mind, which as such and by its own nature must be free from legal compulsion. On the second line, the argument is that the agents which handle the subject-matter, or conduct the activity, are living groups, of the nature of persons, which as such and by their own nature must possess and enjoy the liberty inherent in all personality.

The latter line of defence has often been employed by English thinkers since the beginning of the century. The foundations were laid by Professor Maitland, as long ago as 1900, in the introduction to his translation of a section of Gierke's work on *Das deutsche Genossenschaftsrecht,* which was published under the title of *Political Theories of the Middle Age.* The subsequent development of events—particularly the judgement of the House of Lords, in the year 1904, in the Free Church of Scotland case, and the Osborne judgement of the same House, in the year 1909, in a case concerning the rights of trade unions—led to further building on these foundations; and a general theory began to be advanced of the general rights of groups, both religious and economic, in the system of the modern State. The gist of this theory was (1) that a group, such as a Church or a trade union, is a real person, a group person, with its own group mind, its own group will, and the general attributes of personality; (2) that groups of this order come into existence, and continue to grow, as such real persons, not in virtue of a legal act outside themselves, such as parliamentary authorisation, but in virtue of their own motion and by their own spontaneous action; (3) that being real persons, which have come spontaneously into existence and continue to grow spontaneously, these groups have rights of acting freely for their own purposes, which the State is bound to respect (as it is generally bound to respect all rights of personality), so long as they are not exercised for purposes inimical to its own purpose of maintaining a scheme of law and order.

We may begin by noting that this general theory is double-edged. If it is applied to groups other than the State, it fosters syndicalism, or a general philosophy of the autonomy of groups (and particularly of economic groups) at the expense of the authority of the State. If, on the other hand, it is applied to the State, and if the State is regarded as a *personne morale* with a *volenté générale* transcending and reconciling individual wills, the theory fosters étatisme, and issues in a philosophy of the total and engulfing State whose will is the peace—and the tomb—of its members. If groups are to be the beneficiaries of this theory, the greatest group may well be the greatest, and even the only, beneficiary. We shall, therefore, be wise, before we turn groups into persons (and 'real' persons at that), to inquire what a person is, and in what sense, if any, a group may be called a person. Here we must draw a distinction between the moral world and the legal. In the moral world the only persons are individual human beings. It is they, and they alone, who have minds: they, and they alone, who have wills. In the moral world there are no group persons, no group minds, and no group wills. There are, of course, groups in the moral world. But these groups are not persons. They are bodies ('wholes', as Aristotle would have said) composed of individual persons who hold common ideas and will common purposes, but hold them as individuals and will them as individuals: individual persons who, of course, interact, and are what they are because they interact, but who are still individual persons. The unity of a group, in the moral world, is not the unity of a common mind: it is the unity of a common content of many individual minds.

We may now turn to the legal world. Here we have to notice that the word 'person' has a peculiar sense. A study of etymology will help us to understand this sense. Originally the word *persona* signified an actor's mask, and thence, by an easy transference, the character or *dramatis persona* who wore a particular mask. A further transference carried the word from the stage to the field of law; and *persona* became the legal mask worn, and the legal character sustained, by a legal actor or agent on the scene of the legal State. A still further transference carried the word in time from the legal sphere to the moral; and *persona* became a personage or person who sustained a character and played a part on the general scene of man's moral activity. The dramatic, the legal, and the moral senses of the word have each their own significance; and, in particular, the legal sense has a peculiar significance of its own which must be distinguished from that of the moral. In the legal sense individuals—that is to say men and women who are already persons in the moral sense and agents in the moral world—are further conceived as wearing legal masks; as each sustaining a legal character; as being legal actors or agents who play their part in the 'drama' or action of the legal State; in a word, as being 'persons at law'. But this is not all. In the legal sense, and in the view of the law, a group of individuals, which as a group is not a person in the moral sense or in the moral world, may also wear a legal mask, sustain a legal character, and be a person at law. This is what happens when a group becomes 'corporate' or embodied, and when, as such, it is 'legally authorised to act as a single individual'. It may then hold property, sue and be sued, make and break contracts, suffer and inflict torts, and generally behave and be treated as a quasi-individual. But it remains a quasi-individual, and does not become an individual: it remains in the legal sphere, but it does not enter the moral: it is a person only in the legal, and not in the moral, sense.

How are these quasi-individuals, these purely legal persons, admitted to their position? Obviously, if they exist as persons only within the legal area, they must be admitted into that area by an act of the legal association, or in other words of the State. This is not to say that the act of the legal association—which may take the form of executive warrant or charter, or of legislative authorisation, or of judicial decision—is an act of creation. It is an act of recognition. The group is already there as a fact before it achieves recognition as a person; and groups may continue to remain as facts without being recognised as persons. In the whole of the area of legal personality the State is an organ of selection and recognition. This is true, in a measure, of individuals, as well as of groups. The State makes some sort of selection even among individuals; it determines which of them it will recognise—or, more exactly, which of them it will *not* recognise—as legal persons in its legal scheme. In England, for instance, an 'idiot' is not a legal person, and in France a person punished with civil death (*mort civile*) forfeits all legal personality. Similarly the State selects among groups, determining which it will accept as legal persons in its scheme; but here—more concerned with positive selection than with negative—it picks and chooses not those which it will not recognise, but those which it *will*. Individuals are legal persons unless they are excepted; groups are legal persons only if they are accepted. No groups, therefore, are legal persons in the absence of specific authority in their favour—authority proceeding from the executive or legislative or judicial organ of the State.

We may now draw the argument to a conclusion, and bring the conclusion to a point by taking a particular example. The conclusion is, on the one hand, that no groups are real persons, possessing real minds and wills of their own apart from the minds and wills of their members; it is also, on the other hand, that some groups are legal persons, vested with legal capacities of acting in the sphere of the State as though they were individuals, and vested accordingly with the consequent position or status of quasi-individuals. Trade unions may serve us as an example. A trade union is not a real person, acting in the moral world. It is not even one of those groups which are legal persons, entitled to act in the legal world as quasi-individuals; for it is not in the eye of the law (though some judicial decisions in the past have tended in this direction) 'corporate' or embodied, and therefore it is not a person at law. But if a trade union is neither a real person nor a legal person, then there is little to be gained from discussing its rights, or the measure of liberty which it should enjoy, or its general relation to the State, *in terms of persons and personality*. If we wish to defend the rights and the liberty of trade unions, we shall do better to adopt the line of defence which starts from the subject-matter of their action and the nature of their activity; which looks pragmatically to what they do, and not metaphysically to what they are. The real question, in any discussion of the relation of trade unions to the State, is not the question whether they are persons, of whatever sort or character. It is the simple question whether the State, in determining its attitude to a group of individuals acting together on the basis of common ideas for the realisation of a common purpose, should leave their activity to operate freely in the voluntary area of social initiative and social experiment, or should draw it into the involuntary area of legal control and legal uniformity. The 'being' of the group (person or not-person? and, if a person, which sort of person, the moral or the legal?) is irrelevant to that question: the one thing relevant is what the group does, what its activity is, and whether that activity can, and should, be regulated by law.

On this basis it may be argued that, as the activity of a trade union is multiple (partly charitable or educational, partly political, and partly—indeed mainly—economic), different considerations will come into play in each different field of activity. So far as the activity of a trade union is charitable or educational, it should, in principle, be left free to operate in the voluntary area, because it is an internal or spiritual activity, a free motion of the mind, which belongs by its nature to that area. So far as the activity is, directly or indirectly, political—so far as it consists in raising political funds to support a political party, or in promoting a strike intended or likely to affect the government of the community by pressure or the community itself by privation and hardship—the activity may, in principle, be brought under legal control and made subject to legal rules. (This is not to deny that, in practice, the State may be wise in abstaining as far as possible from the policy of legal control, and in preferring to trust to voluntary good sense and the voluntary action of public opinion.) Midway between these two activities—the charitable or educational activity, and the activity which is directly or indirectly political—there is the main and general activity of trade unions, the economic activity, which consists in collective bargaining (backed by the power of the strike) about the wages and conditions of labour. Here, if we follow the principle that original decision, at the point where a problem arises, and original experiment for its solution, by the method of trial and error, are the cardinal factors which ought to be respected in the field of economics, the activity of trade unions will be left, as far as possible, to operate freely in the voluntary area. It cannot, indeed, be left utterly free. On the one hand the State is bound to protect the rights of persons, if and so far as they are adversely affected by particular acts of trade unions (such as acts of intimidation) in the course of the general activity of conducting a strike: on the other hand it is bound to ensure the efficient and continuous operation of its own administrative agencies (post office, police, and the general civil service), and it must thus impose some measures of restriction on trade unions formed by its own employees. Generally, however, and apart from such exceptions, the presumption remains in favour of the freedom of the economic activity of trade unions. But it must again be repeated that that presumption is not based on any 'personality' of trade unions, or the nature of that 'personality'. It is based entirely on their activity and the nature of that activity.

Because it is activities that matter, and because one and the same group may have, and indeed is likely to have, different orders of activity at the same time—activity of the voluntary orders in the social sphere, and activity of the controlled order in the legal—it follows that the same group may belong, and indeed is likely to belong, to both spheres simultaneously. A group moves in two worlds, or at any rate shows two faces: it is, as a general rule, both a voluntary group acting freely in the social sphere and a state-regulated group acting under law in the legal. A Free Church lives and moves almost altogether outside the legal sphere: but even a Free Church—or rather the trustees who hold its funds on its behalf—will come into the courts, and be drawn into the legal sphere, if a question arises about the application of its funds and its property. The same may also be said of trade unions: indeed, it may be said even more, because a trade union may not only come into the courts on a question of the proper application of its trust funds, but also on a question of the effect of its acts, or the acts of its representative agents, on the rights of persons whom they may affect. But if we connect we must also distinguish the status of the religious group and the status of the economic. Both move in two worlds; but the one moves more in both than the other. When a religious group has vindicated the position of a Free Church, and established itself and its life in the area of Society, it remains in that area untroubled (unless some rare issue of funds or the like should draw it out into the legal sphere), because its main activity is a practice of spiritual conviction which does not affect other persons—at any rate in the ways of which the State can, or will, take cognizance. No economic group can escape so entirely, or remain so untroubled; for the main activity of economic groups consists in the doing of external acts which may affect other persons adversely. It is true that a trade union has, at its roots, the same sort of desire as a Free Church to defend and maintain a set of inward convictions; but the convictions themselves, even when they reach their highest point of a genuine passion for moral principles, are convictions of a different order from those of a religious society, and the means of their maintenance and defence are mainly material means. The theorists who have connected the cause of religious liberty with that of economic liberty have sometimes forgotten that there is a difference which divides, as well as an analogy which connects, the two causes.

The Idea of a Social Parliament

A distinction has been drawn, in the general course of the argument, between national Society and the national State. The State, we have said, is legal—specifically and essentially legal—and just because it is legal, and therefore also compulsory, it must leave room and scope for the action of voluntary Society, being in its nature 'unable to satisfy the pressure of the varied currents of economic, religious, cultural aspirations by its exclusive action'. At the same time, we have also said, the State is the one and only form of legal organisation, and the only vehicle of legal action. The State is only the agent of law, but it is also the only agent of law; and whenever a legal question arises in any field whatsoever, or a legal rule has to be made on anything whatsoever, it is the State alone which acts and which alone can make the rule.

A question, however, has been raised whether there ought not to be some central organisation of Society: some social parliament, or even some general system of social parliaments, which might be added to the political parliament of the State, and might stand by its side in some sort of relation, whether subordinate and advisory or co-ordinate and concurrent. Hitherto (so the argument runs) there has been only a single mirror—the political mirror—the political parliament which reflects, or as we say 'represents' the legal association as such: ought we not also to have another mirror, or even a set of other mirrors, reflecting some one great aspect of Society as such, or even several of its different aspects?

The suggestion most commonly made is of a single social mirror, an economic council (or economic 'parliament', or economic 'sub-parliament') reflecting the one great aspect of Society implied in the adjective 'economic'. That suggestion acquired vogue, and even seemed likely to be translated into fact, at the close of the war of 1914-18. In Great Britain an industrial conference, convened by the Prime Minister in 1919, proposed the institution of a National Industrial Council, to be elected by the workers and employers in each industry separately, and to be vested with the general power of advising the Government on industrial legislation. The proposal, however, was left in abeyance and Great Britain has remained content with a single political parliament. On the Continent more was attempted, but little, in the issue, achieved. Germany instituted in 1920 a National Economic Council, by the side of the Reichstag, for the purpose of advising the Government on social and economic legislation; but the Council soon dissolved into committees which advised the Government directly, and eventually even the committees ceased to be asked for advice. France instituted in 1926 a National Economic Council, which (after 1936) included 173 members representing economic groups and interests, to study economic problems, to report on them to the Government, and to advise the Government on all economic measures proposed in Parliament. In a different setting the French Economic Council still remains, and its powers have been confirmed and expanded by the new French Constitution of 1946; but it is not clear that it plays any role of importance, or that it has relieved the political Parliament of any part of its burden. Italy, under its Fascist régime, instituted from 1930 onwards a National Council of Corporations, containing representatives of employers and employed and empowered 'to formulate rules for the general co-ordination of the national economy'. The National Council of Corporations stood by the side of the Senate and the Chamber of Deputies (with the latter of which it was eventually merged in 1938), but like so much else in Italian Fascism it served rather as a theatrical property than as an actual institution.

If, as has just been said, Great Britain has in practice remained content with a political Parliament, the idea of a social parliament has continued to be mooted among us in theory. The Guild Socialists, in the early years of the century, advocated the institution of two parliaments—an economic parliament, based on guilds, for economic affairs, and a political parliament, based on local constituencies, for the business of the State. In 1920 the Webbs, in a work entitled *A Constitution for the Socialist Commonwealth of Great Britain,* similarly advocated a plurality of parliaments. Pleading the hypertrophy of a single parliament and—even more—its 'vicious mixture' of functions separate in their nature, they suggested that the old political parliament should henceforth be confined to its proper and original functions of the conduct of external relations and the maintenance of internal law and order. A new social parliament, they proposed, should then be instituted by its side to take over the more modern functions of the management of social policy and the general development of a 'way of life' or 'type of civilisation'. In their ingenious and carefully constructed scheme of parliamentary dyarchy both of these parliaments were to be elected (though not simultaneously, or by the same method) on the basis of geographical constituencies. Both were to co-operate by a system of joint committees; and in the event of a clash a joint session of both was to make the final decision. But as the control of the budget and the power of the purse were to be vested in the social parliament, it would appear that the social parliament was to be the greater of the two. This was an extreme and dubious plan—the more so as it was never made clear how the maintenance of law, entrusted to the political parliament, could be divided from the management of social policy (and from all the making and maintenance of law involved in that management) which was assigned to the social parliament.

Dr. Temple, afterwards Archbishop of Canterbury, was at once more moderate and more extreme in the proposals he made in 1928 in a work on *Christianity and the State*. Pleading the example of the National Assembly of the Church of England (an ecclesiastical parliament competent, under its enabling act of 1919, to deliberate on and make provision for all matters concerning the Church, subject to the consent of both Houses of Parliament in such matters as by the law of the land require parliamentary sanction), he proposed, in addition, (1) an industrial parliament, based on voluntary associations, which should legislate in its own department subject to the veto of the political parliament, and (2) an educational parliament, based on voluntary bodies of teachers and also on local education authorities, which should legislate in its own sphere 'subject', as he wrote, 'in one way or another to parliamentary veto'. This was consequently a proposal for what may be called a set of social parliaments—an ecclesiastical, an industrial, and an educational parliament. In that sense it went beyond the proposal of the Webbs. But Dr. Temple also suggested that the political parliament should impose a limit or veto on the acts of these several social parliaments, and in this respect his proposal was more moderate than that of the Webbs.

Mr. Churchill, in a Romanes lecture delivered at Oxford in 1930, confined himself to industry, and followed in the track of the policy proposed by the industrial conference of 1919. He suggested a House of Industry (but a House on a different level of power from the two existing Houses of Parliament) empowered to prepare and recommend solutions of industrial problems. This would be an advisory body—parallel, let us say, to the French advisory Economic Council. Of late Mr. Amery, in his *Thoughts on the Constitution* of the year 1947, has adopted and expanded Mr. Churchill's suggestion. Pleading, like Dr. Temple, the analogy of the functions and powers of the National Assembly of the Church of England, he proposes a third 'House', or 'sub-parliament', which might frame measures altering or amplifying Acts of Parliament, subject to the consent of the two existing Houses. This third House would be based on trade unions and employers' associations, possibly with the addition of representatives of consumers nominated by the Government. It would have the advantage, he argues, of enabling the new principle of 'functional' representation to be tried without destroying the existing geographical principle.

There is here a variety of counsellors, and a multiplicity of consels. In structure, most of the counsellors suggest a social parliament of a new type, based on the functional principle, and representing vocations: the Webbs are perhaps alone in arguing for a social parliament based, like the political, on the principle of local or geographical constituencies. In function, some would vest the social parliament only with the power of advising the political parliament or, alternatively, the executive government: the Webbs, however, would make it a concurrent or even a superior legislature; others, again, would attempt a *via media* and give to the social parliament the position of a subordinate legislature, competent indeed to enact laws but only with the assent of the political parliament. On one issue all would seem to be agreed. They would all institute the social parliament—whatever the basis of its composition, or whatever the extent of its function—by an act of State and by way of a formal amendment of the constitution. They do not consider the possibility that a social parliament may possibly be evolved by an act of Society; that it may, as it were, grow of itself; that it may begin and end in Society, as a purely social organ, simply and solely expressive of social opinions and aspirations.

Nothing need here be said, at any rate for the moment, about the composition of a social parliament. There is a prior question of greater importance—that of its powers. Should it have the powers of a concurrent parliament, or should it have only advisory powers? The first alternative has commended itself to a succession of thinkers, which began with the Guild Socialists, was continued by the Webbs, and may still be traced in the theories and suggestions of Dr. Temple and Mr. Amery. The basis of this first alternative is the policy of functional devolution: the policy of sorting out and separating functions at present combined (or, as the argument goes, 'viciously mixed') in a single parliament, and of remitting some of the functions so sorted out and separated to a new body or bodies. Such a policy raises a grave but also simple issue. What would be left to be old 'political' parliament, if a system were adopted of functional devolution upon another 'social' parliament or set of 'social' parliaments? It is possible to answer that question by saying that law would remain: that though economics and education (the general management of social policy and the general development of a 'way of life' or 'type of civilisation') would be lost to the political parliament, the maintenance of law (along with the conduct of external relations and the control of a system of defence) would be left. But what is law?

Law is not a separate or separable *set* of things in an isolated compartment. It is, as we have already seen, a general *mode of action*. It is a mode of dealing, by uniform rules, with things in general—with things economic and educational, and with all others sorts and sets of things which are capable of being brought under and regulated by a uniform rule or system of rules. Law, in a word, is a general mode of action which ranges over all places where a uniform rule is possible, and which touches, as it ranges, every sort of thing; but if it is general it is also single, and must proceed from a single source. Being general, and ranging everywhere, it ranges over the field of economics. One cannot distinguish law from economics, or say that law belongs to one sort of parliament and economics to another. Being, on the other hand, a single mode, law has a single organ for its making or declaration. The State, in the shape of the political parliament through which it acts, is the only organ and maker of law. The State, on the theory here assumed, is only a legal association; but, by the same token, it is also the only legal association. Because it is that, its political parliament is the one adjustment-centre. There cannot be a plurality of adjustment-centres. If there were, they would themselves need to be adjusted. There must be some one, single, final adjustment-centre; and that adjustment-centre is necessarily compelled by its nature not only to adjust finally all sovereign issues (issues, that is to say, which demand the exercise of sovereignty), but also to take the initiative in formulating their adjustment. A magnetic attraction draws such issues directly to the one final authority. Men will always seek to go straight to it, and the institution of other instances will not defeat or deflect the attraction. That attraction will be especially strong in the field of economics. Economic issues, in these troubled days, are the issues which specially demand adjustment. They are swept particularly, and swept directly, to the final adjustment-centre; and that centre is accordingly compelled, both by its own nature and by their urgency, to take the initiative in their adjustment, and to act with an original efficiency as well as a formal finality.

The powers of a social parliament will not therefore be powers of legislation. They will, at the most, be powers of advice to the one and only legislative authority—or, more exactly, for even 'advice' is too strong a term, they will be powers of expressing social opinion and formulating social aspiration at the bar of that authority. Now a State-created body, acting in the framework and as a part of the State, is not the natural or logical vehicle for the exercise of those powers. Society is something different from the State, and the formulation of social opinion is something different from the formulation of legal rules. If Society is the area of voluntary formations and voluntary action, we should naturally expect a social parliament (or a complex of social parliaments, corresponding to the complexity of society) to form itself voluntarily, and not to be formed by an act of State-creation. We should also expect it, when it is formed, to move in the area of Society and to proceed by the method of social action: to express social opinion and aspiration, and to serve as an indication of the trend of thought in general Society. It will thus be a new form (and yet, perhaps, by no means so new as its advocates think) of that play of national or public opinion which, as we have seen, is always at work behind the political parliament, and which is always affecting and qualifying the action of that parliament.

We must not exaggerate the peculiarity or the novelty of the idea of a social parliament. It is an idea which is neither so peculiar nor so novel as many are inclined to think. There already exists, and has long existed among us, a whole complex of what may be called 'social parliaments'. There are the 'social parliaments' of the organised professions (though there is as yet no federal parliament of all the professions); there is the 'social parliament' of the occupations, in the shape of the Trades Union Congress; there are the 'social parliaments' of the employers in the shape of their federations and unions; there are the 'social parliaments' of the different churches; there are a number of 'social parliaments' (partly professional, but some of a wider scope) in the field of education. The novelty of the idea of a social parliament, in the form in which it has become recently current, consists in the suggestion of a new *joint* social parliament in the field of industrial production, representing both workers and employers, and drawing together the separate 'social parliaments' in which the two sides have hitherto acted. This would, indeed, be something new, though there have been tentative movements towards it during the last thirty years. But the question is whether such a new joint social parliament cannot form itself, and is not likely to form itself, by the method of voluntary action. We may safely answer that the fertility of social invention is not exhausted; that the idea of the voluntary formation of such a new joint body has already been mooted between workers and employers; and that in the new conditions of production and the new social temper of our time the idea may thrive to fruition. We have already formed a number of specialised social parliaments for ourselves by the method of voluntary action. There is no reason, in the nature of things, why we should not form for ourselves, by the same voluntary method, a new social parliament, of a greater scope and of wider dimensions, in the shape of a joint industrial parliament.

But such a new social parliament, so formed, will be a parliament of Society (otherwise it will not be a 'social parliament'): it will not be a parliament of the State, or a 'third House', or anything else which is *in pari materia* with the organs and organisation of the legal community. It will be simply an organ, larger and more catholic in its scope than the previous organs, but not different from them in its nature, for the expression of social opinions and social aspirations. We must beware of importing into our thought about social parliaments any idea of a policy of devolution; any idea that the State should remit to social organs its own specific and inalienable political function of preparing, formulating, and enunciating all the rules of law. Devolution is a current word. It is the reverse side of the word 'congestion', which is often applied to the parliament and the general government of the State. It is possible that there *is* congestion of the State; but if there is the remedy has to be found within the State. Devolution of the legal powers of the territorial State, if it should be attempted, will naturally be territorial devolution—devolution, that is to say, on the territorial sub-divisions of the State, which are of the same nature as itself. It will be devolution on national areas, if such areas are contained in the State. It will be devolution on provincial, regional, and local areas of one order or other—in a word, on areas of neighbourhood. (Neighbourhood is the great bond of men, uniting people of all sorts, for purposes of all sorts, in common areas of residence which are the areas of those general contacts and general relations that really need adjustment.) But even devolution of this order, devolution of the territorial order, logical as it may seem, may not be practicable in a country such as Great Britain. Here a large population is massed together, upon a small soil, in a system of relations so inextricably interwoven, from one end of the country to the other, that any legal rule must always be a rule which also runs from end to end. It is difficult, after all, to think even of a system of provincial or regional sub-legislatures in the conditions of such a texture.

How much more difficult, then, will it be to think of a system of social sub-legislatures, or to advocate a policy of functional devolution—devolution, that is to say, on social-economic groups pursuing social and economic aims in the area of Society. Here we cannot even plead the claims of logic in our favour, as we can for territorial devolution. On the contrary, we are involved in a confusion of ideas. Social groups belong to the area of Society; they are not subdivisions of the State. No social group, and no assembly representing such a group or a number of such groups, is fitted by its nature to act as an organ of the legal and rule-making association which we call the State. It is true that the opinion of a social group, or of an assembly representing such a group, may properly affect the State, because it is a part and a form of that encompassing body of general social opinion which is always playing upon, always affecting, and always qualifying the action of the legal association. But it is also true that a social group in itself, and any assembly representing such a group or a number of such groups, is not, and is not by its nature fitted to be, a law-making, or even a law-formulating, or indeed in any sense a legal body, as all organs of the legal association must be.

There is not only a confusion of ideas, and a defect of logic, in the idea of functional devolution of the powers of the State. There are also grave practical difficulties. One of these practical difficulties is the difficulty of space. The members of social groups (doctors, miners, teachers, transport-workers, lawyers, agricultural workers) are necessarily scattered in space, and separated by interstices. But the State, and each division of the State, is by its nature a territorial continuum. It is based on contiguity in space, and on the fact and feeling of neighbourhood. To combine in a single scheme the functional and the territorial would be to mix and confound the discrete and the continuous. There is a second and greater difficulty—a difficulty not of material space, but of mental sentiment and moral solidarity. Functions, when they are complementary and are consciously felt to be complementary, *may* serve to draw men together in the sense of a common need and the feeling of mutual dependence. But it is also true, and even more true, that they also serve to divide, and that each industry, trade, occupation, and profession develops its own special interest, its own peculiar bias, and its own exclusive group-interest. It would be far from easy for the State to devolve upon such bodies the performance of any of the common duties which it owes to the whole territorial community. The essence of the State, and equally of the divisions of the State, is a common territorial citizenship, which unites the residents in a common area for the common handling of the common questions that concern them all in their common capacity as neighbours.

But while there is reason to doubt the idea that the State should devolve any part of its powers upon social groups, there is little reason for doubting that the modern State owes a large and generous measure of respect to such group in the exercise of their own intrinsic and native powers. It would not show that respect—indeed it would do the opposite—if it sought to incorporate social groups in its own organisation, and to make them part of its own legal system. There are other and more generous methods which the State can adopt. In the first place, it can recognise frankly that there is a whole area of social action parallel to, if different from, its own area of legal action: an area of voluntary action, of tentative non-official effort, of many-sided initiative and manifold experiment. In other words, it can recognise that it is not only concerned with individuals ('that State and the Individual' is not the whole of the matter), but also with societies: it can admit that it is in its nature not only an association composed of individuals, but also an association composed of associations (*consociatio consociationum*). Accordingly it can respect and protect the liberty and the rights of groups, as well as the liberty and the rights of individuals. In the second place, and as a part of such respect and protection, it can develop a general law of associations and their rights, side by side with its private law of persons and the rights of persons. It can construct, as a modern jurist has said, a system of 'public law on the lines of a comprehensive treatment of the rights and duties of various social organisations—...ecclesiastical, professional, educational, literary—that have stepped in between the individual and the State and are daily growing in importance in their task of organising scattered individuals into conscious and powerful groups'. In the third place, and as a still farther extension of its respect for and its protection of the life of voluntary societies, it may even give positive aid and encouragement to their activities. Just as the modern State increasingly aids and encourages the development of individuals by the provision of what are called public social services, so it can also aid and encourage the development of societies, when they are doing good work for the benefit of the general community, by fostering their expansion and even by giving them financial aid. The policy of financial subsidies adopted by the British Government during the last thirty years towards the societies, called universities, that serve the advancement of learning and the general promotion of higher education, may be cited as a notable example of the respect which the modern State can show, and the encouragement it can give, to societies which render voluntary service, in their own way, for the benefit of the general community.